$\mathcal{A}$MERICA

STUDY GUIDE

VOLUME II/ FIFTH EDITION

AMERICA

A NARRATIVE HISTORY

TINDALL and SHI

STUDY GUIDE

VOLUME II / FIFTH EDITION

CHARLES W. EAGLES
UNIVERSITY OF MISSISSIPPI

W · W · NORTON & COMPANY · NEW YORK · LONDON

Composition and layout by Roberta Flechner Graphics.

ISBN 0-393-97354-9 (pbk.)

W. W. Norton & Company, Inc.
500 Fifth Avenue, New York, N.Y. 10110

W. W. Norton & Company Ltd.
10 Coptic Street, London WC1A 1PU

4 5 6 7 8 9 0

CONTENTS

INTRODUCTION

This *Study Guide* is designed to help you learn the important concepts in *America: A Narrative History,* Fifth Edition, by George B. Tindall and David Shi. It is not intended as a replacement for the textbook, but as an aid to be used along with the text. When used conscientiously, this *Study Guide* will help you to understand the major themes in American history and to do well on quizzes based on your reading.

STRUCTURE OF THIS STUDY GUIDE

Each chapter of the *Study Guide* contains the following sections:

Chapter Objectives
Chapter Outline
Key Items of Chronology
Terms to Master
Vocabulary Building
Exercises for Understanding:
    Multiple-Choice Questions
    True-False Questions
    Essay Questions
Document(s) or Reading(s)

The purpose of each of the sections, along with the instructions for its use, is explained below.

Chapter Objectives

For each chapter you will find about five objectives, or key concepts, on which you should focus your attention as you read. You should read the whole of each chapter, taking in details as well as major themes, but by keeping the chapter objectives in mind, you will avoid getting bogged down and missing the key ideas.

Chapter Outline

Skim this outline carefully before you begin reading a chapter. The outline provides a more detailed overview than do the objectives. Often headings in the outline are worded to suggest questions about the material. For example, "Impact of the Civil War" and "Developing a plan for Reconstruction" raise the questions "What was the impact of the Civil War? and "What were the plans for Reconstruction?" Look for the answers to such questions as you read the text. This approach will help those of you who are new to reading history.

Key Items of Chronology

Each chapter of this *Study Guide* will include a list of dates. You need not learn every date you encounter in the chapter, but if you learn the key ones listed here and any other dates emphasized by your instructor, you will have the sound chronological framework so important for understanding historical events.

Keep in mind that dates, while important, are not the sole subject matter of history. Seldom will any of the quizzes in this *Study Guide* ask for recall of dates. On the other hand, answers to essay questions, and term papers should include important dates to show that you are familiar with the chronology of your subject.

Terms to Master

This section of the *Study Guide* gives you a list of important terms to study. (Remember, of course, that your instructor may emphasize additional terms that you should learn.) After reading each chapter, return to the list of terms and write a brief definition of each. If you cannot recall the term readily, turn to the relevant pages in the textbook and reread the discussion of the term. If you need or want to consult another source, go to the annotated bibliography at the end of the relevant chapter, or ask your instructor for suggestions.

Vocabulary Building

This is a section of the *Study Guide* that you may or may not need. If you do not know the meaning of the words or terms listed in Vocabulary Building, look them up in a dictionary before you begin reading a chapter. By looking up such words and then using them yourself, you will increase your vocabulary.

When the terms in Vocabulary Building are not readily found in the standard dictionary or when their use in the Tindall text lends them a special meaning, we have defined them for you. We've used the *American Heritage Dictionary,* Second College Edition, as a guide to determine which terms should be defined here for you.

Exercises for Understanding

You should reserve these exercises to use as a check on your reading after you study the chapter. The multiple-choice and true-false questions included here will test your recall and understanding of the facts in the chapter. The answers to these questions are found at the end of each *Study Guide* chapter.

Essay Questions

The essay questions that come next may be used in several ways. If you are using this *Study Guide* entirely on your own, you should try to outline answers to these questions based on your reading of the chapter. In the early stages of the course you may want to consider writing formal answers to these essay questions just as you would if you encountered them on an exam. The questions will often be quite broad and will lead you to think about material in the chapter in different ways. By reviewing the essay questions in this *Study Guide* before attending class, you will better understand the class lecture or discussion.

Documents and Readings

All the chapter s in this *Study Guide* contain a section of documents or readings. The documents are sources from the time period of the chapter (primary sources), chosen to illumine some aspect of the period covered in the text. The readings are excerpts form works of historians (secondary sources), chosen either to illustrate the approach of a master historian or to offer varying interpretations of an event. Study the documents or readings after you have completed the chapter, and consult the headnotes given in this *Study Guide* before each document. Then attempt to answer the questions that follow the documents.

STUDYING HISTORY

The term "history" has been defined in many ways. One way to define it is "everything that has happened in the past." But there are serious problems with this definition. First, it is simply impossible to recount *everything* that has happened in the past. Any single event, such as your eating dinner, is a combination of an infinite number of subevents, ranging from the cultivation of vegetables to the mechanisms involved in digestion. Each of these is itself composed of an unlimited number of subevents. The past, which includes everything that has happened, is shapeless; history is a way of lending shape to the past by focusing on significant events and their relationships. Your "history" of last night's dinner will include only the significant elements, perhaps who your companions were and why you got together, not where the spinach was grown.

Second, the historical record is limited. As you will discover, there is much we don't know about everyday life in seventeenth-century America. History must be based on fact and evidence. The historian then, using the evidence available, fashions a story in which certain past events are connected and take on special meaning or significance. If we accept this definition, we will recognize that much history is subjective, or influenced by the perspective and bias of the historian attempting to give meaning to events.

This is why there is so much disagreement about the importance of some past events. You may have been taught in high school that it was important simply to learn dates and facts: that the Declaration of Independence was adopted on July 4, 1776, or that Franklin Roosevelt was inaugurated on March 4, 1933. But these facts by themselves are limited in meaning. They gain significance when they become parts of larger stories, such as why the American colonies revolted against England or how the United States responded to the Great Depression. When historians construct stories or narratives in which these facts or events take on special significance, room for disagreement creeps in.

Since it is valid for historians to disagree, you should not automatically accept what any one historian writes. You should learn to apply general rules of logic and evidence in assessing the validity of different historical interpretations. This *Study Guide* will at times give you an opportunity to assess different interpretations of events. By doing this, you will learn to question what you read and hear, to think critically.

HOW TO READ A TEXTBOOK

Reading a textbook should be both pleasurable and profitable. The responsibility for this is partly the author's and partly yours, the reader's.

George Tindall and David Shi have written a text that should teach and entertain. In order to get the most out of it, you must read actively and critically. One way to avoid passive, mindless reading is to write, underline, or highlight material by hand. Thus simply by highlighting or underlining pertinent passages in the textbook, you will later be better able to recall what you have read and you will be able to review quickly important material. The key to effective highlighting is to be judicious about what you choose to mark. You should highlight key words and phrases, not whole sentences unless all the words are important. For example, the two paragraphs below from chapter 3 of the textbook (pp. 858–59) show the way we would highlight them:

During the second half of the nineteenth century, an **unrelenting stream of migrants** flowed into the largely Indian and Hispanic West. Newspaper editors described western migration as a "flood tide." Millions of Anglo-Americans, African Americans, Mexicans, and European and Chinese immigrants transformed the patterns of western society and culture. **Most of the settlers were relatively prosperous white, native-born farming families.** Because of the expense of transportation, land, and supplies, the very poor could not afford to relocate. **Three-quarters of the western migrants were men.**

The largest number of foreign immigrants came from **northern Europe and Canada.** In the northern plains, Germans, Scandinavians, and Irish were especially numerous. Not surprisingly, these foreign settlers tended to **cluster together according to ethnic and kinship ties.** Norwegians and Swedes, for example, often gravitated toward others from the same home province or parish to form cohesive rural communities. In the new state of Nebraska in 1870, a quarter of the 123,000 residents were foreign-born. In North Dakota in 1890, 45 percent of the residents were immigrants. Compared to European immigrants, those **from China and Mexico were much less numerous** but nonetheless significant. More than 200,000 Chinese arrived in California between 1876 and 1890.

Probably no two persons would agree on exactly what words in the passage should be underlined, but you can readily see that we have emphasized only the major points concerning English justice.

Highlighting like this can be helpful, but even more useful in increasing your retention of the material is to jot down brief notes about what you read. For example, from the passage above you might give some key features of immigration patterns in the Indian and Hispanic West: the fact that three-quarters of the migrants were men, the fact that most foreign immigrants came from northern Europe and Canada, and the tendency of foreign settlers to cluster together according to ethnic and kinship ties.

Taking notes makes it easier to commit important points to memory. This will help especially when you review for a test.

ACKNOWLEDGMENTS

I wish to thank George B. Tindall and David Shi for having written the excellent text around which I developed this *Study Guide*. My hope is that the text and the *Study Guide* will combine to promote in students a clear understanding of the history of the United States. I owe a great debt to Steven Forman, our editor at W. W. Norton & Company, who has used considerable skill in fashioning the final product. I hope the Fifth Edition of this *Study Guide* will be as useful to students as the previous editions proved to be.

C.W.E.

$\mathcal{A}$MERICA

STUDY GUIDE

18 ∽

RECONSTRUCTION: NORTH AND SOUTH

CHAPTER OBJECTIVES

After you complete the reading and study of this chapter, you should be able to

1. Describe the impact of the Civil War on both the South and the North and on the status of freed blacks.
2. Explain the circumstances that led to Radical Reconstruction.
3. Assess the nature and extent of Radical Reconstruction.
4. Explain the process that returned control of the South to the conservatives.
5. Discuss the contributions and failures of the Grant administration.
6. Explain the outcome of the election of 1876 and the effects of that election and the special arrangements made to conclude it.
7. Appraise the overall impact of Reconstruction.

CHAPTER OUTLINE

I. Questions raised by Reconstruction
   A. Treatment of ex-Confederates
   B. New southern governments
   C. Rebuilding southern economy
   D. Role and rights of former slaves

II. Impact of the Civil War
   A. Change in political power
      1. More friendly to business
      2. Legislative accomplishments
   B. Effects of the South
      1. Physical and economic devastation
      2. White women and work
      3. Bitterness of whites
      4. The former slaves
         a. Free but landless
         b. Freedmen's Bureau

III. Developing a plan of Reconstruction
   A. Loyal counties of Virginia
   B. Military governors in Tennessee, Arkansas, and Louisiana
   C. Lincoln's plan of Reconstruction
      1. Provisions
      2. Implementation in Tennessee, Arkansas, and Louisiana
      3. Congressional reaction
      4. Wade-Davis Bill and its veto
      5. Lincoln's final statement on Reconstruction
      6. Assassination of Lincoln
   D. Johnson and Reconstruction
      1. Johnson's background
      2. Radicals' perception of him
      3. Johnson's plan

    a. Union indestructible
    b. Amnesty and pardon
    c. End of land distribution
    d. State governments
E. Southern reactions
    1. Intransigence
    2. Black codes
F. Radicals and Reconstruction
    1. Motivation
    2. Conquered provinces argument
    3. Forfeited rights theory
G. Johnson vs. Congress
    1. Veto of Freedmen's Bureau extension
    2. Assault on Radicals
    3. Veto of Civil Rights Act overridden
H. Fourteenth Amendment

IV. Congressional Reconstruction triumphant
  A. Actions in Congress early in 1867
    1. Extension of suffrage in the District of Columbia
    2. Requirement that new Congress convene
    3. Command of the Army Act
    4. Tenure of Office Act
    5. Military Reconstruction Act
      a. Key provisions for black suffrage and the Fourteenth Amendment
      b. Tennessee exempted
      c. Military districts
  B. Later Reconstruction Acts to plug loopholes
  C. Constitutional issues and the Supreme Court
    1. Congress removes to the right of the Supreme Court to decide *Ex parte McCardle*
    2. *Texas* v. *White* upheld congressional Reconstruction
  D. The impeachment and trial of Johnson
    1. Failure of early efforts to impeach him
    2. Violation of Tenure of Office Act
    3. The articles of impeachment
    4. The Senate trial
    5. Ramifications of the impeachment

E. Radical rule in the South
    1. Readmission of southern states
    2. Duration of Radical control
    3. Role of the Union League prior to Reconstruction

V. African Americans in the postwar South
  A. Role of military service in developing African-American leadership
  B. Independent African-American churches
  C. African-American fraternal and benevolent societies
  D. Affirmation of African-American family life
  E. Development of schools
    1. White elite's fear of the effects of education
    2. Use of northern assistance

VI. Southern Politics
  A. African Americans in southern politics
    1. Characteristics of African-American activity
    2. Disagreements among African Americans
    3. Extent of African-American control
  B. Carpetbaggers and scalawags
  C. New state constitutions
  D. Achievements of the Radical governments
  E. The measure of corruption and abuse in Radical governments
  F. The development of white terror techniques
    1. Objections to black participation in government
    2. The Ku Klux Klan
    3. Enforcement Acts to protect black voters
  G. The return of conservative control
    1. Reasons for abandonment of the Radical programs
    2. Duration of Radical control

VII. The Grant years
  A. The election of 1868
    1. Reasons for support of Grant
    2. The Grant ticket and platform

3. Democratic programs and candidates
4. Results
B. The character of Grant's leadership
C. Early appointments
D. Proposal to pay the government debt
E. Scandals
   1. Jay Gould's effort to corner the gold market
   2. The Crédit-Mobilier exposure
   3. Other scandals
   4. Grant's personal role in the scandals
F. Reform and the election of 1872
   1. Liberal Republicans nominate Greeley in 1872
   2. Grant's advantages
G. Economic panic
   1. Causes for the depression
   2. Severity of the depression

H. Democratic control of the House in 1874
I. Reissue of greenbacks
J. Resumption of specie payments approved in 1875

VIII. Election of 1876
A. Elimination of Grant and Blaine
B. Republicans nominate Hayes
C. Democrats nominate Tilden
D. Views of the parties
E. Results of the popular vote
F. Role of the Electoral Commission
G. Wormley House bargain
   1. Promises of each side
   2. Promises filled and unfilled
H. The end of Reconstruction
   1. The crumbling of African-American rights
   2. An enduring legacy

KEY ITEMS OF CHRONOLOGY

Lincoln's plan for Reconstruction announced	1863
Creation of Freedmen's Bureau	1865
Thirteenth Amendment ratified	1865
Assassination of Lincoln	April 14, 1865
Johnson's plan for Reconstruction announced	May 29, 1865
Veto of Freedmen's Bureau Extension Bill	February 1866
Congress overrode Johnson's veto of Civil Rights Bill	April 1866
Ku Klux Klan organized in the South	1866
Military Reconstruction Act	March 2, 1867
Johnson replaced Stanton with Grant as secretary of war	August 1867
Johnson named Thomas secretary of war	February 1868
House voted to impeach Johnson	February 1868
Trial of Johnson in Senate	March 5 to May 26, 1868
All southern states except Virginia, Mississippi, and Texas readmitted to Congress	June 1868
Fourteenth Amendment ratified	1868
Texas v. *White* decision of Supreme Court	1869
Grant administrations	1869–1877
Mississippi, Texas, and Virginia readmitted	1870
Fifteenth Amendment ratified	1870
Resumption Act	1875

TERMS TO MASTER

Listed below are some important terms or people with which you should be familiar after you complete the study of this chapter. Identify each name or term.

1. Freedmen's Bureau
2. "forty acres and a mule"
3. Wade-Davis Hill
4. "iron clad oath"
5. Black Codes
6. Radicals
7. Fourteenth Amendment
8. Military Reconstruction
9. Command of the Army Act
10. Tenure of Office Act
11. *Ex parte McCardle*
12. carpetbaggers and scalawags
13. Tweed ring
14. Ku Klux Klan
15. "Ohio Idea"
16. Liberal Republicans
17. Jay Gould
18. Crédit-Mobilier
19. Samuel J. Tilden
20. Compromise of 1877

VOCABULARY BUILDING

Listed below are some words or phrases used in this chapter. Look in the dictionary for the meaning of each term not defined here for you.

1. ravage
2. consensus
3. profundity
4. marauding
5. avenge
6. amnesty
7. infamous
8. edict
9. mulatto
10. inversion
11. entity
12. litigation
13. abridge
14. boor
15. imbecile
16. impeach
17. indictable
18. rudiments
19. derisive
20. prototype

EXERCISES FOR UNDERSTANDING

When you have completed reading the chapter, answer each of the following questions. If you have difficulty, go back to the text and reread the section of the chapter related to the question.

Multiple-Choice Questions

Select the letter of the response that best completes the statement.

1. During the Civil War, the national government became
   A. more friendly to business interests.
   B. more supportive of farm interests.
   C. less involved in matters unrelated to the war.
   D. dominated by military leaders.
2. Johnson's plan of Reconstruction was like Lincoln's except that it required
   A. that a majority of voters take an oath of allegiance rather than 10 percent as did Lincoln's plan.
   B. that voters also repudiate the Fourteenth Amendment in their new governments.
   C. that persons who owned property worth $20,000 apply personally to the president for a pardon.
   D. an iron-clad oath from all participants in the new governments.
3. The Radical Republicans argued that control of the southern states was
   A. up to the states themselves.
   B. a matter of presidential prerogative.
   C. an issue for Congress to deal with.
   D. not at issue since they had not really left the Union.
4. The Constitution guaranteed all persons "the equal protection of the laws" as a result of

A. the Thirteenth Amendment.

B. the Fourteenth Amendment.

C. the Fifteenth Amendment.

D. the Supreme Court's decision in *Ex parte McCardle*.

5. The African American's role in Reconstruction did *not* involve

   A. learning leadership skills in the Union army.

   B. supporting the integration of southern schools.

   C. starting new marriages after their unions under slavery ended.

   D. establishing many independent black churches.

6. Carpetbaggers and scalawags generally

   A. belonged to the Ku Klux Klan.

   B. lost the right to vote under Radical Reconstruction.

   C. supported the Republican party.

   D. all of the above

7. U. S. Grant was guilty of

   A. refusing to turn documents over to Congress for their investigation.

   B. trying to block the implementation of Reconstruction laws.

   C. choosing his appointees unwisely.

   D. taking funds from the federal treasury.

8. The election of 1876 resulted in

   A. an agreement to give the Republicans control of every disputed elector.

   B. disputed elections in Georgia, Mississippi, and Oregon.

   C. control of Congress by the Democrats.

   D. a near tie in the popular vote for president.

9. Radical Republican governments lasted

   A. all over the South until the Hayes election in 1877.

   B. longest in the deep South where the heaviest African-American population was.

   C. only five years, until 1872, in Virginia and Tennessee.

   D. longest in Mississippi, Florida, and Georgia.

True-False Questions

Indicate whether each statement is true or false.

1. The Freedmen's Bureau distributed lands to all former slaves, but many recipients quickly sold the land to their former masters.

2. The Black Codes were laws passed by the Radical Reconstruction governments to give equal rights to former slaves.

3. Charles Sumner and Thaddeus Stevens were Radical Republicans.

4. Many Radical Republicans first reacted warmly to Andrew Johnson because they thought he was one of them.

5. President Andrew Johnson was impeached and removed from office.

6. The Tenure of Office Act required that the president get the permission of the Senate to remove any officeholder whose appointment had been confirmed by the Senate.

7. President Grant supported using greenbacks to pay off the national debt.

8. In the election of 1872 the Democrats and Liberal Republicans both nominated the same man for president.

9. The Compromise of 1877 brought "redemption" to the South.

10. The Grant administration made no effort to combat the violence of the KKK in the South.

Essay Questions

1. In 1865, what effects of the Civil War were obvious in southern society?

2. How were the Reconstruction plans of Lincoln and Johnson similar to and different from each other?

3. How were the Radical southern governments unusual and what did they accomplish?

4. Why did President Johnson and the Radical Republicans disagree? Could a compromise have been reached?

5. What was the Compromise of 1877 and why was it important?

6. Compare and contrast politics in the North and the South after the Civil War.
7. Assess the significance of the Fourteenth Amendment, discussing why it was needed, its major provisions, and its long-range impact.

8. Discuss the impeachment of Andrew Johnson, including the charges against the president, the outcome of the proceedings, and the implications of the outcome for the future.

READINGS

Reading 1. William A. Dunning Explains the Failure of Reconstruction in Terms of Corruption and Failure of the Governments

Like other significant periods in U.S. history, the Reconstruction Era has gone through cycles of interpretation. Some of the earliest scholarly work on the period was carried out by William A. Dunning and his students, who believed that the Radicals in Congress sought to impose their rule on the South for selfish motives of personal gain. Dunning's synthesis of Reconstruction, written in the early 1900s when he was a professor at Columbia University, presented a southern point of view. Dunning also directed a group of scholars who investigated developments in the southern states from a similar point of view. In the excerpts below from one of his articles, Dunning, while explaining the failure of Reconstruction, reveals his attitude about the corruption and inadequacy of Reconstruction governments and his reservations about the abilities of African Americans.

The leading motive of the reconstruction had been, at the inception of the process, to insure to the freedmen an effective protection of their civil rights,—of life, liberty, and property. In the course of the process, the chief stress came to be laid on the endowment of the blacks with full political rights,—with the electoral franchise and eligibility to office. And by the time the process was complete, a very important, if not the most important part had been played by the desire and the purpose to secure to the Republican party the permanent control of several Southern states in which hitherto such a political organization had been unknown. This last motive had a plausible and widely accepted justification in the view that the rights of the negro and the "results of the war" in general would be secure only if the national government should remain indefinitely in Republican hands, and that therefore the strengthening of the party was a primary dictate of patriotism.

Through the operation of these various motives successive and simultaneous, the completion of the reconstruction showed the following situation: (1) the negroes were in the enjoyment of the equal political rights with the whites; (2) the Republican party was in vigorous life in all the Southern states, and in firm control of many of them; and (3) the negroes exercised an influence in political affairs out of all relation to their intelligence or property, and, since so many of the whites were defranchised, excessive even in proportion to their numbers. At the present day, in the same states, the negroes enjoy practically no political rights; the Republican party is but the shadow of a name; and the influence of the negroes in political affairs is nil. This contrast suggests what has been involved in the undoing of reconstruction.

Before the last state was restored to the Union the process was well under way through which the resumption of control by the whites was to be effected. The tendency in this direction was greatly promoted by conditions within the Republican party itself. Two years of supremacy in those states which had been restored in 1868 had revealed unmistakable evidences of moral and political weakness in the governments. The personnel of the party was declining in character through the return to the North of the more substantial of the carpetbaggers, who found Southern conditions, both social and industrial, far from what they had anticipated, and through the very frequent instances in which the "scalawags" ran to open disgrace. Along with this deterioration in the white element of the party, the negroes who rose to prominence and leadership were very frequently of a type which acquired and practiced the tricks and knavery rather than the useful arts of politics, and the vicious courses of these negroes strongly confirmed the prejudices of the whites. But at the same time that the incapacity of the party in power to administer any government was becoming demonstrable the problems with which it was required to cope were made by its adversaries such as would have taxed the capacity of the most efficient statesmen the world could produce. . . . No attention was paid to the claim that the manifest inefficiency and viciousness of the Republican governments afforded a partial, if not wholly adequate explanation of their overthrow. Not even the relative quiet and order that followed the triumph of the whites in these states were recognized as justifying the new regime.

[From William A. Dunning, "The Undoing of Reconstruction," *Atlantic Monthly,* October 1901, pp. 437–38.]

Reading 2. La Wanda Cox Questions Whether Reconstruction Could Have Been Effective

In a strong departure from Dunning's racial arguments, most historians in recent years have come to see the failure of Reconstruction as the refusal to establish a sound basis for black equality. According to this view, Reconstruction as a reform movement aiming to improve the status of former slaves was undermined by events at the end of the nineteenth century. Several key historians have argued that the declining fortunes of blacks in the 1890s stemmed from the political failure to provide land for the freed slaves. In the excerpt below, La Wanda Cox, writing in 1981, takes issue with that view, finding other reasons for the failure of Reconstruction. As you read, carefully identify each of her other arguments.

. . . Yet there can be no question but that the equality of citizenship embodied in national and state law during the 1860s lay shattered and apparently unmendable as the South entered the twentieth century. Most former slaves and their children still lived in agrarian dependence and poverty, poorly educated, increasingly disfranchised and segregated, with little protection against a new surge of white violence.

All accounts of Reconstruction recognize the intensity of white southern resistance to the new status of blacks imposed by Republicans upon the defeated South. Curiously, in explaining the outcome, generally characterized by modern historians as the failure of Reconstruction (though with qualification and some dissent), they tend to place major responsibility not upon the South but upon "the North." By "the North" they usually mean the Republican party, which held national political power, and sometimes say as much. Their explanation is not free of moral stricture, often patently implicit when not expressly stated. Since the mid-1960s there has seldom been missing from accounts of the "First Reconstruction" the pejorative term "betrayal." . . .

Failure to enforce black civil and political rights in the South is often attributed to a lack of will on the part of Republican leaders and their constituencies due to their racial views. The explanation may not be susceptible of definite disproof, but it has not been proven and probably cannot be. Many factors entered into the abandonment of the cause of the black man in the South, and Republicans gave up neither quickly nor easily. The voting record of regular Republicans in Congress through 1891 remained remarkably consistent and cohesive behind efforts to strengthen federal enforcement of Reconstruction legislation. Democratic party obstruction was equally consistent and created a major roadblock. Republicans enacted a drastic enforcement law in 1870 and another in 1871. For most of the twenty years after the elections of 1870 they did not have the power in Congress to pass additional legislation supportive of black rights but they kept the issue alive. It is true that as early as 1872 some Republicans, notably those who joined the Liberal Republican movement, broke with the policy of national action in support of black rights. But race prejudice was neither a conscious nor a major determinant of their new attitude toward federal intervention in the South. Indeed, the Liberal Republican Platform of 1872 tried to reconcile a policy of national retreat with loyalty to the Reconstruction amendments. When Republicans regained control of both houses of Congress in 1890–1891 by only a narrow margin, they passed in the house an enforcement bill to protect black voters but narrowly lost it in the Senate by the perfidy of a few who broke ranks to gain support for silver legislation. On the local front in the northern states, in keeping with party tradition, the Republican record on black rights remained stronger than that of their opponents.

In 1877 when President Hayes withdrew federal troops and acquiesced to "home rule" for the South, racism was not the key to presidential decision. . . . The will to continue the battle was undermined by growing doubt of the wisdom of immediate universal black enfranchisement, increasingly seen as the source of corruption There was revulsion against the turmoil of disputed elections and the force used to settle them. Many Republicans were discouraged as state after state came under "Redeemer" control, or distracted by the pressure of problems closer at home. There was a general desire in the North for the peace and national reconciliation that Grant had invoked but could not attain as president. Whatever part race prejudice played in weakening Republican support for continuing military intervention, its role was peripheral rather than central.

A critical question needs to be addressed. Could a greater use of force have brought white southerners to accept civil and political rights for blacks? Neither history nor theory can answer this question with certainty. A number of historians have implied that direct coercion could have effected a fundamental change, that Reconstruction was the nation's great missed opportunity. . . . Given the nation's traditional commitment to civilian control and majority rule, "the use of force was self-defeating."

Force *and* consent, how to achieve the one by use of the other, posed a dilemma which by the 1870s strained the bounds of the possible. The outcome would have been only a little less problematic had Reconstruction been formulated in early 1865 and backed by force, i.e., by force alone. Particularly vulnerable is the assumption that by eliminating the power of the landed aristocracy, resistance would have been broken and a new order of equal rights for blacks securely established. There would still have remained for the South as a whole a white majority with prejudices and interests inimicable to the advancement of blacks. . . .

Certainly by the mid-1870s the use of coercion had intensified a deep and bitter reaction. Instead of passive resignation, coercion led to a "negative consensus" that rejected the legitimacy of national authority, over the status of blacks, fed resistance and united white southerners to an unprecedented degree. It is well to be reminded that the coercion used had been considerable. . . .

The force employed in the 1870s was grossly insufficient for the task at hand. Too often local officials and courts sidestepped justice for blacks without interference. Troops stationed in the South were woefully inadequate in number to contain violent resistance wherever it erupted. . . .

Nonetheless, the direct coercion mobilized by the national government in the 1860s and 1870s was substantial, far greater than any similar action in support of desegregation and black voting in the 1950s and '60s. It was large enough to give strong support to the contention that a century ago the amount of force necessary to realize equal civil and political rights in the South was impossible to sustain in a nation whose democratic traditional and constitutional structure limited the use of power, exalted the rule of law, and embodied the concept of government by the consent of the governed. Neither national institutions nor public opinion could be expected to have sustained a military intervention of indefinite length and of sufficient strength to crush all local resistance. And by the mid-1870s, the issue at stake no longer appeared clear-cut, even to northern Republicans.

. . . No explanation for the tragic outcome of the postwar decades for black America has been more generally accepted in modern scholarship than that Reconstruction failed because the federal government did not provide land for the freedman. The thesis has been sharply challenged, and the challenge has not been met. The work of historians and economists in exploring afresh the roots of poverty, particularly of black poverty, in the postbellum South afford some relevant perspectives. Between 1974 and 1979 six book-length studies appeared with significant bearing on the problem of black poverty, and others were in progress; conference papers and published articles also reflected the vigor of scholarly interest in the question.

No consensus has developed either as explanation for the continuing dependence and poverty of southern blacks or as an analysis of the potential economic effect of land distribution. However, four of five econometricians who addressed the latter question concluded that grants of land, while desirable and beneficial, would not have solved the predicament of the freedmen and their children. . . .

More than a land program was needed to insure the freedman's economic future. Although areas of land with high fertility prospered, it seems doubtful that income from cotton between the close of the war and the turn of the century, even if equitably distributed, could have sustained much beyond a marginal level of existence for those who worked the cotton fields whether as wage earner, cropper, tenant, or small owner. And the lower South because of its soils and climate, . . . had no viable alternative to cotton as a commercial crop until the scientific and technological advances of the twentieth century. Nor could nonmarket subsistence farming offer much by way of material reward. The "more" that was needed can be envisaged in retrospect, and was glimpsed by contemporaries, but it is not clear how it could have been achieved. . . . Despite scholarship, new and old, there is no certain explanation of why the South failed to catch up with the North. If historians and economists should agree upon a diagnosis, it is unlikely that they will uncover a remedy that could have been reorganized and implemented a century ago. . . .

. . . More than a land program, the civil and political rights Republicans established in law, had they been secured in practice, could have mitigated the discrimination that worsened their condition and constricted whatever opportunities might otherwise have existed for escape from poverty. . . .

The priority Republicans gave to civil and political rights in their fight to establish a meaningful new status for ex-slaves had been too readily discounted by historians. Small landholdings could not have protected blacks from intimidation, or even from many forms of economic coercion. They would not have brought economic power. In the face of overwhelming white opposition, they could not have safeguarded the new equality of civil and political status. Where blacks voted freely, on the other hand, there was always the potential for sharing political power and using it as a means to protect and advance their interests. There is considerable evidence that this did happen. Local officials elected by black votes during the years of Republican control upheld blacks against planters, state legislators repealed Black Codes, shifted the burden of taxation from the poor, granted agricultural laborers a first lien in crops, increased expenditures for education. . . . And beyond immediate gains, black votes meant support for educational facilities through which blacks could acquire the literacy and skills essential for advancement.

Security for black civil and political rights required acceptance by white southerners. An acquiescence induced by a judicious combination of force and consent needed for its perpetuation reinforcement by self-interest. The most effective vehicle of self-interest would have been a Union-Republican party able to command substantial continuing support from native whites. The Republican party that gained temporary dominance through the congressional legislation of 1867 enfranchising blacks failed to meet the test of substantial white support. Despite a strong white following in a few states, its scalawag component from the start was too limited to offset the opposition's attack on it as the party of the black man and the Yankee. And white participation diminished as appeals to race prejudice and sectional animosity intensified.

The potential for a major second party among southern whites existed in the aftermath of Confederate defeat. The Democratic party was in disarray, discredited for having led the South out of the Union and having lost the war Old Whig loyalties subsumed by the slavery issue had nonetheless endured; southern unionism had survived in varying degrees from wartime adherence to the Union to reluctant support of the Confederacy. . . .

Had party recruitment and organization, with full presidential support, begun at the end of hostilities and escaped the period of confusion and bitterness that thinned the ranks of the willing during the conflict between Johnson and Congress, the result could have been promising. . . .

Even under the guidance of a Lincoln, the building of a permanent biracial major party in the South was by no means assured. A broad enduring coalition of disparate elements would face the necessity of reconciling sharply divergent economic interests. Agricultural workers sought maximum autonomy, more than bare necessities, and an opportunity for land ownership while planter-merchants strove to control labor and maximize profit. The burden of increased taxation to meet essential but unaccustomed social services, particularly for blacks, meant an inescapable clash of class and racial interests. Concessions by the more privileged were especially difficult in a South of limited available resources and credit, impoverished by war and enmeshed in inflated costs, crop disasters, and falling cotton prices. By the mid-1870s a nationwide depression intensified regional problems. Efforts to promote a more varied and vigorous economy by state favor, credit, and appropriation became a political liability as the primary effect appeared to be the proliferation of civic corruption and entrepreneurial plunder.

The years of political Reconstruction, to borrow an apt phrase from Thomas B. Alexander's study of Tennessee offered no "narrowly missed opportunities to leap a century forward in reform." Not even a Lincoln could have wrought such a miracle. To have secured something less, yet something substantially more than blacks had gained by the end of the nineteenth century, did not lie beyond the limits of the possible given a president who at war's end would have joined party in an effort to realize "as nearly as we can" the fullness of freedom for blacks.

[From La Wanda Cox, *Lincoln and Black Freedom: A Study in Presidential Leadership* (Columbia: University of South Carolina Press, 1981), pp. 155–56, 162–64, 165–69, 174–83.]

Reading 3. Eric Foner Contends That Reconstruction Did Not Go Far Enough

Historical scholarship on the Reconstruction era continues to grow at a remarkable rate. In the following excerpt Eric Foner summarizes some of the most recent scholarship and suggests a new way to view Reconstruction.

Despite the excellence of recent writing and the continual expansion of our knowledge of the period, historians of Reconstruction today face a unique dilemma. An old interpretation has been overthrown, but a coherent new synthesis has yet to take its place. The revisionists of the 1960s effectively established a series of negative points: the Reconstruction governments were not as bad as had been portrayed, black supremacy was a myth, the Radicals were not cynical manipulators of the freedmen. Yet no convincing overall portrait of the quality of political and social life emerged from their writings.

. . . a new portrait of Reconstruction ought to begin by viewing it not as a specific time period, bounded by the years 1865 and 1877, but as an episode in a prolonged historical process—American society's adjustment to the consequences of the Civil War and emancipation.

. . . the focal point of Reconstruction was the social revolution known as emancipation. Plantation slavery was simultaneously a system of labor, a form of racial domination, and the foundation upon which arose a distinctive ruling class within the South. Its demise threw open the most fundamental questions of economy, society, and politics. A new system of labor, social, racial, and political relations had to be created to replace slavery.

Few modern scholars believe the Reconstruction governments established in the South in 1867 and 1868 fulfilled the aspirations of their humble constituents. While their achievements in such realms as education, civil rights, and the economic rebuilding of the South are now widely appreciated, historians today believe they failed to affect either the economic plight of the emancipated slave or the ongoing transformation of independent white farmers into cotton tenants. Yet their opponents did perceive the Reconstruction governments in precisely this way—as representatives of a revolution that had put the bottom rail, both racial and economic, on top. This perception helps explain the ferocity of the attacks leveled against them and the pervasiveness of violence in the postemancipation South.

The spectacle of black men voting and holding office was anathema to large numbers of Southern whites. Even more disturbing, at least in the view of those who still controlled the plantation regions of the South, was the emergence of local officials, black and white, who sympathized with the plight of the black laborer. . . . During presidential Reconstruction, and after "Redemption," with planters and their allies in control of politics, the law emerged as a means of stabilizing and promoting the plantation system. If Radical Reconstruction failed to redistribute the land of the South, the ouster of the planter class from control of politics at least ensured that the sanctions of the criminal law would not be employed to discipline the black labor force.

An understanding of this fundamental conflict over the relation between government and society helps explain the pervasive complaints concerning corruption and "extravagance" during Radical Reconstruction. Corruption there was aplenty; tax rates did rise sharply. More significant than the rate of taxation, however, was the change in its incidence. For the first time, planters and white farmers had to pay a significant portion of their income to the government, while propertyless blacks often escaped scot-free. Several states, moreover, enacted heavy taxes on uncultivated land to discourage land speculation and force land onto the market, benefiting it was hoped, the freedmen.

As time passed, complaints about the "extravagance" and corruption of Southern governments found a sympathetic audience among influential Northerners. The Democratic charge that universal suffrage in the South was responsible for high taxes and governmental extravagance coincided with a rising conviction among the urban middle classes of the North that city government had to be taken out of the hands of the immigrant poor and returned to the "best men"—the educated, professional, financially independent citizens unable to exert much political influence at a time of mass parties and machine politics. Increasingly the "respectable" middle classes began to retreat from the very notion of universal suffrage. The poor were no longer perceived as honest producers, the backbone of the social order; now they became the "dangerous classes," the "mob." As the historian Francis Parkman put it, too much power rested with "masses of imported ignorance and hereditary ineptitude." To Parkman the Irish of the Northern cities and the blacks of the South were equally incapable of utilizing the ballot: "Witness the municipal corruptions of New York, and the monstrosities of negro rule in South Carolina." Such attitudes helped to justify Northern inaction as, one by one, the Reconstruction regimes of the South were overthrown by political violence.

In the end, then, neither the abolition of slavery nor Reconstruction succeeded in resolving the debate over the meaning of freedom in American life. Twenty years before the American Civil War, writing about the prospect of abolition in France's colonies, Alexis de Tocqueville had written, "If the Negroes have the right to become free, the [planters] have the incontestable right not to be ruined by the Negroes' freedom." And in the United States, as in nearly every plantation society that experienced the end of slavery, a rigid social and political dichotomy between former master and former slave, an ideology of racism, and a dependent labor force with limited economic opportunities all survived abolition. Unless one means by freedom the simple fact of not being a slave, emancipation thrust blacks into a kind of no-man's land, a partial freedom that made a mockery of the American ideal of equal citizenship.

Yet by the same token the ultimate outcome underscores the uniqueness of Reconstruction itself. Alone among the societies that abolished slavery in the nineteenth century, the United States, for a moment, offered the freedmen a measure of political control over their own destinies. However brief its sway, Reconstruction allowed scope for a remarkable political and social mobilization of the black community. It opened doors of opportunity that could never be completely closed. Reconstruction transformed the lives of Southern blacks in ways immeasurable by statistics and unreachable by law. It raised their expectations and aspirations, redefined their status in relation to the larger society, and allowed space for the creation of institutions that enabled them to survive the repression that followed. And it established constitutional principles of civil and political equality that, while flagrantly violated after Redemption, planted the seeds of future struggle.

[From Eric Foner, "The New View of Reconstruction," *American Heritage* 34, no. 6 (October–November 1983): 13–15.]

Questions for Reflection

What good, if any, does Dunning seem to imply came from Reconstruction? What appear to be Dunning's views of African Americans? What does Dunning mean by "The failure of Radicalism is thus a part of the wider failure of bourgeois liberalism to solve the problems of the new age which was dawning"?

Explain how Cox's view of the failure of Reconstruction is different from Dunning's.

Why does she say that the use of more force would not have solved the problems of Reconstruction? What issue does she contend was more important than the need to provide land for former slaves? What is the basis for her argument? Do you agree with her view? Explain.

Cox seems to imply that if Lincoln had lived, Reconstruction would have developed more effectively. What is her basis for that view? Why does she think that even Lincoln would have had difficulty in making Reconstruction succeed?

According to Eric Foner, how did Reconstruction lead to the ouster of the planter class from control of politics and why was that important? How did attitudes toward blacks in Reconstruction interact with attitudes toward immigrants and other oppressed groups in the North? What reason does Foner give for the failure of Reconstruction governments to give blacks long-term freedom?

All three of these writers assert that Reconstruction failed from one perspective or another. How do *you* think the problems of Reconstruction in the South could have been better solved?

ANSWERS TO MULTIPLE-CHOICE AND TRUE-FALSE QUESTIONS

Multiple-Choice Questions

1-A, 2-C, 3-C, 4-B, 5-B, 6-C, 7-C, 8-A, 9-B

True-False Questions

1-F, 2-F, 3-T, 4-T, 5-F, 6-T, 7-F, 8-T, 9-T, 10-F

19 ∽

NEW FRONTIERS: SOUTH AND WEST

CHAPTER OBJECTIVES

*After you complete the reading and study of
this chapter, you should be able to:*

1. Explain the concept of the New South, its
   development, and how it affected the
   South after the Civil War.
2. Account for the rise of the Bourbons to
   power in the South and explain their
   impact on the South.
3. Discuss the causes and process of disfranchisement of blacks in the South.
4. Compare the views of Washington and Du
   Bois on the place of blacks in American
   life.
5. Describe the Indian wars and explain the
   new Indian policy of 1887.
6. Account for the rise and decline of the cattle industry.
7. Describe the problems of farming on the
   western frontier.
8. Explain the importance of Turner's theory
   of the significance of the frontier in American history.

CHAPTER OUTLINE

  I. The New South
    A. Concept of the New South

      1. Henry Grady's background
      2. His vision
      3. Other prophets of the New South
        Creed
    B. Economic growth
      1. Growth of cotton textile manufac-
        turing
      2. Development of the tobacco
        industry
        a. John Ruffin Green and Bull's
          Head
        b. Duke family
        c. Techniques used by Buck
          Duke for growth
        d. Creation and breakup of the
          American Tobacco Company
      3. Coal production
      4. Lumbering
      5. Other products
      6. Beginnings of petroleum and
        hydroelectric power
    C. Agriculture in the New South
      1. Limited diversity in agriculture
      2. Seaman A. Knapp and agricultur-
        al education
      3. Features of sharecropping and
        tenancy
      4. Impact of the crop lien system
    D. Role of the Bourbon Redeemers
      1. Nature of the Bourbons

2. Bourbon economic policies
    a. Laissez-faire
    b. Retrenchment in government spending
    c. Assistance of private philanthropy
    d. Convict lease system
    e. Repudiation of Confederate debts in some states
    f. Positive contributions of the Bourbons
E. Role of the Democratic party in the New South
    1. Nature of the mongrel coalition
    2. Basis for independent political movements
    3. Efforts for Republican and independent collaboration
F. Race relations
    1. Bourbon–African-American political compatibility
    2. Variety of color lines in social relations
    3. Disfranchisement of blacks
        a. Impetus for action
        b. Techniques used
        c. Results
    4. Spread of segregation
        a. Railway cars
        b. Civil rights cases, 1883
        c. *Plessy* v. *Ferguson,* 1896
        d. Other areas
    5. Violence against blacks
G. Black responses to racism
    1. Booker T. Washington
        a. Accommodation to segregation
        b. 1895 speech in Atlanta
    2. W. E. B. Du Bois
        a. Criticisms of Washington
        b. "Ceaseless agitation"
H. Importance of the Bourbons

II. The New West
A. Views of western history
B. The West after the Civil War
    1. Frontiers of settlement
    2. Great American Desert
C. Migration to the West
    1. Native-born Americans

2. Foreign immigrants
3. Exodusters
    a. "Pap" Singleton
    b. Kansas and Oklahoma
    c. "Buffalo soldiers"
D. The mining frontier
    1. Pattern of mining development
    2. Locations of major mineral discoveries
    3. Development of new states
E. Displacement of the Indians
    1. Agreement for tribal limitations, 1851
    2. Conflicts that arose during the Civil War
    3. Establishment of the Indian Peace Commission, 1867
        a. Policy of two large reservations
        b. Agreements with the Indians in 1867 and 1868
    4. Continued resistance of Indians
        a. The Great Sioux War
        b. Massacre at Little Bighorn
        c. Conquest of Sioux and others
        d. Significance of Chief Joseph and Nez Percé
        e. Ghost Dance movement
    5. Impact of annihilation of buffalo herds
    6. Stirrings for reform in Indian policy
        a. Eastern view of Indian slaughter
        b. Role of Helen Hunt Jackson
    7. Dawes Severalty Act, 1887
        a. Concept of new policy
        b. Provisions of Dawes and subsequent acts
        c. Impact of new policy
F. Cattle industry in the West
    1. Development of the open range
    2. War's increased demand for beef
    3. Renewal of long drives after the Civil War
        a. Joseph McCoy
        b. Features of the cow town
    4. Trade with the East
        a. Refrigerated train cars

b. Marketing campaigns
5. Joseph Glidden and barbed wire
6. Boom and bust on the open range
G. The farming frontier
1. Land policy after the Civil War
2. Changed institutions beyond the 100th meridian
3. Efforts for reclamation of arid lands
4. An assessment of land distribution
5. Farm life on the Great Plains

a. Difficulties
b. Importance of women
c. Advances in equipment
d. Bonanza farms
e. Diversified small farms
H. Violence on the frontier
1. Functions of violence
a. Resolve disputes
b. Protection
c. Masculine honor
2. Variety of violent conflicts

KEY ITEMS OF CHRONOLOGY

Homestead Act	1862
First of the long drives	1866
Report on the Condition of the Indian Tribes	1867
Indian Peace Commission settlements	1867–1868
Battle of Little Bighorn	1876
Civil rights cases	1883
Dawes Severalty Act	1887
Mississippi Constitution incorporates disfranchisement of blacks	1890
Census shows frontier closed	1890
Cripple Creek gold strike	1891–1894
Turner frontier thesis presented	1893
B. T. Washington's "Atlanta Compromise" speech	1895
Plessy v. *Ferguson*	1896
Disfranchisement of blacks essentially completed in southern states	1910

TERMS TO MASTER

Listed below are some important terms or people with which you should be familiar after you complete the study of this chapter. Explain the significance of each name or term.

1. Henry W. Grady
2. James Buchanan Duke
3. sharecropping
4. crop lien system
5. Bourbons
6. Peabody Fund for Education
7. convict lease system
8. Mississippi Plan for disfranchisement
9. grandfather clauses
10. Jim Crow laws
11. *Plessy* v. *Ferguson*
12. Booker T. Washington
13. W. E. B. Du Bois
14. Exodusters
15. Indian Peace Commission
16. George A. Custer
17. Chief Joseph
18. *A Century of Dishonor*
19. Dawes Severalty Act
20. Homestead Act of 1862

VOCABULARY BUILDING

Listed below are some words or phrases used in this chapter. Look up each word in your dictionary unless the meaning is given here.

1. oligarch
2. corollary
3. profusion
4. forge (n.)
5. peonage
6. privation
7. proliferate
8. sanctity
9. paragon
10. capricious
11. venality
12. proviso
13. oblique
14. inexorable
15. nomadic
16. lucrative
17. countenance (v.)
18. arduous
19. tutelage
20. prolific

EXERCISES FOR UNDERSTANDING

When you have completed reading the chapter, answer each of the following questions. If you have difficulty, go back and reread the section of the chapter related to the question.

Multiple-Choice Questions

Select the letter of the response that best completes the statement.

1. The New South Creed was *not*
   A. a pessimistic, defeatist view of the South's future.
   B. given classic expression by Henry W. Grady.
   C. a call for diversified industry.
   D. an inspiration to southerners in the late nineteenth century.
2. The most significant impact of the crop lien system in the South was that it
   A. made possible cash payments for goods.
   B. provided a source of labor in the post-Reconstruction South.
   C. made possible low-interest-rate loans for blacks.
   D. encouraged keeping the South on the one crop, cotton.
3. In the 1890s the disfranchisement of blacks was
   A. advocated by the Populists.
   B. supported by the Fifteenth Amendment.
   C. blocked by Bourbons.
   D. often achieved by literacy tests and poll taxes.
4. A program of "ceaseless agitation" for blacks—including education, voting, and an end to segregation—was proposed by
   A. Henry Grady.
   B. Booker T. Washington.
   C. W. E. B. Du Bois.
   D. Jim Crow.
5. Southern blacks who migrated to Kansas were called
   A. Redeemers.
   B. sodbusters.
   C. Exodusters.
   D. Jim Crows.
6. One key to the growth of the cattle industry was
   A. moving slaughter houses to the East.
   B. refrigerated railroad cars.
   C. better marketing techniques.
   D. B and C but not A
7. The institutions of the West were shaped most by
   A. the climate.
   B. the influence of Indian culture.
   C. violence.
   D. government policies.
8. The frontier thesis of Frederick Jackson Turner emphasized
   A. the importance of Indians in American history.
   B. the democratic values found on the frontier.
   C. the role of women in the West.
   D. the diversity in the West.

True-False Questions

Indicate whether each statement is true or false.

1. James B. Duke played a key role in the development of the cigarette industry.
2. The Peabody and Slater Funds provided subsidies to southern industrial development.
3. The Bourbon Redeemers reduced government services.
4. The *Plessy* v. *Ferguson* decision included a ruling that states could not interfere with the rights of blacks.
5. The "Buffalo Soldiers" rode buffaloes instead of horses.
6. In the West, land reclamation required irrigation.
7. The decline of buffalo herds played a significant role in ending Indian resistance in the West.
8. Most of the individual violence in the West occurred in towns and communities.

Essay Questions

1. What were the economic, political, and racial policies of the Bourbon Redeemers in the South?
2. How did relations between African Americans and whites change after the Civil War?
3. Explain how the sharecropping and tenant systems worked in southern agriculture.
4. Contrast the visions of Booker T. Washington and W. E. B. Du Bois for freed blacks.
5. How did the cattle industry grow and how did it affect both the West and the East?
6. Describe the effects on Indians of the expansion of white settlements in the West.
7. Compare the treatment of Indians in the West to African Americans in the South.
8. How helpful is Turner's frontier thesis in explaining what is distinctive about the United States?

MAP EXERCISE

Match the following places with ten of the locations numbered on the map below.

A. Henry Grady's home
B. where *Plessy* v. *Ferguson* began
C. location of James Duke's cigarette factories
D. site of the Comstock Lode
E. one of last two of forty-eight original states admitted to Union
F. where Battle of Wounded Knee occurred
G. state that led in disfranchisement of blacks
H. home of Mormons
I. Washington's Tuskegee Institute
J. Little Bighorn

DOCUMENTS

Document 1. An Act to Secure Homesteads to Actual Settlers on the Public Domain

Congress passed the Homestead Act in 1862 to provide public lands to settlers.

Be it enacted, That any person who is the head of a family, or who has arrived at the age of twenty-one years, and is a citizen of the United States, or who shall have filed his declaration of intention to become such, as required by the naturalization laws of the United States, and who has never borne arms against the United States Government or given aid and comfort to its enemies, shall, from and after the first of January, eighteen hundred and sixty-three, be entitled to enter one quarter-section or a less quantity of unappropriated public lands, upon which said person may have filed a pre-emption claim, or which may, at the time the application is made, be subject to pre-emption at one dollar and twenty-five cents, or less, per acre; or eighty acres or less of such unappropriated lands, at two dollars and fifty cents per acre, to be located in a body, in conformity to the legal subdivisions of the public lands, and after the same shall have been surveyed: *Provided,* That any person owning or residing on land, may, under the provisions of this act, enter other land lying contiguous to his or her said land, which shall not, with the land so already owned and occupied, exceed in the aggregate one hundred and sixty acres.

Sec. 2. That the person applying for the benefit of this act shall, upon application to the register of the land office in which he or she is about to make such entry, make affidavit before the said register or receiver that he or she is the head of a family, or is twenty-one or more years of age, or shall have performed service in the Army or Navy of the United States, and that he has never borne arms against the Government of the United States or given aid and comfort to its enemies, and that such application is made for his or her exclusive use and benefit, and that said entry is made for the purpose of actual settlement and cultivation, and not, either directly or indirectly, for the use or benefit of any other person or persons whomsoever; and upon filing the said affidavit with the register or receiver, and on payment of ten dollars, he or she shall thereupon be permitted to enter the quantity of land specified: *Provided, however,* That no certificate shall be given or patent issued therefor until the expiration of five years from the date of such entry; and if, at the expiration of such time, or at any time within two years thereafter, the person making such entry—or if he be dead, his widow; or in case of her death, his heirs or devisee; or in case of a widow making such entry, her heirs or devisee, in case of her death—shall prove by two credible witnesses that he, she, or they have resided upon or cultivated the same for the term of five years immediately succeeding the time of filing the affidavit aforesaid, and shall make affidavit that no part of said land has been alienated, and that he has borne true allegiance to the Government of the United States; then, in such case, he, she, or they if at that time a citizen of the United States, shall be entitled to a patent, as in other cases provided for by law: And *provided, further,* That in case of the death of both father and mother, leaving an infant child or children under twenty-one years of age, the right and fee shall inure to the benefit of said infant child or children; and the executor, administrator, or guardian may, at any time within two years after the death of the surviving parent, and in accordance with the laws of the State in which such children for the time being have their domicile, sell said land for the benefit of said infants, but for no other purpose; and the purchaser shall acquire the absolute title by the purchase, and be entitled to a patent from the United States, on payment of the office fees and sum of money herein specified. . . .

[From *U.S. Statutes at Large,* XII, 392ff.]

Document 2. Life on Prairie Farms

In 1893 E. V. Smalley described the social isolation experienced by many farmers on the plains in the late nineteenth century.

. . . the life of a poor settler on a homestead claim in one of the Dakotas or Nebraska. Every homesteader must live upon his claim for five years to perfect his title and get his patent; so that if there were not the universal American custom of isolated farm life to stand in the way, no farm villages would be possible in the first occupancy of a new region in the West without a change in our land laws. If the country were so thickly settled that every quarter section of land (160 acres) had a family upon it, each family would be half a mile from any neighbor, supposing the houses to stand in the centre of the farms, and in any case the average distance between them could not be less. But many settlers own 320 acres, and a few have a square mile of land, 640 acres. Then there are school sections, belonging to the State, and not occupied at all, and everywhere you find vacant tracts owned by Eastern speculators or by mortgage companies, to which former settlers have abandoned their claims, going to newer regions, and leaving their debts and their land behind. Thus the average space separating the farmsteads is, in fact, always more than half a mile, and many settlers must go a mile or two to reach a neighbor's house. This condition obtains not on the frontiers alone, but in fairly well peopled agricultural districts.

If there be any region in the world where the natural gregarious instincts of mankind should assert itself that region is our Northwestern prairies, where a short hot summer is followed by a long cold winter and where there is little in the aspect of nature to furnish food for thought. On every hand the treeless plain stretches away to the horizon line. In summer, it is checkered with grain fields or carpeted with grass and flowers, and it is inspiring in its color and vastness, but one mile of it is almost exactly like another, save where some watercourse nurtures a fringe of willows and cottonwoods. When the snow covers the ground the prospect is bleak and dispiriting. No brooks babble under icy armor. There is no bird life after the wild geese and ducks have passed on their way way south. The silence of death rests on the vast landscape, save when it is swept by cruel winds that search out every chink and cranny of the buildings, and drive through each unguarded aperture the dry, powdery snow. In such a region, you would expect the dwellings to be of substantial construction, but they are not. The new settler is too poor to build of brick or stone. He hauls a few loads of lumber from the nearest railway station, and puts up a frail little house of two, three or four rooms that looks as though the prairie winds would blow it away. Were it not for the invention of tarred building-paper, the flimsy walls would not keep out the wind and snow. With this paper the walls are sheathed under the weatherboards. The barn is often a nondescript affair of sod walls and straw roof. Lumber is much too dear to be used for dooryard fences, and there is no inclosure about the house. A barbed-wire fence surrounds the barnyard. Rarely are there any trees for on the prairies trees grow very slowly, and must be nursed with care to get a start. There is a saying that you must first get the Indian out of the soil before a tree will grow at all; which means that some savage quality must be taken from the ground by cultivation.

In this cramped abode, from the windows of which there is nothing more cheerful in sight than the distant houses of other settlers, just as ugly and lonely, and stacks of straw and unthreshed grain, the farmer's family must live. In the summer there is a school for the children, one, two, or three miles away; but in the winter the distances across the snow-covered plains are too great for them to travel in severe weather; the schoolhouse is closed, and there is nothing for them to do but to house themselves and long for spring. Each family must live mainly to itself, and life, shut up in the little wooden farmhouses, cannot well be very cheerful. A drive to the nearest town is almost the only diversion. There the farmers and their wives gather in the stores and manage to enjoy a little sociability The big coal stove gives out a grateful warmth, and there is a pleasant odor of dried codfish, groceries, and ready-made clothing. The women look at the display of thick cloths and garments, and wish the crop had been better, so that they could buy some of the things of which they are badly in need. The men smoke corncob pipes and talk politics. It is a cold drive home across the wind-swept prairies, but at least they have had a glimpse of a little broader and more comfortable life than that of the isolated farm.

There are few social events in the life of these prairie farmers to enliven the monotony of the long winter evenings; no singing schools, spelling-schools, debating clubs, or church gatherings.

Neighborly calls are infrequent, because of the long distances which separate the farmhouses, and because too, of the lack of homogeneity of the people. They have no common past to talk about. They were strangers to one another when they arrived in this new land, and their work and ways have not thrown them much together. Often the strangeness is intensified by the differences of national origin. There are Swedes, Norwegians, Germans, French Canadians, and perhaps even such peculiar people as Finns and Icelanders, among the settlers, and the Americans come from many different States. It is hard to establish any social bond in such a mixed population, yet one and all need social intercourse, as the thing most essential to pleasant living, after food, fuel, shelter, and clothing. An alarming amount of insanity occurs in the new prairie States among farmers and their wives. In proportion to their numbers, the Scandinavian settlers furnish the largest contingent to the asylums. The reason is not far to seek. These people came from cheery little farm villages. Life in the fatherland was hard and toilsome, but it was not lonesome. Think for a moment how great the change must be from the white-walled, red-roofed village of a Norway fiord, with its church and schoolhouse, its fishing-boats on the blue inlet, and its green mountain walls towering aloft to snow fields, to an isolated cabin on a Dakota prairie, and say if it is any wonder that so many Scandinavians lose their mental balance.

[From E. V. Smalley, "The Isolation of Life on Prairie Farms," *Atlantic Monthly,* 72 (1893): 378–83.]

Document 3. Wheat Farming in Iowa

Herbert Quick remembers the economic trials his family experienced as wheat farmers in Iowa.

We grew wonderful wheat at first; the only problem was to get it to market and to live on the proceeds when it was sold. My father hauled his wheat from the Iowa River to Waterloo, and even to Iowa City, when it was the railhead for our part of the country; hauled it slowly over mere trails across the prairie. It took him three days to market a load of wheat in Waterloo. . . .

But the worst, however, was yet to come. A harvest came when we found that something was wrong with the wheat. No longer did the stalks stand clean and green as of old until they went golden in the sun. The broad green blades were spotted red and black with rust. Still it grew tall and rank; but as it matured it showed signs of disease. The heads did not fill well. Some blight was at work on it. However, we thought next year all would be well again. And when it grew worse year by year, it became a blight not only on the life of the grain but on human life as well. Wheat was almost our sole cash crop. If it failed, what should we do? And it was failing!

We were incurring, of course, the penalty for a one-crop system. We ought to have known that it was inevitable. . . .

This . . . gave me my first contact with the phenomenon which puzzles so many city people. If the farmers are losing money on a certain crop, why in the world don't they change to something else? It is not so easy to change as the city man may think. The wheat growers of the Central States at the time of this writing have been losing money on their wheat for years; but if they endeavor to change, they are confronted by a great problem. Such a change means the adoption of an entirely new rotation of crops. They have for years used a three- or four-year rotation—wheat, then corn, then clover. The sowing of the wheat gives them the chance to put in their fertilizer. They are used to this system. Any change from it involves the risking of a new crop on which losses are also probable. . . .

The fields of grain had always been a delight to me. . . . But now all the poetry went out of it. There was no joy for the soul of the boy who was steeped in such poetry as he could stumble upon, in these grainfields threatened by grasshoppers, eaten by chinchbugs, blackened with molds and rusts, their blades specked as with the shed blood of the husbandman, their gold dulled by disease, their straw crinkling down in dead brittleness instead of rising and falling and swaying with the beautiful resiliency of health and abundance. . . .

All this time, while we were playing the role of the tortured victims in the tragedy of the wheat, we were feeling our way toward some way out. We knew that our fields would grow great crops of maize—it was a good corn country. But if there was more than one person who grew and fed cattle for the market there I did not know of it. The average small farmer grew into the combination of hogs and corn. Gradually we changed over from wheat farming to big cornfields and populous hog lots. And then the price of both corn and pork went down, down, down, until corn sold for less than ten cents a bushel in our depreciated money and hogs for even less than three cents a pound. We had not found out about the balanced ration and the hog's need of pasture; and after a few generations of a diet of corn, the swine lost vitality and the crop of young pigs failed save where there was milk for them. The villain of misfortune still pursued us. . . .

Gradually we worked out a better *modus vivendi*—worked it out in a welter of debt and a depression which has characterized the rural mind to this day. Corn and hogs came to pay us as little as had wheat; yet for a while they were our only recourse, for the soil refused to grow wheat. For a long time there was plenty of open prairie on which cattle could be grazed freely. . . . Then the expanding acres of wheat land cut us off from any extended range of free grass. We had no fencing until barbed wire came in. So our cows were picketed on the prairie, led to water and cared for much as the Danes handle their cows now.

In spite of these difficulties, however, it gradually dawned upon us that by the sale of butter we were getting a little money from time to time. And though eggs were sometimes as low as eight cents a dozen, they brought in some funds. The skim milk restored our hogs to health. Without conscious planning, we were entering the business of mixed farming. My mother's butter was famed in all the nearby villages. In view of all the pains she took with it, it should have been; for she met the hot weather of our Iowa summers by hanging both cream and butter down the well where it was cool. Finally a creamery was started in Holland, a small town near us; and by this time we had a nice little herd of cows. A tank was made where water could be pumped through it and in this we set our cans of milk; and the cream hauler of the creamery came, skimmed off the cream, gave us tickets for it and hauled it away, thus giving us the cash when we went to town and saving the women the work of making the butter. It was the first contact of the factory system with the Iowa farm.

All this made life easier both as to labor and money. But it was not our only amelioration. We began to have a better food supply. . . . our strawberries, raspberries, grapes, gooseberries, currants and cherries yielded abundantly. I had a patch of raspberries which I pruned and tended on a system of my own which gave us all we could consume and furnished dividends for our friends. In place of the old regimen of dried fruits and just dry groceries, we were surfeited on jams, jellies, preserves and other delicious viands; and with our supply of milk and cream, found the pioneer epoch definitely past so far as the larder was concerned. The prairie had been tamed. Iowa had been civilized. Our eighty-acre farm was furnishing us a real living for the first time. . . .

The farmer is often accused by the city dweller of being a confirmed calamity howler. He is. He is such because almost every calamity which comes on the land hits him sooner or later. Whenever any other industry shifts from under an economic change it shifts it in part upon the farmer, and the farmer is unable to shift it in his turn; while most other shiftees can, by adding to prices or wages, get from under the load. The farmer is so placed that there is nothing beyond him but the wall. He is crushed against it. There is nothing under him but the earth. He is pressed into it. He is the end of the line in the economic game of crack the whip, and he is cracked off.

[From Herbert Quick, *One Man's Life* (Indianapolis, Ind., 1925), pp. 207–9, 212–17.]

Questions for Reflection

How did the government promote settlement of the public lands in the West? Do you think that farming in the Midwest and West was as attractive as many of the settlers probably expected? What problems did the new farmers experience? Were the advantages, which Smalley and Quick may not mention, that compensated for the difficulties? How and why has the life of farmers changed in the last hundred years?

ANSWERS TO MULTIPLE-CHOICE AND TRUE-FALSE QUESTIONS AND MAP EXERCISES

Multiple-Choice Questions

1-A, 2-D, 3-D, 4-C, 5-C, 6-B, 7-A, 8-B

Map Exercise

A-8, B-4, C-1, D-2, E-9, F-7, G-12, H-5, I-14, J-13

True-False Questions

1-T, 2-F, 3-T, 4-F, 5-F, 6-T, 7-T, 8-T

20 ∾

BIG BUSINESS AND ORGANIZED LABOR

CHAPTER OBJECTIVES

After you complete the reading and study of this chapter, you should be able to:

1. Describe the economic impact of the Civil War.
2. Delineate the important factors in the growth of the economy in the late nineteenth century.
3. Describe the role of the major entrepreneurs like Rockefeller, Carnegie, and Morgan.
4. Account for the limited growth of unions in this period, and the success of the Knights of Labor and the American Federation of Labor.
5. Discuss the major labor confrontations in the period.
6. Explain the limited appeal of socialism for American labor.

CHAPTER OUTLINE

I. Post–Civil War economy
   A. General characteristics
      1. Growth
      2. Increasingly urban-industrial society
      3. Corporate dominance
      4. Tensions and dissent
   B. Railroad building
      1. Early federal aid to the railroads
      2. The transcontinental plan
         a. Central Pacific
         b. Union Pacific
         c. Chinese labor
      3. Other transcontinentals
      4. Financing the railroads
         a. Crédit-Mobilier fraud
         b. Government returns from the financial assistance given
      5. Jay Gould's work
      6. Cornelius Vanderbilt
   C. New products and inventions
      1. Refrigerated railway car
      2. Flour milling
      3. Paper making
      4. Other improvements and innovations
      5. Development of the telephone
      6. Edison's work with electricity
   D. Entrepreneurs of the era
      1. Rockefeller and the oil industry
         a. Background
         b. Concentration on refining and transportation
         c. Development of the trust

      d. Evolution of the holding
         company
   2. Andrew Carnegie and the Gospel
     of Wealth
      a. Background
      b. Concentration on steel
      c. Philosophy for big business
   3. J. P. Morgan and investment
     banking
      a. Background
      b. Concentration on railroad
         financing
      c. Control of organizations
      d. Consolidation of the steel
         industry
   4. Sears and Roebuck and retailing
      a. Montgomery Ward
      b. Retail by mail
      c. Creation of national market

II. Developments in labor
  A. Wealth and income
    1. Standard of living
    2. Disparities between rich and poor
    3. Degree of social mobility
    4. Increase in manufacturing wages
  B. Lives of workers
    1. Living and working conditions
    2. Bureaucracy's impersonal control
  C. Violence in union activity
    1. The Molly Maguires
    2. The railroad strike of 1877

    3. "Sand Lot" incident
  D. Efforts at union building
    1. National Labor Union
    2. Knights of Labor
      a. Early development
      b. Emphasis on the union
      c. Role of Terrence Powderly
      d. Victories of the Knights
      e. Haymarket Affair
      f. Lasting influence of the
         Knights of Labor
    3. American Federation of Labor
      a. Development of craft unions
      b. Role of Samuel Gompers
      c. Focus on the eight-hour day
      d. Growth of the union
  E. Violence in the 1890s
    1. Homestead Strike, 1892
    2. Pullman Strike, 1894
      a. Causes
      b. Role of the government
      c. Impact on Eugene V. Debs
  F. Socialism and American labor
    1. Daniel DeLeon and Eugene Debs
    2. Social Democratic party
      a. Early work
      b. Height of influence
    3. Rise of the IWW
      a. Sources of strength
      b. Revolutionary goals
      c. Causes for decline

KEY ITEMS OF CHRONOLOGY

National Labor Union formed	1866
Completion of the first transcontinental railroad	1869
Standard Oil of Ohio incorporated	1870
Telephone patented	1876
Incandescent light bulb invented	1879
Terrence Powderly became president of the Knights of Labor	1879
First electric current supplied to 85 customers in New York City	1882
Creation of the Standard Oil Trust	1882
Haymarket Affair	1886
Founding of the American Federation of Labor	1886

Pullman Strike	1894
U.S. Steel Corporation formed	1901
IWW founded	1905

TERMS TO MASTER

Listed below are some important terms or people with which you should be familiar after you complete the study of this chapter. Explain the significance of each name or term.

1. transcontinental railroads
2. Crédit-Mobilier
3. Jay Gould
4. Cornelius Vanderbilt
5. Alexander Graham Bell
6. Thomas Alva Edison
7. "Battle of the Currents"
8. John D. Rockefeller
9. Gospel of Wealth
10. Horatio Alger
11. J. Pierpont Morgan
12. holding company
13. social mobility
14. vertical integration
15. industrial and craft unions
16. Knights of Labor
17. American Federation of Labor
18. Haymarket Affair
19. anarchism
20. Samuel Gompers
21. Pullman Strike
22. Eugene V. Debs
23. Wobblies

VOCABULARY BUILDING

Listed below are some words or phrases used in this chapter. Look up each word in your dictionary unless the meaning is given here.

1. trebled
2. trunk
3. judicious
4. pristine
5. incandescent
6. trust

7. clout
8. rationale
9. benefactors
10. detriment
11. cornucopia
12. wholesale
13. harbor (v.)
14. animosity
15. impromptu
16. plunder
17. carnage
18. sporadic
19. reprieve
20. tedium

EXERCISES FOR UNDERSTANDING

When you have completed reading the chapter, answer each of the following questions. If you have difficulty, go back and reread the section of the chapter related to the question.

Multiple-Choice Questions

Select the letter of the response that best completes the statement.

1. The first transcontinental railroad was built by
   A. the federal government.
   B. private companies granted a monopoly by the government.
   C. private companies with no federal assistance.
   D. private companies with government subsidies.
2. John D. Rockefeller stands out among business leaders because of his
   A. innovative organization called vertical integration.
   B. Gospel of Wealth philosophy.
   C. cooperation with labor unions.

D. dominance of investment banking.
3. Consolidation of the steel industry in the U.S. Steel Corporation was the achievement of
   A. Cornelius Vanderbilt.
   B. Andrew Carnegie.
   C. J. P. Morgan.
   D. John D. Rockefeller.
4. The "Battle of the Currents" involved
   A. the transcontinental railroads.
   B. Thomas Edison and George Westinghouse.
   C. Alexander Graham Bell.
   D. Jay Gould and Cornelius Vanderbilt.
5. Sears, Roebuck and Company became the nation's largest retailer by
   A. creating a national market.
   B. selling directly to the consumer at low prices.
   C. distributing goods through the mails.
   D. all of the above
6. The social costs of industrialization included
   A. closer relationships between workers and factory owners.
   B. numerous job-related injuries and deaths.
   C. rising wages for workers.
   D. healthier working conditions for most workers.
7. The Knights of Labor
   A. organized only skilled workers.
   B. shunned politics and strikes.
   C. was damaged by the Haymarket affair.
   D. all the above
8. American workers tended to reject unions because
   A. they believed they would only be workers for a short time until they could own their own farms or move up otherwise.
   B. they were so strongly committed to a system of equality and uniform wages for all.

C. they did not like the association with immigrants in unions.
D. they thought all unions were corrupt.

True-False Questions

Indicate whether each statement is true or false.

1. The first big business with large-scale bureaucracies was in the steel industry.
2. By 1900, seven railroad groups controlled two-thirds of the nation's railroad mileage.
3. Andrew Carnegie wrote "The Gospel of Wealth."
4. The first major interstate labor strike was the Homestead Strike in 1894.
5. In 1900 the average worker in manufacturing worked only about 45 hours per week.
6. Terence V. Powderly led the Knights of Labor.
7. Samuel Gompers was an anarchist labor leader.
8. The Pullman Strike disrupted rail traffic.

Essay Questions

1. List and explain the factors that promoted the growth of industry in the United States in the late nineteenth century.
2. Compare and contrast the achievements of the American economy of Rockefeller, Carnegie, Morgan, and Sears as entrepreneurs.
3. Why was the Pullman Strike of 1894 important?
4. How did the methods and goals of the Knights of Labor differ from those of the American Federation of Labor?
5. Why did socialism, anarchism, and forms of radicalism appeal to some but not all American workers?

DOCUMENTS

Document 1. John D. Rockefeller on Industrial Combinations

As the textbook describes, Rockefeller's Standard Oil dominated the oil-refining business. The following defense of big business is part of Rockefeller's written responses in 1900 to questions asked by congressional representatives about trusts and industrial combinations.

10. Q. What are, in your judgment, the chief advantages from industrial combinations—(a) financially to stockholders; (b) to the public?—A. All the advantages which can be derived from a cooperation of persons and aggregation of capital. Much that one man can not do alone two can do together, and once admit the fact that cooperation, or, what is the same thing, combination, is necessary on a small scale, the limit depends solely upon the necessities of business. Two persons in partnership may be a sufficiently large combination for a small business, but if the business grows or can be made to grow, more persons and more capital must be taken in. The business may grow so large that a partnership ceases to be a proper instrumentality for its purposes, and then a corporation becomes a necessity. In most countries, as in England, this form of industrial combination is sufficient for a business coextensive with the parent country, but it is not so in this country. Our Federal form of government, making every corporation created by a State foreign to every other State, renders it necessary for persons doing business through corporate agency to organize corporations in some or many of the different States in which their business is located. Instead of doing business through the agency of one corporation they must do business through the agencies of several corporations. If the business is extended to foreign countries, and Americans are not to-day satisfied with home markets alone, it will be found helpful and possibly necessary to organize corporations in such countries, for Europeans are prejudiced against foreign corporations as are the people of many of our States. These different corporations thus become cooperating agencies in the same business and are held together by common ownership of their stocks.

It is too late to argue about advantages of industrial combinations. They are a necessity. And if Americans are to have the privilege of extending their business in all the States of the Union, and into foreign countries as well, they are a necessity on a large scale, and require the agency of more than one corporation. Their chief advantages are:

(1) Command of necessary capital.

(2) Extension of limits of business.

(3) Increase of number of persons interested in the business.

(4) Economy in the business.

(5) Improvements and economies which are derived from knowledge of many interested persons of wide experience.

(6) Power to give the public improved products at less prices and still make a profit for stockholders.

(7) Permanent work and good wages for laborers.

I speak from my experience in the business with which I have been intimately connected for about 40 years.

11. Q. What are the chief disadvantages or dangers to the public arising from them?—A. The dangers are that the power conferred by combination may be abused; that combinations may be formed for speculation in stocks rather than for conducting business, and that for this purpose prices may be temporarily raised instead of being lowered. These abuses are possible to a greater or less extent in all combinations, large or small, but this fact is no more of an argument against combinations than the fact that steam may explode is an argument against steam. Steam is necessary and can be made comparatively safe. Combination is necessary and its abuses can be minimized; otherwise our legislators must acknowledge their incapacity to deal with the most important instrument of industry. Hitherto most legislative attempts have been an effort not to control but to destroy; hence their futility.

12. Q. What legislation, if any, would you suggest regarding industrial combinations?—A. First. Federal legislation under which corporations may be created and regulated, if that be possible. Second. In lieu thereof, State legislation as nearly uniform as possible encouraging combinations of persons and capital for the purpose of carrying on industries, but permitting State supervision, not of a character to hamper industries, but sufficient to prevent frauds upon the public.

[From U. S. Industrial Commission, *Preliminary Report on Trusts and Combinations,* 56th Cong., 1st sess. (30 Dec. 1899) Document No. 476, Part 1, pp. 796–97.]

Document 2. Henry D. Lloyd on the Lords of Industry

Not everyone agreed with Rockefeller's defense of big business. Below is an excerpt from a criticism of large corporations and their effects on American life by a journalist and writer, Henry D. Lloyd.

Last July Messrs. Vanderbilt, Sloan, and one or two others out of several hundred owners of coal lands and coal railroads, met in the pleasant shadows of Saratoga to make "a binding arrangement for the control of the coal trade." "Binding arrangement" the sensitive coal presidents say they prefer to the word "combination." The gratuitous warmth of summer suggested to these men the need the public would have of artificial heat, at artificial prices, the coming winter. It was agreed to fix prices, and to prevent the production of too much of the raw material of warmth, by suspensions of mining. In anticipation of the arrival of the cold wave from Manitoba, a cold wave was sent out all over the United States, from their parlors in New York, in an order for half-time work by the miners during the first three months of this year, and for an increase of prices. These are the means this combination uses to keep down wages—the price of men, and keep up the price of coal—the wages of capital. Prices of coal in the West are fixed by the Western Anthracite Coal Association, controlled entirely by the large railroads and mine-owners of Pennsylvania. This association regulates the price west of Buffalo and Pittsburgh and in Canada. Our annual consumption of anthracite is now between 31,000,000 and 32,000,000 tons. The West takes between 5,000,000 and 6,000,000 tons. The companies which compose the combination mine, transport, and sell their own coal. They are obliterating other mine-owners and the retailer. The Chicago and New York dealer has almost nothing to say about what he shall pay or what he shall charge, or what his profits shall be. The great companies do not let the little men make too much. Year by year the coal retailers are sinking into the status of mere agents of the combination, with as little freedom as the consumer.

The coal combination was . . . investigated by the New York legislature in 1878, after the combination had raised the prices of coal in New York to double what they had been. The legislature found that private mine-operators who were not burdened like the great companies with extravagant and often corrupt purchases of coal lands, heavily watered stock, and disadvantageous contracts, forced on them by interested directors, and who have only to pay the actual cost of producing the coal, "can afford to sell at a much less price than the railroad coal-producing companies, and would do so if they could get transportation from the mines to the market." This is denied them by the great companies. "The private operators," says the report, "either find themselves entirely excluded from the benefits of transportation by reason of the high freights, or find it for their interest to make contracts with the railroads, by which they will not sell to others, and so the railroads have and will keep the control of the supply of the private operators." To those who will not make such contracts, rates are fixed excluding them from the market, with the result, usually, of forcing them to sell their property to the lords of the pool. "The combination," the committee declared, "can limit the supply, and thereby create such a demand and price as they may deem advisable." The committee found that coal could be laid down on the dock in New York, after paying all charges, for an average of $3.20 a ton. It was at that time retailing in the city for $4.90 to $5.25 a ton. "The purposes of the combination are solely to advance the price of coal, and it has been successful to the amount of seventy-five cents to one dollar a ton. Its further advance is only a question whether the combination can continue to repress the production." An advance of only twenty five cents a ton would on 32,000,000 tons be $8,000,000 a year, which is not a bad thing—for the combination. [If] any individual or corporate producer, show[s] any backwardness about accepting the invitation to join "the pool," they are whipped in with all the competitive weapons at command, from assault and battery to boycotting and conspiracy. The private wars that are ravaging our world of trade give small men their choice between extermination and vassalage. Combine or die! Competitors swear themselves on the Bible into accomplices, and free and equal citizens abandon their business privacy to pool commissioners vested with absolute power, but subject to human frailties. Commerce is learning the delights of universal suffrage, and in scores of trades supply and demand are adjusted by a majority vote. In a society which has the wherewithal to cover, fatten and cheer every one, Lords of Industry are acquiring the power to pool the profits of scarcity and to decree famine. They cannot stop the brook that runs the mill, but they can chain the wheel; they cannot hide the coal mine, but they can close the shaft three days every week. To keep up gold-digging rates of dividends, they declare war against plenty. On all that keeps him alive the workman must pay them their prices, while they lock him out of the mill in which alone his labor can be made to fetch the price of life. Only society can compel a social use of its resources; the man is for himself.

[From Henry D. Lloyd, "Lords of Industry," *North American Review* 138 (June 1894): 535–53.]

Questions for Reflection

Rockefeller and Lloyd take opposing views of the advantages and disadvantages of big business. How do their positions reflect different sets of values, different beliefs about what is important?

How would Lloyd respond to Rockfeller's specific argument for the advantages of industrial combinations? On the other hand, how would Rockefeller rebut Lloyd's claims about the detrimental effects of trusts?

Are their positions still relevant to today's debates about the U.S. economy? Has either position become dominant in the twentieth century?

ANSWERS TO MULTIPLE-CHOICE AND TRUE-FALSE QUESTIONS

Multiple-Choice Questions

1-D, 2-A, 3-C, 4-B, 5-D, 6-B, 7-C, 8-A

True-False Questions

1-F, 2-T, 3-T, 4-F, 5-F, 6-T, 7-F, 8-T

21 ∞

THE EMERGENCE OF URBAN AMERICA

CHAPTER OBJECTIVES

After you complete the reading and study of this chapter, you should be able to:

1. Discuss the important intellectual trends in the period 1877–1890.
2. Describe city growth in the late nineteenth century.
3. Account for the new immigration and the reaction that it engendered.
4. Trace major developments in higher education after the Civil War.
5. Discuss the development of an urban popular culture.
6. Explain the concepts of Social Darwinism and Reform Darwinism.
7. Describe the local-color, realist, and naturalist movements in literature.
8. Explain the social gospel and describe its manifestations.

CHAPTER OUTLINE

I. Urbanization
   A. In westward movement
   B. Influence of industry and transportation
   C. Vertical growth and elevators
   D. Horizontal growth
      1. Electric streetcars
      2. Subways
      3. Bridges
   E. Urban politics
      1. Political machines
      2. Services
      3. Graft
II. Immigration
   A. Sources of immigration
      1. Rural America
      2. Abroad
   B. Reasons for immigration to the United States
      1. Pull factors
      2. Push factors
   C. 1880s change in immigration
   D. Reception of immigrants
      1. Castle Garden
      2. Statue of Liberty
      3. Ellis Island
   E. Immigrant life
      1. Jobs
      2. Ethnic neighborhoods
      3. Tenement housing
   F. Nativist responses
      1. Objections to new immigrants
      2. American Protective Association
   G. Efforts at immigration restriction
III. Education
   A. Growth of public schooling

B. Vocational education
   1. Manual training in high schools
   2. Morrill Act and land-grant colleges
C. Higher education
   1. Increase in college population
   2. Growth of elective system
   3. More opportunities for women
   4. Graduate education
      a. German model
      b. Johns Hopkins University

IV. Popular culture
  A. Distinctive urban culture
    1. Middle-class and white
    2. Affluent leisure
  B. Wild West shows
  C. Vaudeville
  D. Outdoor recreation
    1. Parks
    2. Tennis
    3. Bicycling
  E. Ethnic and working-class recreation
  F. Spectator sports
    1. Urban location
    2. Football
    3. Basketball
    4. Baseball

V. Theories of society
  A. Darwinism and its impact
    1. Social Darwinism
      a. Herbert Spencer
      b. William Graham Sumner
    2. Lester Frank Ward and Reform Darwinism
  B. Effects of Darwinism in academia
    1. Scientific history
    2. Emergence of sociology
    3. Changes in economics
    4. Pragmatism
      a. William James
      b. John Dewey and instrumentalism
  C. Literature
    1. Local colorists
      a. Bret Harte
      b. Hamlin Garlin
      c. George Washington Cable
      d. Joel Chandler Harris
      e. Thomas Nelson Page

    2. Mark Twain
    3. William Dean Howells
    4. Henry James
    5. Literary Naturalism
      a. Frank Norris
      b. Stephen Crane
      c. Jack London
      d. Theodore Dreiser
  D. Social Criticism
    1. Henry George and the single tax
    2. Henry Demarest Lloyd and cooperation
    3. Thorstein Veblen and conspicuous consumption
    4. Edward Bellamy and the utopian novel

VI. The religious response: social gospel
  A. Abandonment of inner-city churches
  B. Development of the institutional church
    1. YMCA and the Salvation Army
    2. Institutional churches
  C. Washington Gladden
  D. Walter Rauschenbusch
  E. Catholic responses to modernity
    1. *Syllabus of Errors*
    2. *Rerum Novarum*

VII. Early efforts at urban reform
  A. The settlement house movement
    1. Nature of settlement houses
    2. Social control
  B. Women's jobs and rights
    1. Growth of the female labor force
    2. Women's suffrage
      a. Conflicts in the movement
      b. Gains in the states
    3. Other women's efforts
  C. Efforts to regulate business
    1. State regulatory commissions
    2. Development of substantive due process
    3. Supreme Court acceptance of the view
      a. In cases against regulatory units
      b. In cases against labor
    4. The status of laissez-faire at the end of the century

KEY ITEMS OF CHRONOLOGY

Morrill Act	1862
First professional baseball team	1869
Start of *Popular Science Monthly*	1872
Founding of Johns Hopkins University	1876
Henry George's *Progress and Poverty*	1879
Chinese Exclusion Act	1882
Lester Ward's *Dynamic Sociology*	1883
Mark Twain's *Huckleberry Finn*	1883
Santa Clara County v. *Southern Pacific Railroad Co.*	1886
First electric elevator	1889
Electric streetcar systems in cities	1890s
Steven Crane's *Maggie: A Girl of the Streets*	1893
Smith v. *Ames*	1898
Veblen's *The Theory of the Leisure Class*	1899
National College Athletics Association formed	1910

TERMS TO MASTER

Listed below are some important terms or people with which you should be familiar after you complete the study of this chapter. Explain the significance of each name or term.

1. Louis Sullivan
2. "streetcar suburbs"
3. dumbbell tenements
4. the "new" immigration
5. American Protective Association
6. Morrill Act of 1862
7. Johns Hopkins University
8. professionalism
9. popular culture
10. "Buffalo Bill" Cody
11. vaudeville
12. Frederick Law Olmstead
13. James Naismith
14. Social Darwinism
15. William Graham Sumner
16. Lester Frank Ward
17. pragmatism
18. John Dewey
19. local-color movement
20. Henry James
21. naturalism
22. Henry George
23. Edward Bellamy
24. Social Gospel
25. settlement houses
26. Susan B. Anthony
27. due process

VOCABULARY BUILDING

Listed below are some words or phrases used in this chapter. Look up each word in your dictionary unless the meaning is given here.

1. epitomize
2. proletariat
3. sinister
4. medley
5. lien
6. fraught
7. debilitating
8. remit
9. poignant
10. nondescript
11. discretionary
12. exemplar
13. scoff
14. licentious

15. odium
16. regatta
17. expatriate
18. panacea
19. spate
20. blandishment

EXERCISES FOR UNDERSTANDING

When you have completed the reading of the chapter, answer each of the following questions. If you have difficulty, go back and reread the section of the chapter related to the question.

Multiple-Choice Questions

Select the letter of the response that best completes the statement.

1. Urban political machines did *not*
   A. help immigrants cope with city life.
   B. operate honestly.
   C. provide needed city services.
   D. aid the poor and needy.
2. In the 1880s, the source of foreign immigration to the United States shifted from
   A. Europe to Asia and Africa.
   B. northeastern Europe to Latin America.
   C. Canada and the British Empire to Asia.
   D. northwestern Europe to southeastern Europe.
3. The most democratic sport in America was
   A. lawn tennis.
   B. baseball.
   C. football.
   D. croquet.
4. In the 1890s Dr. James Naismith
   A. advocated the social gospel movement.
   B. developed the Johns Hopkins University graduate program on the German model.
   C. invented basketball.
   D. was a major naturalist writer.
5. Lester Frank Ward stressed
   A. the power of folkways in determining social conditions.
   B. the potential of human intelligence in

planning change.
   C. the importance of heredity in human progress.
   D. the similarity of social evolution and biological evolution.
6. Henry James was
   A. the author of *Pragmatism.*
   B. responsible for reviving the Olympics.
   C. leading Protestant minister in the late nineteenth century.
   D. the father of the psychological novel.
7. The social gospel of Washington Gladden encouraged
   A. assistance to middle-class Christians.
   B. a focus on personal sins and saving souls.
   C. community services and helping the poor.
   D. the laissez-faire business philosophy.
8. Women's suffrage gained important victories in the late 1800s
   A. in the urban Northeast.
   B. among white southerners.
   C. in the West.
   D. everywhere with the Nineteenth Amendment.

True-False Questions

Indicate whether each statement is true or false.

1. In 1890 eighty percent of New Yorkers were foreign born.
2. Immigrants to the United States included Knute Rockne, Al Jolson, and Felix Frankfurter.
3. The modern American university was based on a German model.
4. Social Darwinism supported government regulation of business.
5. Buffalo Bill Cody was a major vaudeville attraction.
6. William Graham Sumner wrote *The Rise of Silas Lapham.*
7. Women's suffrage was achieved first in the urban states of the Northwest.
8. In the last two decades of the nineteenth century, laissez-faire values became stronger and more influential.

Essay Questions

1. Who peopled the growing U.S. cities and why did they move there?
2. What were the new problems found in urban areas, and how did politicians and reformers try to deal with them?
3. What were the significant elements of the distinctive urban culture that developed in the late nineteenth century?

4. How did Darwinism, pragmatism, and literary naturalism resemble each other and how did they differ?
5. What was the settlement-house movement and what were its effects?
6. How did the U.S. Supreme Court block the regulation of business in the 1880s and 1890s?

DOCUMENT

Document 1. The Working Girls of Boston

In 1884 the Massachusetts Bureau of Statistics of Labor reported the findings of a study of more than one thousand young women working in Boston.

Sanitary Surroundings at Home

. . . In numerous cases . . . girls were found living for the sake of economy in very limited quarters, which could not be conducive to good sanitary conditions. In some instances, girls were found living in small attic rooms, lighted and ventilated by the skylight only; the furnishings generally consisted of a small single bed, bureau and chair, with no wardrobe, except one curtained in the corner. In other cases, girls were forced to content themselves with small side rooms without a chance for a fire, which in some cases was sadly needed. One girl had a small side room in the third story of a respectable house, but said she could not expect much more at the present cost of living; still others were reported as living together with other members of the family in a tenement of one back room and side bedroom; another, as one of 18 families in a single building with hardly the necessary articles of furniture; another, occupying the third story of a house which seemed the poorest on the street. On the other hand, girls were found living in large rooms, quite well and sometimes handsomely furnished, in some instances with side rooms adjoining, not perhaps because they could really afford such quarters, but because they preferred to economize in other ways, in order to have some of the comforts, in look at least, of home.

In a few cases where girls reported their health as being poor, or not good, they also complained of the poor board provided, as well as the unpleasant surroundings at home; one girl made the statement that her home was pleasant and healthy, but to the agent of the bureau the reverse seemed to be the case, for the hall was dirty, the floor covered with a worn-out rag carpet while the air was filled with disagreeable odors; the girl appeared to be in poor health, untidily dressed, and dirty. Another was found living in the upper story of a cheap tenement house, directly in the rear of a kerosene factory having a tall chimney that constantly puffed out thick black smoke, which together with the offensive smell of the kerosene, forced the occupants always to keep the kitchen windows closed. In another case, one of the girls said that she spent all her spare time and Sundays with her sister in another part of the city, as her home was very unpleasant and uncomfortable; she also said the Board of Health had visited the house last year and recommended many alterations, but she did not know whether they were attended to or not. Another girl was found living in four small rooms as one of a family of 12, in a house located very near a stable and having bad drainage. One other girl complained of the odor from the watercloset in the halls, and said it was anything but agreeable.

In a house where a considerable number of girls are cared for, it was found that there was no elevator in the building, and some of the girls were obliged to go up five flights of stairs to reach their rooms, two or three girls being placed in each room; the upper story of the building was without heat, and in winter was said to be like an ice house; radiators are placed at the ends of halls, and transoms open into the rooms, but these have no particular effect on the temperature of the rooms and there are no other ways of heating; extra charge is made for rooms heated directly by the register and even then such rooms are not always to be obtained, they being generally occupied, and there being but a few of them. . . .

Effect of Work on Health

Long hours, and being obliged to stand all day, are very generally advanced as the principal reasons for any lack or loss of health occasioned by the work of the girls. The nature of the work is mentioned as a cause for decline, which together with the other causes described will be found to be prevalent in all the various branches of their work.

Feather sorters, cotton sorters, and workers on any material which in its nature is apt to give off a "dust," complain of the disagreeable if not actually injurious effect on the health of persons so employed.

Taking the question by industries and occupations in detail, we find in "Personal Service," that the restaurant employees generally complain of long hours, no dinner hour to speak of, and the great strain upon them from being busy all day on their feet. They all complain of a low state of health, and are pretty much tired out on reaching home. . . .

In "Trade," a bookkeeper was found who had ruined her eyes, by bringing her books home nights and working until twelve and one o'clock. Among the saleswomen, "standing all day" is generally reported as being very trying on their health and strength. In one store, no stools are provided, the girls being obliged to go to one end of the store to sit down.

. . . A good many saleswomen consider their work very hard, and that it has a bad effect on their health; in one instance, a girl says she has paid out over $500 in doctor's bills during the past few years. In one store, it is very unsatisfactory in this respect; no talking is allowed, only half enough time is given for dinner, and being obliged to walk home at night, the girl is completely exhausted; on Sunday she brings dinner and supper. . . .

In bakeries the strain of long hours and standing is especially felt by the salesgirls, while in other branches of business the health of many girls is so poor as to necessitate long rests, one girl being out a year on this account. Another girl in poor health was obliged to leave her work, while one other reports that it is not possible for her to work the year round as she could not stand the strain, not being at all strong. A girl, who had worked in one place for three years, was obliged to leave on account of poor health, being completely run down from badly ventilated workrooms, and obliged to take an eight months' rest; she worked a week when not able, but left to save her life. She says she has to work almost to death to make fair compensation (now $12 per week).

Under "Manufactures," in *Bookbinderies* and in the manufacture of *Brushes,* girls complain of their health being run down on account of work, or from over-work. In *Boots and shoes,* the work is very hard, the girls being obliged to be on their feet all day, and in cases where they have to walk any great distance to their homes they become very tired at night.

In the manufacture of *Buttons,* the girls say the work is rather dangerous, as they are liable to get their fingers jammed under the punch, or caught in the die when it comes down to press the parts of the button together. A man (although not a surgeon) is provided to dress wounds three times for each individual without charge; afterwards, the person injured must pay all expenses. There are 35 machines in use, and accidents are of very frequent occurrence. . . .

In making *Paper boxes,* the girls are obliged to stand, a practice they think is very injurious. The coloring matter in materials used in the construction and covering of boxes is considered dangerous to health by some, one girl being at home sick three months from blood poisoning caused by work. . . .

In the *Clothing* business, the general testimony is that the work is very hard, and is the cause of a great deal of sickness among the working girls so employed. The tax on the strength is very great, and it would seem that unless a girl is strong and robust, the work soon proves too severe for her, and if followed thereafter results disastrously. The running of heavy sewing machines by foot power soon breaks down a girl's health, as several girls have testified. One girl says that steam was introduced six month's ago to her great satisfaction, as she thinks foot power machines too severe for female operators. The girls think all the machines should be run by steam.

Other girls object to standing so much, and say that being on their feet all day and then walking to their homes makes them very tired at night.

The effect of the work on the health of the working girls engaged in tailoring is very apparent from their testimony. A girl who used to bring her work home, says she overtaxed her strength and is now sick.

Others tell the same story, and say that overwork, and the desire to do more than strength would allow, has very seriously affected their health, in one case, the overstraining of the nerves causing deafness, while another girl says, "overwork, cold dinners, and constant application, has brought on chronic rheumatism." . . .

In one or two cases, the girls report that the sewing has affected the eyes, compelling the use of glasses at all times and blue glasses on the street.

Under *Food preparations,* a girl engaged in salt packing is troubled with asthma and bronchitis, she was told at the hospital that the salt would eat into her lungs, as they are diseased; she would leave, if she could find other work.

In the manufacture of confectionery, on account of hot temperatures of rooms, etc., the work is not considered healthy. Some of the girls say work is very severe, they being on their feet all day, while others are out sick, being run down from work.

In the cleaning and packing of fish, the girls say that the fishermen put cayenne pepper and saltpetre on the fish, and girls in handling get their hands and fingers blistered, and often the outside skin taken off; the effect being the same as though they were obliged to keep their hands in a strong caustic solution. One girl says she has tried rubber gloves, but without success. Another girl (a fish packer) says in consequence of the steam necessary to be used the atmosphere is very damp. She says other girls are obliged to stand in cold water all day, having their hands exposed to cold water, and when one was questioned as to what shop she worked in, she answered, "they're not shops, they're working stalls where we are." The same complaint as to standing all day is noticed in this branch of business.

In *Type foundries,* the workroom is always filled with a fine lead dust, caused by "rubbing"; in some shops, this is quite perceptible when standing at one end of the room. . . .

In *Straw goods,* the girls very generally speak of the unhealthy nature of their business. In working on dyed braids, especially green, there is according to the testimony of one girl, a very fine dust which produces a hacking which is almost constant, and to persons of consumptive tendencies, very injurious. Girls are advised by physicians in such cases to abandon the work. . . . Some throat or lung trouble is very prevalent among the girls working on straw, and the hacking cough peculiar to the business is well-nigh universal. A great many girls are said to die of consumption, while many are often subject to severe cases of sickness, the direct result of work. . . .

The individual testimony regarding shops and their surroundings, and the effect of work upon health, has been given, as nearly as possible, in the language of the person interviewed. This testimony is that of the few, the great majority being in good health and in good surrounding.

It is in evidence from other sources that in a few stores, and in some of considerable size, the water-closet accommodations are very deficient, in one instance 60 women being obliged to use one closet.

The evil effect of waiting for the use of a closet common to so large a number is apparent. Many of these women are constantly under the care of physicians for some disease growing out of the condition or things described. . . .

[From Carroll Wright, "The Working Girls of Boston," in the 15th *Annual Report of the Massachusetts Bureau of Statistics of Labor, for 1884,* reprint ed. (Boston, 1889), pp. 64–66, 69–75, as reprinted in Nancy F. Cott et al., eds., *Roots of Bitterness: Documents of the Social History of American Women* (Boston: Northeastern University Press, 1996), pp. 325-29.]

Questions for Reflection

What were the living and working conditions of the working girls? To what extent were they the results of industrialization and urbanization? What possible solutions to their problems existed? Do similar conditions exist today? If not, why not, and when did they cease to exist?

ANSWERS TO MULTIPLE-CHOICE AND TRUE-FALSE QUESTIONS

Multiple-Choice Questions

1-B, 2-D, 3-B, 4-C, 5-B, 6-D, 7-C, 8-C

True-False Questions

1-T, 2-T, 3-T, 4-F, 5-F, 6-F, 7-F, 8-F

22

GILDED-AGE POLITICS
AND AGRARIAN REVOLT

CHAPTER OBJECTIVES

After you complete the reading and study of this chapter, you should be able to:

1. Discuss the major features of politics in the late nineteenth century.
2. Describe the political alignments and issues in the "third political system."
3. Explain the major issues in the presidential elections of 1888, 1892, and 1896.
4. Account for the rise of the farmer protest movement of the 1890s.
5. Explain the impact of populism on the American scene.

CHAPTER OUTLINE

I. Nature of Gilded Age politics
  A. Locus of real power
  B. Mediocre men in public office .
  C. Political parties
    1. Evasive stands on most issues
    2. Some distinction on tariff issue
    3. Patronage important to each party
    4. Coalitions of diverse interests in each party
    5. Reasons for evasiveness of parties
        a. Fear of repetition of split of 1860
        b. Even division between parties in popular vote (1868–1912)
    6. Few decisive new programs
    7. Availability of candidates outweighed ability
    8. Close alliance of business and politics characterized the age
  D. "Third political system"
    1. Not in mold of self-interest and economic motivation
    2. Higher voter participation
    3. Public belief in the reality of the issues
    4. Importance of state and local politics
    5. Intense cultural conflicts
    6. Republican party characterized
    7. Democratic party characterized
    8. Resurgence of nativism
    9. Revival of prohibitionism

II. Hayes administration
  A. His background and upright character
  B. Republican party splits between Stalwarts and Half-Breeds
  C. Need for civil service reform
    1. Hayes's payment of political debts

CHAPTER TWENTY-TWO

2. Supporters of reform
D. Hayes's executive rules for merit appointments
E. Problems with the New York customs house
F. Hayes's limited version of government activism

III. Election of 1880
  A. Republican nomination
    1. Grant candidacy
    2. Garfield's nomination as a dark horse
  B. Democratic nomination of Winfield Scott Hancock
  C. Closest election results of the century

IV. The Garfield-Arthur administration
  A. Garfield's background
  B. His clash with Boss Platt over appointments
  C. His assassination
  D. Arthur's background
  E. His strong actions as president
    1. Prosecution of Star Route Frauds
    2. Veto of Rivers and Harbors Bill
    3. Veto of Chinese Exclusion Act
    4. Support of Pendleton Civil Service Act, 1883
    5. Support for tariff reduction
      a. Effects of treasury surplus
      b. Mongrel Tariff of 1883
  F. Scurrilous campaign of 1884
    1. Reasons Arthur was not a candidate
    2. Republican nomination of Blaine and Logan
      a. Blaine's background
      b. Effect of Mulligan letters
      c. Emergence of Mugwumps
    3. Democratic nomination of Cleveland
      a. Cleveland's political background
      b. His illegitimate child
      c. "Rum, Romanism, and Rebellion"
    4. Election results

V. Cleveland's presidency
  A. Cleveland's view of the role of government
  B. Actions on civil service
  C. Stand for conservation
  D. Stand against veterans' pensions
  E. Effort to return Confederate battle flags
  F. Effort for railroad legislation
  G. Stand for tariff reform
  H. Election of 1888
    1. Cleveland renominated
    2. Republican nomination of Benjamin Harrison
    3. Campaign focuses on the tariff
    4. Personal attacks
    5. Results

VI. Republican reform under Harrison
  A. Harrison's bland personality
  B. His appointments
  C. Republican control of Congress, 1889–1891
  D. Passage of the Sherman Anti-Trust Act, 1890
  E. Sherman Silver Purchase Act, 1890
  F. Effect of the McKinley Tariff, 1890
  G. Democratic congressional victories of 1890
    1. Ostensible reaction to heavy spending of Republicans
    2. Impact on the election of prohibition and social issues

VII. Problems of farmers
  A. Multiple farm interests
    1. Regions
    2. Size of farm
    3. Owners or tenants
  B. Worsening economic and social conditions
    1. Causes for declining agricultural prices
      a. Overproduction
      b. Worldwide competition
    2. Railroads as villains
    3. Effects of the tariff on farmers
    4. Problems of currency deflation

a. Decrease of currency in circulation
b. Impact of greenbacks
c. Reasons for the focus on free silver
5. Problems of geography and climate
6. Isolation of farmers
C. Patrons of Husbandry
1. Development of the Grange
2. Effects of Granger political activity
D. Rise of the Greenback party
E. Farmers' Alliances
1. Membership
2. Appeal of alliances
3. Alliance programs
4. Political activity
5. Colorful leaders
F. Formation of the Populist party

1. Development of the party
2. Platform stands
3. Presidential nominees
4. Victory of Cleveland in 1892

VIII. Depression of 1893
A. Nature of the depression
B. Reactions to the depression
C. Results of the 1894 elections

IX. Focus on silver
A. Causes and effects of the gold drain
B. Agitation for free silver
1. American Bimetallic League
2. *Coin's Financial School*
C. Effect on nominations of 1896
1. Republican actions
2. Democratic candidate
3. Populist position
D. Campaign of 1896 and its results
E. Postelection shift to gold

KEY ITEMS OF CHRONOLOGY

Patrons of Husbandry founded	1867
Munn v. *Illinois*	1877
Bland-Allison Act	1878
President James A. Garfield assassinated	1881
Pendleton Civil Service Act	1883
Mongrel Tariff Act	1883
Interstate Commerce Act	1887
Sherman Anti-Trust Act	1890
Sherman Silver Purchase Act	1890
McKinley Tariff Act	1890
Populist party founded	1892
Economic depression	1893
Cleveland administrations	1885–1889; 1893–1897
William Jennings Bryan's "Cross of Gold" speech	1896

TERMS TO MASTER

Listed below are some important terms or people with which you should be familiar after you complete the study of this chapter. Explain the significance of each name or term.

1. Stalwarts and Half-Breeds
2. Bland-Allison Act
3. Star Route Frauds
4. Pendleton Civil Service Act (1883)
5. Mongrel Tariff of 1883
6. James G. Blaine

7. Mugwumps
8. "bloody shirt"
9. *Wabash Railroad* v. *Illinois*
10. Sherman Anti-Trust Act
11. Sherman Silver Purchase Act
12. McKinley Tariff Act
13. greenbacks
14. "free and unlimited coinage of silver"
15. 16:1
16. Patrons of Husbandry
17. Farmers' Alliances
18. subtreasury plea
19. Populist party
20. Jacob S. Coxey
21. William Jennings Bryan

VOCABULARY BUILDING

Listed below are some words or phrases used in this chapter. Look up each word in your dictionary unless the meaning is given here.

1. humbuggery
2. heterogeneous
3. nativism
4. *de facto*
5. renounce
6. faction
7. pastel
8. mandate
9. stalwart
10. sop
11. scurrilous
12. integrity
13. festoon
14. insolent
15. dubious

EXERCISES FOR UNDERSTANDING

When you have completed reading the chapter, answer each of the following questions. If you have difficulty, go back and reread the section of the chapter related to the question.

Multiple-Choice Questions

Select the letter of the response that best completes the statement.

1. From the 1870s to the 1890s, the Republican Party generally
   A. agreed with the Democrats on tariff policy.
   B. supported a protective tariff.
   C. favored a low tariff.
   D. evaded the tariff issue altogether.
2. The Democratic party generally consisted of
   A. nativists, blacks, and Catholics.
   B. Catholics, reformers, and prohibitionists.
   C. moral reformers, Protestants, and political insiders.
   D. southern whites, immigrants, and political outsiders.
3. Passage of the Pendleton Civil Service Act was spurred in part by the
   A. assassination of James Garfield.
   B. compromise of 1877.
   C. panic of 1873.
   D. election of Grover Cleveland in 1884.
4. As president, Cleveland did *not*
   A. try to add pensions for Confederate veterans.
   B. restore to the public domain exploited public lands in the West.
   C. work to reduce the tariff.
   D. create an agency to regulate railroads and other interstate commerce.
5. In the 1870s middle-sized farmers
   A. feared inflation.
   B. wanted lower commodity prices and low tariffs.
   C. advocated the free coinage of silver.
   D. all the above
6. The basic problem of farmers in the late nineteenth century was
   A. the high rates charged by the railroads.
   B. the overproduction of agricultural products.
   C. inflation.
   D. the high prices for manufactured goods caused by high tariffs.

7. The Farmers' Alliance movement
   A. was a powerful national organization.
   B. stressed economic and political programs only.
   C. was succeeded by the Patrons of Husbandry.
   D. appealed to marginal farmers.
8. In 1896, William Jennings Bryan
   A. opposed repeal of the Sherman Silver Purchase Act.
   B. ran for president on the Republican ticket.
   C. carried the midwestern states from Ohio to Iowa.
   D. all the above

5. In 1887 the first regulatory agency, the Interstate Commerce Commission, was created.
6. The Populist party was an outgrowth of the Patrons of Husbandry.
7. In the 1870s the Grangers primarily sought inflation of the currency.
8. Silver coinage in the late nineteenth century caused deflation.

True-False Questions

Indicate whether each statement is true or false.

1. The Republican party clearly dominated American politics in the Gilded Age.
2. Party loyalty and voter turnout in the Gilded Age were primarily motivated by intense cultural conflicts among ethnic groups.
3. Roscoe Conkiling and the Stalwarts supported civil service reform.
4. "Ma, ma, where's my pa? Gone to the White House, ha, ha, ha!" referred to Grover Cleveland.

Essay Questions

1. What were the main characteristics of the "third political system"?
2. Which was the most effective and which was the least effective president between Reconstruction and the turn of the century? Justify your choices.
3. Why did some farmers join the Alliance movement? How did they expect the movement to help with their problems?
4. What issues divided the Republicans in the 1870s and 1880s?
5. Explain the specific problems faced by many farmers in the late nineteenth century.
6. Describe the programs advocated by the Populist party in the 1890s. How would you judge their success?

DOCUMENTS

Documents 1 and 2. The Farmers' Situation

Some of the grievances of the United States's farmers in the 1890s are discussed in the first two sections. F. B. Tracy described the conditions in Iowa, and W. A. Peffer (later a Populist senator) assessed the plight of Kansas farmers.

> Nothing has done more to injure the [Western] region than these freight rates. The railroads have retarded its growth as much as they first hastened it. The rates are often four times as large as Eastern rates. . . . The extortionate character of the freight rates has been recognized by all parties, and all have pledged themselves to lower them, but no state west of the Missouri has been able to do so.

In the early days, people were so anxious to secure railways that they would grant any sort of concession which the companies asked. There were counties in Iowa and other Western states struggling under heavy loads of bond-taxes, levied twenty-five years ago, to aid railways of which not one foot has been built. Perhaps a little grading would be done, and then the project would be abandoned, the bonds transferred, and the county called upon by the "innocent purchaser" to pay the debt incurred by blind credulity. I have known men to sacrifice fortunes, brains, and lives in fighting vainly this iniquitous bond-swindle.

Railways have often acquired mines and other properties by placing such high freight rates upon their products that the owner was compelled to sell at the railroad company's own terms. These freight rates have been especially burdensome to the farmers, who are far from their selling and buying markets, thus robbing them in both directions.

Another fact which has incited the farmer against corporations is the bold and unblushing participation of the railways in politics. At every political convention their emissaries are present with blandishments and passes and other practical arguments to secure the nomination of their friends. The sessions of these legislatures are disgusting scenes of bribery and debauchery. There is not an attorney of prominence in Western towns who does not carry a pass or has not had the opportunity to do so. The passes, of course, compass the end sought. By these means, the railroads have secured an iron grip upon legislatures and officers, while no redress has been given to the farmer.

The land question, also, is a source of righteous complaint. Much of the land of the West, instead of being held for actual settlers, has been bought up by speculators and Eastern syndicates in large tracts. They have done nothing to improve the land and have simply waited for the inevitable settler who bought cheaply a small "patch" and proceeded to cultivate it. When he had prospered so that he needed more land, he found that his own labor had increased tremendously the value of the adjacent land. . . .

Closely connected with the land abuse are the money grievances. As his pecuniary condition grew more serious, the farmer could not make payments on his land. Or he found that, with the ruling prices, he could not sell his produce at a profit. In either case he needed money, to make the payment or maintain himself until prices should rise. When he went to the moneylenders, these men, often dishonest usurers, told him that money was very scarce, that the rate of interest was rapidly rising, etc., so that in the end the farmer paid as much interest a month as the moneylender was paying a year for the same money. In this transaction, the farmer obtained his first glimpse of the idea of "the contraction of the currency at the hands of Eastern money sharks."

Disaster always follows the exaction of such exorbitant rates of interest, and want or eviction quickly came. Consequently, when demagogues went among the farmers to utter their calamitous cries, the scales seemed to drop from the farmer's eyes, and he saw gold bugs, Shylocks, conspiracies, and criminal legislation *ad infinitum.* Like a lightning flash, the idea of political action ran through the Alliances. A few farmers' victories in county campaigns the previous year became a promise of broader conquest, and with one bound the Farmers' Alliance went into politics all over the West.

[From F. B. Tracy, "Why the Farmers Revolted," *Forum* 16 (October 1893): 242–43.]

Farmers are passing through the "valley and shadow of death"; farming as a business is profitless; values of farm products have fallen 50 per cent since the great war, and farm values have depreciated 25 to 50 per cent during the last ten years; farmers are overwhelmed with debts secured by mortgages on their homes, unable in many instances to pay even the interest as it falls due, and unable to renew the loans because securities are weakening by reason of the general depression; many farmers are losing their homes under this dreadful blight, and the mortgage mill still grinds. We are in the hands of a merciless power; the people's homes are at stake. . . .

The American farmer of today is altogether a different sort of a man from his ancestor of fifty or a hundred years ago. . . . All over the West, . . . the farmer thrashes his wheat all at one time, he disposes of it all at one time, and in a great many instances the straw is wasted. He sells his hogs, and buys bacon and pork; he sells his cattle, and buys fresh beef and canned beef or corned beef, as the case may be; he sells his fruit, and buys it back in cans. . . . Not more than one farmer in fifty now keeps sheep at all; he relies upon the large sheep farmer for the wool, which is put into cloth or clothing ready for his use. Instead of having clothing made up on the farm in his own house or by a neighbor woman or country tailor a mile away, he either purchases his clothing ready made at the nearest town, or he buys the cloth and has a city tailor make it up for him. Instead of making implements which he uses about the farm—forks, rakes, etc., he goes to town to purchase even a handle for his axe or his mallet; . . . indeed, he buys nearly everything now that he produced at one time himself, and these things all cost money.

Besides all this, and what seems stranger than anything else, whereas in the earlier time the American home was a free home, unencumbered, . . . and whereas but a small amount of money was then needed for actual use in conducting the business of farming, there was always enough of it among the farmers to supply the demand, now, when at least ten times as much is needed, there is little or none to be obtained. . . .

The railroad builder, the banker, the money changer, and the manufacturer undermined the farmer. . . . The manufacturer came with his woolen mill, his carding mill, his broom factory, his rope factory, his wooden-ware factory, his cotton factory, his pork-packing establishment, his canning factory and fruit-preserving houses; the little shop on the farm has given place to the large shop in town; the wagon-maker's shop in the neighborhood has given way to the large establishment in the city where men by the thousand work and where a hundred or two hundred wagons are made in a week; the shoemaker's shop has given way to large establishments in the cities where most of the work is done by machines; the old smoke house has given way to the packing house, and the fruit cellars have been displaced by preserving factories. The farmer now is compelled to go to town for nearly everything that he wants. . . . And what is worse than all, if he needs a little more money than he has about him, he is compelled to go to town to borrow it. But he does not find the money there; in place of it he finds an agent who will "negotiate" a loan for him. The money is in the East . . . five thousand miles away. He pays the agent his commission, pays all the expenses of looking through the records and furnishing abstracts, pays for every postage stamp used in the transaction, and finally receives a draft for the amount of money required, minus these expenses. In this way the farmers of the country today are maintaining an army of middlemen, loan agents, bankers, and others, who are absolutely worthless for all good purposes in the community. . . .

These things, however, are on only the mechanical side of the farmer. His domain has been invaded by men of his own calling, who have taken up large tracts of land and farmed upon the plan of the manufacturers who employ a great many persons to perform the work under one management. This is "bonanza" farming. . . . The aim of some of the great "bonanza farms" of Dakota has been to apply machinery so effectually that the cultivation of one full section, or six hundred and forty acres, shall represent one year's work of only one man. This has not yet been reached, but so far as the production of the grain of wheat is concerned, one man's work will now give to each of one thousand persons enough for a barrel of flour a year, which is the average ration. . . .

The manufacture of oleomargarine came into active competition with farm butter. And about the same time a process was discovered by which a substitute for lard was produced—an article so very like the genuine lard taken from the fat of swine that the farmer himself was deceived by it. . . .

From this array of testimony the reader need have no difficulty in determining for himself "how we got here." The hand of the money changer is upon us. Money dictates our financial policy; money controls the business of the country; money is despoiling the people. . . . These men of Wall Street . . . hold the bonds of nearly every state, county, city and township in the Union; every railroad owes them more than it is worth. Corners in grain and other products of toil are the legitimate fruits of Wall Street methods. Every trust and combine made to rob the people had its origin in the example of Wall Street dealers. . . . This dangerous power which money gives is fast undermining the liberties of the people. It now has control of nearly half their homes, and is reaching out its clutching hands for the rest. This is the power we have to deal with.

[From W. A. Peffer, *The Farmer's Side* (New York, 1891), pp. 42, 56, 58–63, 121–23.]

Document 3. A Response to the Farmers' Protests

William Allen White, editor of the Emporia, Kansas, *Gazette,* wrote "What's the Matter with Kansas?" as he observed the 1896 presidential campaign. He ridiculed the agrarian challenge of the Populist party and helped elect William McKinley.

Today the Kansas Department of Agriculture sent out a statement which indicates that Kansas has gained less than two thousand people in the past year. There are about two hundred and twenty-five thousand families in this state, and there were ten thousand babies born in Kansas, and yet so many people have left the state that the natural increase is cut down to less than two thousand net.

This has been going on for eight years.

If there had been a high brick wall around the state eight years ago, and not a soul had been admitted or permitted to leave, Kansas would be a half million souls better off than she is today. And yet the nation has increased in population. In five years ten million people have been added to the national population, yet instead of gaining a share of this—say, half a million—Kansas has apparently been a plague spot and, in the very garden of the world, has lost population by ten thousands every year.

Not only has she lost population, but she has lost money. Every moneyed man in the state who could get out without loss has gone. Every month in every community sees someone who has a little money pack up and leave the state. This has been going on for eight years. Money has been drained out all the time. In towns where ten years ago there were three or four or half a dozen money-lending concerns, stimulating industry by furnishing capital, there is now none, or one or two that are looking after the interests and principal already outstanding.

No one brings any money into Kansas any more. What community knows over one or two men who have moved in with more than $5,000 in the past three years? And what community cannot count half a score of men in that time who have left, taking all the money they could scrape together?

Yet the nation has grown rich; other states have increased in population and wealth—other neighboring states. Missouri has gained over two million, while Kansas has been losing half a million. Nebraska has gained in wealth and population while Kansas has gone downhill. Colorado has gained every way, while Kansas has lost every way since 1888.

What's the matter with Kansas?

There is no substantial city in the state. Every big town save one has lost in population. Yet Kansas City, Omaha, Lincoln, St. Louis, Denver, Colorado Springs, Sedalia, the cities of the Dakotas, St. Paul and Minneapolis and Des Moines—all cities and towns in the West—have steadily grown.

Take up the government blue book and you will see that Kansas is virtually off the map. Two or three little scrubby consular places in yellow-fever-stricken communities that do not aggregate ten thousand dollars a year is all the recognition that Kansas has. Nebraska draws about one hundred thousand dollars; little old North Dakota draws about fifty thousand dollars; Oklahoma doubles Kansas; Missouri leaves her a thousand miles behind; Colorado is almost seven times greater than Kansas—the whole west is ahead of Kansas.

Take it by any standard you please, Kansas is not in it.

Go east and you hear them laugh at Kansas; go west and they sneer at her; go south and they "cuss" her; go north and they have forgotten her. Go into any crowd of intelligent people gathered anywhere on the globe, and you will find the Kansas man on the defensive. The newspaper columns and magazines once devoted to praise of her, to boastful facts and startling figures concerning her resources, are now filled with cartoons, jibes and Pefferian speeches. Kansas just naturally isn't in it. She has traded places with Arkansas and Timbuctoo.

What's the matter with Kansas?

We all know; yet here we are at it again. We have an old mossback Jacksonian who snorts and howls because there is a bathtub in the State House; we are running that old jay for Governor. We have another shabby, wild-eyed, rattlebrained fanatic who has said openly in a dozen speeches that "the rights of the user are paramount to the rights of the owner": we are running him for Chief Justice, so that capital will come tumbling over itself to get into the state. We have raked the old ash heap of failure in the state and found an old human hoop skirt who has failed as a businessman, who has failed as an editor, who has failed as a preacher, and we are going to run him for Congressman-at-Large. He will help the looks of the Kansas delegation at Washington. Then we have discovered a kid without a law practice and have decided to run him for Attorney General. Then, for fear some hint that the state had become respectable might percolate through the civilized portions of the nation, we have decided to send three or four harpies out lecturing, telling the people that Kansas is raising hell and letting the corn go to weed.

Oh, this is a state to be proud of! We are a people who can hold up our heads! What we need is not more money, but less capital, fewer white shirts and brains, fewer men with business judgment, and more of those fellows who boast that they are "just ordinary clodhoppers, but they know more in a minute about finance than John Sherman"; we need more men who are "posted," who can bellow about the crime of '73, who hate prosperity, and who think, because a man believes in national honor, he is a tool of Wall Street. We have had a few of them—some hundred fifty thousand—but we need more.

We need several thousand gibbering idiots to scream about the "Great Red Dragon" of Lombard Street. We don't need population, we don't need wealth, we don't need well-dressed men on the streets, we don't need cities on the fertile prairies; you bet we don't! What we are after is the money power. Because we have become poorer and ornerier and meaner than a spavined, distempered mule, we, the people of Kansas, propose to kick; we don't care to build up, we wish to tear down.

"There are two ideas of government," said our noble Bryan at Chicago. "There are those who believe that if you legislate to make the well-to-do prosperous, this prosperity will leak through on those below. The Democratic idea has been that if you legislate to make the masses prosperous their prosperity will find its way up and through every class and rest upon them."

That's the stuff! Give the prosperous man the dickens! Legislate the thriftless man into ease, whack the stuffing out of the creditors and tell the debtors who borrowed the money five years ago when money "per capita" was greater than it is now, that the contraction of currency gives him a right to repudiate.

Whoop it up for the ragged trousers; put the lazy, greasy fizzle, who can't pay his debts, on the altar, and bow down and worship him. Let the state ideal be high. What we need is not the respect of our fellow men, but the chance to get something for nothing.

Oh, yes, Kansas is a great state. Here are people fleeing from it by the score every day, capital going out of the state by the hundreds of dollars; and every industry but farming paralyzed, and that crippled, because its products have to go across the ocean before they can find a laboring man at work who can afford to buy them. Let's don't stop this year. Let's drive all the decent, self-respecting men out of the state. Let's keep the old clodhoppers who know it all. Let's encourage the man who is "posted." He can talk, and what we need is not mill hands to eat our meat, nor factory hands to eat our wheat, nor cities to oppress the farmer by consuming his butter and eggs and chickens and produce. What Kansas needs is men who can talk, who have large leisure to argue the currency question while their wives wait at home for the nickel's worth of bluing.

What's the matter with Kansas? :

Nothing under the shining sun. She is losing her wealth, population and standing. She has got her statesmen, and the money power is afraid of her. Kansas is all right. She has started in to raise hell, as Mrs. Lease advised, and she seems to have an overproduction. But that doesn't matter. Kansas never did believe in diversified crops. Kansas is all right. There is absolutely nothing wrong with Kansas. "Every prospect pleases and only man is vile."

[From William Allen White, *The Autobiography of William Allen White* (New York: Macmillan Co., 1946), pp. 280–83.]

Questions for Reflection

What problems faced farmers in the 1890s? Explain the causes of their predicament according to the farmers and their advocates? Did they have an accurate perception of their situation? How does William Allen White answer their arguments? Was there any validity to White's derisive comments? How has the role of the farmer changed since the 1890s?

ANSWERS TO MULTIPLE-CHOICE AND TRUE-FALSE QUESTIONS

Multiple-Choice Questions

1-B, 2-D, 3-A, 4-A, 5-C, 6-B, 7-D, 8-A

True-False Questions

1-F, 2-T, 3-F, 4-F, 5-T, 6-F, 7-F, 8-F

23

AN AMERICAN EMPIRE

CHAPTER OBJECTIVES

After you complete the reading and study of this chapter, you should be able to:

1. Explain why the United States pursued a policy of imperialism.
2. Account for the outbreak of the Spanish-American War.
3. Explain the course of United States relations with Latin America during the late nineteenth century and its impact on later relations with Latin America.
4. Contrast the arguments for and against imperialism in 1899.
5. Explain the development of America's policy to deal with its imperial possessions.
6. Account for the acquisition of the Panama Canal.
7. Assess the foreign policies of Theodore Roosevelt.

CHAPTER OUTLINE

I. Background to a new imperialism
   A. Manifest destiny
   B. European examples
   C. Trade
      1. Access to raw materials
      2. Markets
   D. Needs of a large navy
   E. Intellectual currents
      1. Darwinism
      2. Josiah Strong

II. Expansion in the Pacific
   A. Seward and the purchase of Alaska
   B. Involvement in Samoa
   C. Relations with Hawaii
      1. Reciprocal trade agreement
      2. Economic crisis
      3. Revolution and U.S. intervention
      4. Annexation by the United States.

III. Incidents in the Western Hemisphere
   A. Dispute over sealing in the Bering Sea
   B. Venezuelan boundary dispute
      1. Venezuela's conflict with Britain
      2. United States and arbitration
      3. Final settlement

IV. Development of the Spanish-American War
   A. Effects of American investments and tariffs
   B. Guerrilla warfare by revolutionaries
   C. Wyler's reconcentration policy
   D. Role of the press in the war
      1. Contest between Hearst's *Journal* and Pulitzer's *World*

2. Examples of yellow journalism
E. Cleveland's efforts for compromise
F. Spanish response to McKinley's stance
G. Arousal of public opinion
   1. de Lôme letter (Feb. 9, 1898)
   2. Sinking of the *Maine* (Feb. 15, 1898)
H. Final moves to war
I. Motives for war

V. Fighting the "splendid little war"
A. Naval victory at Manila Bay
B. Cuban blockade
   1. Problems of the army
   2. Rough Riders
   3. Siege of Santiago
C. Terms of the armistice

VI. Results of the war
A. Treaty of Paris
   1. Negotiations
   2. Motives for annexation
   3. Terms of the treaty
B. Other territorial acquisitions
C. Debate over treaty
   1. Anti-imperialist arguments
   2. Bryan's support
   3. Ratification
D. Guerrilla war in Philippines
E. Anti-Imperialist League
F. Organizing acquisitions
   1. Philippines under Taft
   2. Civil government in Puerto Rico
   3. Insular Cases
G. Situation in Cuba
   1. Leonard Wood as governor
   2. Yellow fever
   3. Cuban constitution
   4. Platt Amendment

5. Insurrection of 1906

VII. Imperial rivalries in the Far East
A. Japan's modernization
B. Scramble for spheres of influence in China
C. The Open-Door Policy
   1. British initiatives
   2. Unilateral action
   3. Policies of the Open Door Note
   4. Reactions of other nations
D. The Boxer Rebellion
E. Success of Hay's policy

VIII. Roosevelt and diplomacy
A. Background of TR
B. Imperialism and the 1900 election
C. TR as president
D. The Panama Canal
   1. Need for the canal
   2. Negotiations with the British and French
   3. Difficulties with Colombia
   4. Panamanian revolution
   5. End to negotiations
   6. Construction of the canal
   7. Legacies of the incident
E. Roosevelt Corollary
   1. Problems of debt collection
   2. Formulation of the corollary
F. Russo-Japanese War
   1. Cause of war
   2. TR's efforts for peace
G. United States's relations with Japan
   1. Respect for possessions
   2. Fears of the "yellow peril"
   3. Gentlemen's Agreement of 1907
H. Other diplomatic efforts
   1. Algeciras Conference (1906)
   2. The "Great White Fleet"

KEY ITEMS OF CHRONOLOGY

Purchase of Alaska	1867
Mahan's *The Influence of Seapower upon History*	1890
Venezuelan Boundary Dispute submitted to arbitration	1897
de Lôme letter revealed	February 9, 1898

Maine sunk	February 15, 1898
War formally declared between Spain and the United States	April 1898
Hawaii annexed	July 1898
Armistice	August 1898
Treaty of Paris	December 1898
Anti-Imperialist League formed	1899
Open Door Notes	1899
Assassination of McKinley	1901
Panama Canal acquired	1903
Roosevelt Corollary announced	1904
Gentlemen's Agreement with Japan	1907

TERMS TO MASTER

Listed below are some important terms or people with which you should be familiar after you complete the study of this chapter. Explain the significance of each name or term.

1. "Seward's Folly"
2. Hamilton Fish
3. Alfred Thayer Mahan
4. John Fiske
5. Josiah Strong
6. pelagic sealing controversy
7. Venezuelan Boundary Dispute
8. yellow journalism
9. de Lôme letter
10. Teller Amendment
11. white man's burden
12. doctrine of incorporation
13. Platt Amendment
14. Open-Door Policy
15. Boxer Rebellion
16. Gentlemen's Agreement
17. Roosevelt Corollary

VOCABULARY BUILDING

Listed below are some words or phrases used in this chapter. Look up each word in your dictionary unless the meaning is given here.

1. languid
2. manifest
3. accord
4. sequel
5. tripartite

6. isthmian
7. rebuff
8. impale
9. dilemma
10. ostensibly
11. jingo
12. eclair
13. unilateral
14. ultimatum
15. transpire
16. garrison
17. illimitable
18. tutelary
19. insular
20. indemnity

EXERCISES FOR UNDERSTANDING

When you have completed reading the chapter, answer each of the following questions. If you have difficulty, go back and reread the section of the chapter related to the question.

Multiple-Choice Questions

Select the letter of the response that best completes the statement.

1. The "new imperialism" of the 1890s especially stressed
   A. access to new markets.
   B. converting heathens to Christianity.
   C. annexing territory to the United States.
   D. military conquests of other nations.

2. Albert J. Beveridge, Henry Cabot Lodge, and Theodore Roosevelt agreed on
   A. low tariffs for agricultural products.
   B. obtaining overseas possessions.
   C. opposition to the Spanish-American War.
   D. the need for a small navy.

3. Alfred Thayer Mahan is best known for his writings about the
   A. dangers of annexing the Philippines.
   B. importance of sea power.
   C. irrelevance of an isthmian canal.
   D. sinking of the *Maine.*

4. The Teller Amendment
   A. justified the sinking of the *Maine.*
   B. declared Puerto Rico and Hawaii U.S. possessions.
   C. denied the intention to take Cuba.
   D. laid claim to an isthmian canal route.

5. Admiral Dewey scored an early victory in the Spanish-American War at
   A. Hawaii.
   B. Puerto Rico.
   C. Cuba.
   D. Philippines.

6. Opponents of the Treaty of Paris argued that
   A. foreign involvements would undermine the Monroe Doctrine.
   B. the Philippines would be difficult to defend.
   C. bringing large numbers of aliens into U.S. life would threaten the welfare of the nation.
   D. all the above

7. The proposal that each nation should have equal access to trade with China was known as the
   A. Gentlemen's Agreement.
   B. Open-Door Policy.
   C. Teller Amendment.
   D. white man's burden.

8. During the Spanish-American War, Theodore Roosevelt was
   A. president of the United States.
   B. governor of New York.
   C. secretary of war.
   D. assistant secretary of the Navy.

True-False Questions

Indicate whether each statement is true or false.

1. In the 1880s the major field of United States overseas activity was the Pacific Ocean.
2. Alaska was known as "Blaine's Folly."
3. John Fiske used Darwinian ideas to justify Anglo-Saxon dominance.
4. The Platt Amendment annexed Cuba.
5. The Foraker Act set up a civil government in Cuba.
6. In the Spanish-American War, U.S. forces suffered heavy losses in Cuba.
7. In the Russo-Japanese War, the United States fought with the Japanese.
8. The Roosevelt Corollary applied the Monroe Doctrine to Hawaii.

Essay Questions

1. What forces propelled Americans toward imperialism in the late nineteenth century?
2. Discuss the U.S. military actions in the Spanish-American War.
3. What were the major results of the Spanish-American War?
4. Explain the debate over imperialism after the Spanish-American War.
5. How did United States policy in Latin America change between 1890 and 1912?
6. Compare our foreign policies toward Cuba and China around the turn of the last century.
7. What did Theodore Roosevelt mean by "Speak softly, and carry a big stick"? How did he implement such a policy?

DOCUMENT

Document 1. McKinley's "War" Message to Congress

McKinley's message of April 11, 1898, attempted to summarize U.S. relations with Cuba. Read it carefully to gain an understanding of his perception of events.

Obedient to that precept of the Constitution which commands the President to give from time to time to the Congress information of the state of the Union and to recommend to their consideration such measures as he shall judge necessary and expedient, it becomes my duty now to address your body with regard to the grave crisis that has arisen in the relations of the United States to Spain by reason of the warfare that for more than three years has raged in the neighboring island of Cuba. . . .

Since the present revolution began, in February, 1895, this country has seen the fertile domain at our threshold ravaged by fire and sword in the course of a struggle unequaled in the history of the island and rarely paralleled as to the numbers of the combatants and the bitterness of the contest by any revolution of modern times where a dependent people striving to be free have been opposed by the power of the sovereign state. . . .

Our trade has suffered, the capital invested by our citizens in Cuba has been largely lost, and the temper and forbearance of our people have been so sorely tried as to beget a perilous unrest among our own citizens. . . .

The agricultural population to the estimated number of 300,000 or more was herded within the towns and their immediate vicinage, deprived of the means of support, rendered destitute of shelter, left poorly clad, and exposed to the most unsanitary conditions. As the scarcity of food increased with the devastation of the depopulated areas of production, destitution and want became misery and starvation. Month by month the death rate increased in an alarming ratio. By March, 1897, according to conservative estimates from official Spanish sources, the mortality among the reconcentrados from starvation and diseases thereto incident exceeded 50 per cent of their total number. . . .

The war in Cuba is of such a nature that short of subjugation or extermination, a final military victory for either side seems impracticable. The alternative lies in the physical exhaustion of the one or the other party, or perhaps of both. . . . The prospect of such a protraction and conclusion of the present strife is a contingency hardly to be contemplated with equanimity by the civilized world, and least of all by the United States, affected and injured as we are, deeply and intimately, by its very existence. . . .

The forcible intervention of the United States as a neutral to stop the war, according to the large dictates of humanity and following many historical precedents where neighboring States have interfered to check the hopeless sacrifices of life by internecine conflicts beyond their borders, is justifiable on rational grounds. It involves, however, hostile constraint upon both the parties to the contest as well to enforce a truce as to guide the eventual settlement.

. . . The present condition of affairs in Cuba is a constant menace to our peace and entails upon this Government an enormous expense. With such a conflict waged for years in an island so near us and with which our people have such trade and business relations; when the lives and liberty of our citizens are in constant danger and their property destroyed and themselves ruined; where our trading vessels are liable to seizure and are seized at our very door by war ships of a foreign nation, the expeditions of filibustering that we are powerless to prevent altogether, and the irritating questions and entanglements thus arising—all these and others that I need not mention, with the resulting strained relations, are a constant menace to our peace and compel us to keep on a semi-war footing with a nation with which we are at peace.

These elements of danger and disorder already pointed out have been strikingly illustrated by a tragic event which has deeply and justly moved the American people. I have already transmitted to Congress the report of the naval court of inquiry on the destruction of the battle ship *Maine* in the harbor of Havana during the night of the 15th of February. The destruction of that noble vessel has filled the national heart with inexpressible horror. Two hundred and fifty-eight brave sailors and marines and two officers of our Navy, reposing in the fancied security of a friendly harbor, have been hurled to death, grief and want brought to their homes and sorrow to the nation.

The naval court of inquiry, which, it is needless to say, commands the unqualified confidence of the Government, was unanimous in its conclusion that the destruction of the *Maine* was caused by an exterior explosion—that of a submarine mine. It did not assume to place the responsibility. That remains to be fixed.

In any event the destruction of the *Maine,* by whatever exterior cause, is a patent and impressive proof of a state of things in Cuba that is intolerable. That condition is thus shown to be such that the Spanish Government can not assure safety and security to a vessel of the American Navy in the harbor of Havana on a mission of peace, and rightfully there.

In view of these facts and of these considerations I ask the Congress to authorize and empower the President to take measures to secure a full and final termination of hostilities between the Government of Spain and the people of Cuba, and to secure in the island the establishment of a stable government, capable of maintaining order and observing its international obligations, insuring peace and tranquillity and the security of its citizens as well as our own, and to use the military and naval forces of the United States as may be necessary for these purposes. . . .

The issue is now with the Congress. It is a solemn responsibility. I have exhausted every effort to relieve the intolerable condition of affairs which is at our doors. . . .

Yesterday, and since the preparation of the foregoing message, official information was received by me that the latest decree of the Queen Regent of Spain directs General Blanco, in order to prepare and facilitate peace, to proclaim a suspension of hostilities, the duration and details of which have not yet been communicated to me.

This fact with every other pertinent consideration will, I am sure, have your just and careful attention in the solemn deliberations upon which you are about to enter. If this measure attains a successful result, then our aspirations as a Christian, peace-loving people will be realized. If it fails, it will be only another justification for our contemplated action.

[From James D. Richardson (ed.), *A Compilation of the Messages and Papers of the Presidents, 1789–1897,* vol. 10 (Washington, D.C.: U.S. Government Printing Office, 1899), vol. 10, pp. 139–50.]

Questions for Reflection

Does McKinley anywhere in the message ask Congress to declare war on Spain? How could a declaration of war be justified in light of his request? How accurate was McKinley's description of developments between Cuba and the United States? Can you see any reason why Congress might have been skeptical of McKinley's claim that Spain had offered to cease hostilities in Cuba? Does this document suggest that the United States was justified in becoming involved in the Cuban matter and ultimately in the Spanish-American War?

ANSWERS TO MULTIPLE-CHOICE AND TRUE-FALSE QUESTIONS

Multiple-Choice Questions

1-A, 2-B, 3-B, 4-C, 5-D, 6-C, 7-B, 8-D

True-False Questions

1-T, 2-F, 3-T, 4-F, 5-T, 6-F, 7-F, 8-F

24

THE PROGRESSIVE ERA

CHAPTER OBJECTIVES

After you complete the reading and study of this chapter, you should be able to:

1. Explain the nature and the goals of the progressive movement.
2. Compare the progressive movement with the populist movement.
3. Describe Roosevelt's brand of progressivism.
4. Account for Taft's mixed record as a progressive.
5. Describe Wilson's efforts for progressive reform.
6. Assess the impact of progressivism on U.S. politics, society, and economy.

CHAPTER OUTLINE

I. Progressivism
   A. General features
     1. Aimed against the abuses of the Gilded-Age bosses
     2. More businesslike and efficient than populism
     3. Paradox of regulation of business by business leaders
     4. Not an organized group or party

   B. Antecedents
     1. Populism
     2. Mugwumps
     3. Socialist critiques of living and working conditions
     4. Muckrakers
       a. Henry Demarest Lloyd and Jacob Riis
       b. Golden Age of Muckraking
       c. Brought popular support for reform
       d. Stronger on diagnosis than remedy
   C. Themes of progressivism
     1. Efforts to democratize government
       a. Direct primaries
       b. Initiative, referendum, recall, and other local actions
       c. Direct election of senators
     2. A focus on efficiency and good government
       a. Role of Frederick W. Taylor and scientific management
       b. Shorter ballots
       c. Equalized tax assessments and budget systems
       d. Commission and city-manager forms of city government

e. Use of specialists in govern-
    ment and business
  3. Regulation of giant corporations
      a. One alternative: complete lais-
          sez-faire
      b. Socialist program of public
          ownership at the local level
      c. Trust-busting
      d. Acceptance and regulation of
          big business
      e. Problem of regulating the reg-
          ulators
  4. Impulse toward social justice
      a. Use of private charities and
          state power
      b. Outlawing child labor
      c. Restricting night work and
          dangerous occupations
      d. Erratic course of the Supreme
          Court
      e. Stricter building codes and
          factory inspection acts
      f. Workmen's compensation
          laws
      g. Pressure for prohibition

II. Roosevelt's Progressivism
  A. Cautious executive action
  B. Trust regulation
      1. Opposition to trustbusting
      2. *Northern Securities* case, 1904
  C. Coal strike of 1902
      1. Cause of strike
      2. Roosevelt and arbitration
      3. Effects of strike and settlement
  D. Further regulation of business
      1. More antitrust suits
      2. Expedition and Elkins Acts
      3. Bureau of Corporations
  E. Election of 1904
      1. Republican nomination
      2. Democratic candidate and
          positions
      3. Campaign and result
  F. Reforms in second term
      1. Hepburn Act
      2. Regulation of food and drugs
          a. Upton Sinclair's *The Jungle*
          b. Meat Inspection Act

c. Pure Food and Drug Act
  3. Conservation

III. Taft's Administration
  A. Successor to TR in 1908
      1. William Howard Taft
      2. Democrats and Bryan
      3. Election outcome
  B. Taft's background and character
  C. Dollar Diplomacy
      1. Railroads in China
      2. In Latin America
  D. Tariff reform
      1. Preference for lower rates
      2. Problems in Senate
      3. Reactions to compromise
  E. Ballinger-Pinchot controversy
      1. Ballinger's actions to undo Roo-
          sevelt policies
      2. Roles of Pinchot and Glavis
      3. Impact of the affair
  F. Taft's role in the rebellion against
      Speaker Cannon
  G. Elections of 1910
  H. Roosevelt's response on his return to
      the United States
      1. Development of the New Nation-
          alism
      2. Clash over the U.S. Steel suit
      3. TR enters the race
  I. Taft's achievements
      1. In conservation
      2. Mann-Elkins Act
      3. Other laws
      4. Constitutional amendments
  J. The election of 1912
      1. The Republican nomination of
          1912
          a. Roosevelt's primary victories
          b. Taft's nomination
      2. Creation of the Progressive party

IV. Wilson's Progressivism
  A. Wilson's rise to power
      1. His background
      2. Student of politics
      3. President of Princeton
      4. Governor of New Jersey
      5. His nomination

B. Election of 1912
   1. New Nationalism versus New Freedom
   2. Wilson's election
   3. Significance of the election of 1912
      a. High-water mark for progressivism
         i. First presidential primaries used
         ii. Unique for focus on vital alternatives and for high tone
      b. Democrats back into office
      c. Brought southerners into control
      d. Began to alter the Republican party toward conservatism
C. Wilsonian reform
   1. Wilson's style
   2. Courting public support
   3. Tariff reform
      a. Personal appearance before Congress
      b. Efforts to obtain Senate support
      c. Tariff changes in the Underwood-Simmons Act
      d. Income tax provisions
   4. Banking and currency reform
      a. Work of the National Monetary Commission
      b. Compromises required
      c. Federal Reserve System
      d. Defects corrected by the new system
   5. Efforts for new antitrust laws
      a. New Freedom approach

   b. Shift to Federal Trade Commission Act, September 1914
   c. Clayton Anti-Trust Act, October 1914
      i. Practices outlawed
      ii. Provisions for labor and farm organizations
   d. Disappointments with administration of the new laws
6. The limits of Wilson's progressivism
   a. Social justice
   b. African Americans
7. Wilson's return to reform
   a. Plight of the Progressive party
   b. Appointment of Brandeis to the Supreme Court
   c. Support for land banks and long-term farm loans
   d. Other efforts for cheap rural credit
   e. Farm demonstration agents and agricultural education
   f. Federal Highways Act
   g. Labor reform legislation

V. The limits of Progressivism
   A. Acceptance of the public-service concept of the state
   B. Elements of paradox
      1. Disfranchisement of southern African Americans
      2. Manipulation of democratic reforms
      3. Decision making by faceless bureaucratic experts
      4. Decline of voter participation
      5. From optimism to war

KEY ITEMS OF CHRONOLOGY

Roosevelt administration	1901–1909
Anthracite coal strike	1902
Northern Securities case	1904
Elkins Act	1904
Hepburn Act	1906
Pure Food and Drug Act	1906
Mann-Elkins Act	1910

The Principles of Scientific Management	
published	1911
Wilson administration	1913–1921
Underwood-Simmons Tariff Act	1913
Federal Reserve Act	1913
Federal Trade Commission Act	1914
Clayton Anti-Trust Act	1914
Sixteenth Amendment (income tax) ratified	1913
Seventeenth Amendment (direct Senate election) ratified	1913
Adamson Act	1916

TERMS TO MASTER

Listed below are some important terms or people with which you should be familiar after you complete the study of this chapter. Explain the significance of each name or term.

1. muckrakers
2. initiative and referendum
3. Frederick W. Taylor
4. *Northern Securities* case
5. anthracite coal strike
6. "stream of commerce" doctrine
7. Elkins Act
8. Hepburn Act
9. Upton Sinclair
10. dollar diplomacy
11. Ballinger-Pinchot controversy
12. New Nationalism
13. New Freedom
14. Louis Brandeis
15. Federal Reserve System
16. Federal Trade Commission
17. Clayton Anti-Trust Act
18. child labor

VOCABULARY BUILDING

Listed below are some words or phrases used in this chapter. Look up each word in your dictionary unless the meaning is given here.

1. ferment
2. paradox
3. resonant
4. catalyst
5. elicit

6. intrastate
7. arbitration
8. irrevocable
9. bolster
10. proclivity
11. invincible
12. irk
13. clamor
14. injunction
15. adroit
16. guise
17. exonerate
18. impeccable
19. volatility
20. inchoate

EXERCISES FOR UNDERSTANDING

When you have completed reading the chapter, answer each of the following questions. If you have difficulty, go back and reread the section of the chapter related to the question.

Multiple-Choice Questions

Select the letter of the response that best completes the statement.

1. Antecedents contributing to the rise of Progressivism included all of the following *except*
   A. Mugwump reformers.
   B. populism.
   C. isolationism.
   D. socialism.

2. One of the muckrakers' major achievements was to
   A. stir up popular support for reform.
   B. propose solutions to corruption and evil.
   C. help individual reformers run successfully for office.
   D. oppose the popular elections of U.S. senators.

3. Robert LaFollette and the "Wisconsin Idea" emphasized
   A. efficient government.
   B. breaking up trusts.
   C. racial integration.
   D. laissez-faire policies.

4. Municipally owned utilities and transportation systems were examples of
   A. laissez-faire economics.
   B. government regulation.
   C. socialism.
   D. trust-busting.

5. To achieve domestic reforms, Theodore Roosevelt depended on
   A. legislation.
   B. executive action.
   C. judicial decisions.
   D. voluntary actions by groups and businesses.

6. In *The Jungle* Upton Sinclair sought to
   A. defend slaughterhouse workers.
   B. promote socialism.
   C. criticize urban living conditions.
   D. praise new immigrant workers.

7. "Hamiltonian means to achieve Jeffersonian ends" summarizes the 1912 views of
   A. Woodrow Wilson.
   B. William Howard Taft.
   C. Theodore Roosevelt.
   D. Eugene V. Debs.

8. The Clayton Anti-Trust Act attempted to regulate trusts by
   A. defining actions of unfair competition.
   B. placing control in a small group of regulators.
   C. taking control of trusts from the courts.

   D. repealing the Sherman Anti-Trust Act.

True-False Questions

Indicate whether each statement is true or false.

1. In the 1902 coal strike, TR militarized the mines.
2. The city manager was an attempt to make local government more democratic.
3. TR and Taft agreed on conservation policies.
4. Taft brought more antitrust suits in four years than TR did in eight years.
5. Dollar diplomacy was one aspect of the New Nationalism.
6. In the 1912 election, Woodrow Wilson defeated TR and Taft.
7. The Underwood-Simmons Tariff of 1913 sought to restore competition by lowering import duties.
8. President Wilson supported racial segregation.

Essay Questions

1. What were the antecedents to progressivism and why were they important?
2. Explain the various solutions that progressives proposed to deal with the problems of giant corporations.
3. Why was William Howard Taft not as effective a president as either TR or Wilson?
4. Who were the candidates and what were their positions on the issues in the 1912 presidential election?
5. Was Theodore Roosevelt or Wilson the more successful progressive president? Explain your answer.
6. "The great fundamental contribution of progressive politics was the firm establishment and general acceptance of the public-service concept of the state." Explain.

DOCUMENTS

Document 1. "The Treason of the Senate"

In 1906, the muckraker David Graham Phillips wrote an attack on Senator Nelson W. Aldrich (Republican, Rhode Island), which was part of his exposé "The Treason of the Senate." The following is an excerpt from Phillips's essay on Aldrich in *Cosmopolitan* magazine.

Rhode Island is the smallest of our states in area and thirty-fourth in population—twelve hundred and fifty square miles, less than half a million people, barely seventy thousand voters with the rolls padded by the Aldrich machine. But size and numbers are nothing; it contains as many sturdy Americans proportionately as any other state. Its bad distinction of supplying the enemy with a bold leader is due to its ancient and aristocratic constitution, changed once, away back before the middle of the last century, but still an archaic document for class rule. The apportionment of legislators is such that one-eleventh of the population, and they the most ignorant and most venal, elect a majority of the legislature—which means that they elect the two United States senators. Each city and township counts as a political unit; thus, the five cities that together have two-thirds of the population are in an overwhelming minority before twenty almost vacant rural townships—their total population is not thirty-seven thousand—where the ignorance is even illiterate, where the superstition is mediaeval, where tradition and custom have made the vote an article of legitimate merchandising.

The combination of bribery and party prejudice is potent everywhere; but there come crises when these fail "the interests" for the moment. No storm of popular rage, however, could unseat the senators from Rhode Island. The people of Rhode Island might, as a people and voting almost unanimously, elect a governor; but not a legislature. Bribery is a weapon forbidden those who stand for right and justice—who "fights the devil with fire" gives him choice of weapons, and must lose to him, though seeming to win. A few thousand dollars put in the experienced hands of the heelers, and the senatorial general agent of "the interests" is secure for another six years.

The Aldrich machine controls the legislature, the election boards, the courts—the entire machinery of the "republican form of government." In 1904, when Aldrich needed a legislature to reelect him for his fifth consecutive term, it is estimated that carrying the state cost about two hundred thousand dollars—a small sum, easily to be got back by a few minutes of industrious pocket-picking in Wall Street. . . .

And the leader, the boss of the Senate for the past twenty years has been—Aldrich! . . .

The greatest single hold of "the interests" is the fact that they are the "campaign contributors"—the men who supply the money for "keeping the party together," and for "getting out the vote." Did you ever think where the millions for watchers, spellbinders, halls, processions, posters, pamphlets, that are spent in national, state and local campaigns come from? Who pays the big election expenses of your congressman, of the men you send to the legislature to elect senators? Do you imagine those who foot those huge bills are fools? Don't you know that they make sure of getting their money back, with interest, compound upon compound? Your candidates get most of the money for their campaigns from the party committees; and the central party committee is the national committee with which congressional and state and local committees are affiliated. The bulk of the money for the "political trust" comes from "the interests." "The interests" will give only to the "political trust." And that means Aldrich and his Democratic (!) lieutenant, Gorman of Maryland, leader of the minority in the Senate. Aldrich, then, is the head of the "political trust" and Gorman is his right-hand man. When you speak of the Republican party, of the Democratic party, of the "good of the party," of the "best interests of the party;" of "wise party policy," you mean what Aldrich and Gorman, acting for their clients, deem wise and proper and "Republican" or "Democratic." . . .

No railway legislation that was not either helpful to or harmless against "the interests"; no legislation on the subject of corporations that would interfere with "the interests," which use the corporate form to simplify and systematize their stealing; no legislation on the tariff question unless it secured to "the interests" full and free license to loot; no investigations of wholesale robbery or of any of the evils resulting from it—there you have in a few words the whole story of the Senate's treason under Aldrich's leadership, and of why property is concentrating in the hands of the few and the little children of the masses are being sent to toil in the darkness of mines, in the dreariness and unhealthfulness of factories instead of being sent to school; and why the great middle class—the old-fashioned Americans, the people with the incomes of from two thousand to fifteen thousand a year—is being swiftly crushed into dependence and the repulsive miseries of "genteel poverty."

[From David Graham Phillips, "The Treason of the Senate," *Cosmopolitan*, April 1906, pp. 628–38.]

Document 2. "Wall Street and the House of Dollars"

Also appearing in *Cosmopolitan* was the following by Ernest Crosby.

This is the situation. Here we are, a great and vigorous people, generating power enough to run a dozen governments and our government has got away from us, and switched us off, and our nominal representatives are getting their motive power elsewhere. There in the Senate Chamber is the center of the conspiracy which has defrauded

us of our rights. It will soon be with us as it was with the Roman oligarchy. *"Senatus Populusque Romanus,"* they used to say, when they
spoke of the state. "S.P.Q.R."—"The Senate and the Roman People,"
and the Senate came first. It is "The Senate and the American People"
to-day, and we may soon improve on the Roman legend and drop the
"People" altogether, and then, politically speaking, the Senate will be
the Whole Thing. But they tempered the asperities of oligarchy in
Rome by naming tribunes of the people who had the courage to call a
halt when the Senate went too far, and to maintain the rights of the
people against their rulers. We need such tribunes in this country, and
their aim should be to bring the senators back to their allegiance. Legislative elections have proved to be almost invariably corrupt and the
sure means of handing over the selection to the money power. The
senators as a rule are either direct representatives of the trusts or political bosses by the grace of the trusts. The problem before us is to
select our own bosses for ourselves and make the senators *our* representatives, and to cut off the connection which binds them to interests
which are diametrically opposed to ours. Popular election seems to be
the obvious reform. The electors of a whole state cannot be handled
as a legislature can be. The people should rise in their wrath and
demand this change. The world of finance has its own proper functions to accomplish, but it should have no place in the management of
our government. Let the people once more become the Real Thing.

[From Ernest Crosby, "Wall Street and the House of Dollars," *Cosmopolitan,* April 1906, p. 610.]

Document 3. The Seventeenth Amendment

In May 1912 Congress adopted and submitted to the states for ratification what became
the Seventeenth Amendment to the Constitution. It provided for the popular election of
U.S. senators and was declared ratified on May
31, 1913.

Amendment XVII.

The Senate of the United States shall be composed of two senators
from each State, elected by the people thereof, for six years; and each
Senator shall have one vote. The electors in each State shall have the
qualifications requisite for electors of the most numerous branch of
the State legislature.

When vacancies happen in the representation of any State in the
Senate, the executive authority of such State shall issue writs of election to fill such vacancies: *Provided,* That the legislature of any State
may empower the executive thereof to make temporary appointments
until the people fill the vacancies by election as the legislature may
direct.

This amendment shall not be so construed as to affect the election
or term of any senator chosen before it becomes valid as part of the
Constitution.

Questions for Reflection

Would David Graham Phillips have supported the Seventeenth Amendment? How did reformers think direct election of U.S. Senators would change the way government functioned? In what ways did the Seventeenth Amendment reflect the general values of progressives?

Three-quarters of a century later, what has been the effect of the Seventeenth Amendment on U.S. politics? Has the Senate been dramatically changed and improved? Do wealthy business leaders and industrialists continue to exert undue influence?

ANSWERS TO MULTIPLE-CHOICE AND TRUE-FALSE QUESTIONS

Multiple-Choice Questions

1-C, 2-A, 3-A, 4-C, 5-B, 6-B, 7-C, 8-A

True-False Questions

1-F, 2-F, 3-F, 4-T, 5-F, 6-T, 7-T, 8-T

25 ∽

AMERICA AND THE GREAT WAR

CHAPTER OBJECTIVES

*After you complete the reading and study of
this chapter, you should be able to:*

1. Describe Wilson's idealistic diplomacy and
   show the clash of ideals and reality in
   Mexico.
2. Explain early U.S. reaction to the World
   War.
3. Account for the entry of the United States
   into World War I.
4. Explain the status of civil liberties during
   World War I and during the Red Scare
   afterward.
5. Explain the process and product of peacemaking after World War I.
6. Account for the failure of the United States
   to ratify the peace treaty after World War I.
7. Describe the problems of reconversion
   from World War I to civilian life.

CHAPTER OUTLINE

I. Wilson and foreign affairs
   A. His background in diplomacy
   B. His idealism in diplomacy
   C. Bryan's cooling-off treaties
   D. Wilson's revocation of dollar diplo-
      macy in China

   E. Intervention in Mexico
      1. Overthrow of Diaz
      2. Nonrecognition of the Huerta
         government
      3. Invasion at Vera Cruz
      4. Carranza's government
      5. Pursuit of Pancho Villa
   F. Problems in the Caribbean

II. World War I and early U.S. neutrality
   A. Outbreak of the war
   B. Initial U.S. response
      1. Declaration of neutrality
      2. Attitudes of hyphenated
         Americans
      3. Views of other U.S. groups
      4. Effect of propaganda on Ameri-
         cans
   C. Extension of economic credit to the
      Allies
   D. Problems of neutrality
      1. Conflicts over neutral rights at sea
      2. British declaration of the North
         Sea war zone and other
         restrictions
      3. German use of submarines
      4. Sinking of the *Lusitania*
         a. U.S. protests
         b. Bryan's resignation
         c. *Arabic* pledge
      5. House's futile mediation efforts

6. *Sussex* pledge
E. Debate over preparedness
   1. Demands for stronger army and navy
   2. Antiwar advocates
   3. National Defense Act of 1916
   4. Move for a stronger navy
   5. Efforts to obtain revenue for preparedness
F. Election of 1916
   1. Republicans nominated
   2. Progressive party disbanded
   3. Democratic program
   4. Issues of the campaign
   5. Results of the election
G. Steps toward war
   1. Wilson's effort to mediate
   2. Wilson's assertion of terms of peace
   3. German decision for unrestricted submarine warfare
   4. Diplomatic break with Germany
   5. Efforts to arm U.S. merchant ships
   6. Zimmerman telegram
   7. Russian Revolution

III. U.S. entry into the war
A. Declaration of war
   1. Loss of U.S. vessels
   2. Wilson's call for war
   3. Reasons for U.S. entry
B. Early U.S. role
   1. Limited expectations from the United States
   2. Contributions to naval strategy
   3. Financial assistance to the Allies
   4. First contingents of troops
C. Mobilizing a nation
   1. Raising the armed forces
     a. Conscription
     b. Progressive virtues
   2. Use of "war socialism" to regulate the economy
   3. War Industries Board
   4. New labor sources
     a. African Americans
       i. Great Migration
       ii. Racial conflicts

     b. Women
   5. War propaganda
   6. Civil liberties in the war
     a. Popular disdain for all things German
     b. Espionage and Sedition Acts
       i. Terms of the acts
       ii. Prosecutions
       iii. Impact of the acts
       iv. *Schenck* v. *United States*

IV. U.S. military role
A. Allies on defensive through 1917
B. German offensives after Russian withdrawal
C. Instances of significant U.S. participation in the war
D. Intervention in Russia
E. Development of the Fourteen Points
F. Overtures toward peace
G. Terms of the armistice

V. Fight for the peace
A. Wilson's role
   1. Decision to attend the conference
   2. Effects of congressional elections of 1918
   3. Wilson's reception in Europe
   4. Structure of the conference
B. Emphasis on the League of Nations
   1. Article X of the Covenant
   2. Machinery of the League
C. Early warning from Lodge
D. Amendments made to respond to critics at home
E. Compromises on national self-determination
F. Agreement for reparations
G. Obtaining the German signature
H. Wilson's loss at home
   1. Support for the peace
   2. Opposition to the peace
   3. Lodge's reaction
   4. Wilson's speaking tour
   5. Wilson's stroke
   6. Failure of the Senate votes
   7. Formal ending of the war

VI. Conversion to peace
A. Lack of leadership

B. Unplanned mobilization
C. Spanish flu
D. Economic transition
  1. Drop in farm prices
  2. Labor unrest
     a. Seattle General Strike
     b. Steel Strike
     c. Boston Police Strike

E. Race riots
F. Red Scare
  1. Fear of radicals
  2. Bombs in the mail
  3. Deportation of aliens
  4. Evaporation of the Red Scare
  5. Legacy of the Red Scare

KEY ITEMS OF CHRONOLOGY

Huerta in power in Mexico	February 1913
Invasion of Vera Cruz	April 1914
Outbreak of World War I	August 1914
Lusitania sunk	May 1915
Arabic pledge from Germany	September 1915
Sussex pledge	April 1916
Germany resumed unrestricted submarine warfare	February 1917
United States declared war	April 1917
Creation of War Industries Board	July 1917
Armistice	November 1918
Paris Peace Conference	January–May 1919
Senate votes on treaty	November 1919 and March 1920
Red Scare	1919–1920

TERMS TO MASTER

Listed below are some important terms or people with which you should be familiar after you complete the study of this chapter. Explain the significance of each name or term.

1. Victoriano Huerta
2. hyphenated America
3. Central Powers
4. *Lusitania*
5. *Arabic* and *Sussex* pledges
6. Revenue Act of 1916
7. Zimmerman telegram
8. War Industries Board
9. Committee on Public Information
10. Espionage and Sedition Acts
11. *Schenck* v. *United States*
12. Fourteen Points
13. Big Four
14. Henry Cabot Lodge
15. reparations
16. irreconciliables
17. Boston Police Strike
18. A. Mitchell Palmer
19. Red Scare

VOCABULARY BUILDING

Listed below are some words or phrases used in this chapter. Look up each word in your dictionary unless the meaning is given here.

1. crass
2. enunciate
3. spawn
4. reparations
5. abatement
6. capstone

7. edifice
8. exact (v.)
9. fain
10. envoy
11. unabated
12. exigency
13. harangue
14. ardently
15. indemnity
16. abdication
17. lambast
18. peevish
19. virulent
20. pandemic

EXERCISES FOR UNDERSTANDING

When you have completed the reading of the chapter, answer each of the following questions. If you have difficulty, go back and reread the section of the chapter related to the question.

Multiple-Choice Questions

Select the letter of the response that best completes the statement.

1. In Mexico, President Wilson
   A. adhered to dollar diplomacy.
   B. followed an idealistic policy of "missionary diplomacy."
   C. intervened with the U.S. military.
   D. none of the above
2. For two years after the war began in Europe, the Wilson administration pursued a policy that stressed
   A. secret aid to Britain.
   B. neutrality.
   C. opposition to Britain's "freedom of the seas" policy.
   D. support for Germany if it would stop the U-boat attacks.
3. In World War I, President Wilson did *not* say:
   A. "It would be an irony of fate if my administration had to deal chiefly with foreign affairs."

B. Americans must be "impartial in thought as well as action."
   C. money "is the worst of all contrabands because it commands everything else."
   D. the U.S. was "contending for nothing less high and sacred than the rights of humanity."
4. During the war, a major change in the American population involved
   A. women permanently changing their employment patterns.
   B. blacks migrating from the South to the North.
   C. Mexican Americans moving back to Mexico.
   D. all of the above
5. The wartime Espionage and Sedition Acts
   A. were upheld by the Supreme Court.
   B. led to the persecution of more than 1,500 people.
   C. hit hard at socialists and radicals.
   D. all the above
6. The irreconcilables were primarily
   A. midwestern and western progressives.
   B. representatives of hyphenated Americans.
   C. conservative Republicans.
   D. southern Democrats
7. After World War I, the Senate
   A. ratified the Treaty of Versailles.
   B. ratified the treaty except for the League of Nations.
   C. accepted the League of Nations but defeated the Treaty of Versailles.
   D. defeated the Treaty of Versailles.
8. One-half million Americans died
   A. of Spanish influenza in 1918–1919.
   B. in World War I.
   C. in race riots after World War I.
   D. during the postwar Red Scare.

True-False Questions

Indicate whether each statement is true or false.

1. Unlike Taft, Wilson rarely sent U.S. troops into the Caribbean to protect interests.

2. As a result of the *Arabic* pledge, Germany virtually abandoned submarine warfare.
3. The Zimmerman telegram revealed Germany's policy of unrestricted submarine warfare.
4. Probably the decisive reason the United States entered World War I was the issue of submarine warfare.
5. "He kept us out of war" was the slogan of the Republicans in 1916.
6. With the Fourteen Points, Wilson sought to keep Russia in the war and to create disunity among the Central Powers.
7. Wilson thought Germany's admission of war guilt was the most important part of the peace negotiations.
8. The United States did not intervene in the Russian revolution.

Essay Questions

1. Compare Wilson's policies toward Mexico and toward Germany from 1913 to 1917.
2. Was the United States really neutral between 1914 and 1917? Explain.
3. What military role did the United States play in World War I?
4. Generally, what were the Fourteen Points? Why were they important and controversial?
5. Assess the U.S. contribution to the Allied victory in World War I.
6. What was the Red Scare after World War I and what caused it?

DOCUMENTS

Document 1. Woodrow Wilson's Speech to Congress

On April 20, 1914, in an address to Congress on the crisis developing in Mexico, President Wilson asked for authority to act against Mexico.

Gentlemen of the Congress: It is my duty to call your attention to a situation which has arisen in our dealings with General Victoriano Huerta at Mexico City which calls for action, and to ask your advice and cooperation in acting upon it. On the 9th of April a paymaster of the U.S.S. Dolphin landed at the Iturbide Bridge landing at Tampico with a whaleboat and boat's crew to take off certain supplies needed by his ship, and while engaged in loading the boat was arrested by an officer and squad of men of the army of General Huerta. . . . Admiral Mayo regarded the arrest as so serious an affront that he was not satisfied with the apologies offered, but demanded that the flag of the United States be saluted with special ceremony by the military commander of the port.

The incident cannot be regarded as a trivial one, especially as two of the men arrested were taken from the boat itself—that is to say, from the territory of the United States—but had it stood by itself it might have been attributed to the ignorance or arrogance of a single officer. Unfortunately, it was not an isolated case. A series of incidents have recently occurred which cannot but create the impression that the representatives of General Huerta were willing to go out of their way to show disregard for the dignity and rights of this Government and felt perfectly safe in doing what they pleased, making free to show in many ways their irritation and contempt.

The manifest danger of such a situation was that such offenses might grow from bad to worse until something happened of so gross and intolerable a sort as to lead directly and inevitably to armed conflict. It was necessary that the apologies of General Huerta and his representatives should go much further, that they should be such as to attract the attention of the whole population to their significance, and such as to impress upon General Huerta himself the necessity of seeing to it that no further occasion for explanations and professed regrets should arise. I, therefore, felt it my duty to sustain Admiral Mayo in the whole of his demand and to insist that the flag of the United States should be saluted in such a way as to indicate a new spirit and attitude on the part of the Huertistas.

Such a salute, General Huerta has refused, and I have come to ask your approval and support in the course I now propose to pursue.

This Government can, I earnestly hope, in no circumstances be forced into war with the people of Mexico. Mexico is torn by civil strife. If we are to accept the tests of its own constitution, it has no government. General Huerta has set his power up in the City of Mexico, such as it is, without right and by methods for which there can be no justification. Only part of the country is under his control. If armed conflict should unhappily come as a result of his attitude of personal resentment toward this Government, we should be fighting only General Huerta and those who adhere to him and give him their support, and our object would be only to restore to the people of the distracted Republic the opportunity to set up again their own laws and their own government.

But I earnestly hope that war is not now in question. I believe I speak for the American people when I say that we do not desire to control in any degree the affairs of our sister Republic. Our feeling for the people of Mexico is one of deep and genuine friendship, and everything that we have so far done or refrained from doing has proceeded from our desire to help them, not to hinder or embarrass them. We would not wish even to exercise the good offices of friendship without their welcome and consent. The people of Mexico are entitled to settle their own domestic affairs in their own way, and we sincerely desire to respect their right. The present situation need have none of the grave implications of interference if we deal with it promptly, firmly, and wisely.

No doubt I could do what is necessary in the circumstances to enforce respect for our Government without recourse to the Congress, and yet not exceed my constitutional powers as President; but I do not wish to act in a manner possibly of so grave consequence except in close conference and cooperation with both the Senate and House. I, therefore, come to ask your approval that I should use the armed forces of the United States in such ways and to such an extent as may be necessary to obtain from General Huerta and his adherents the fullest recognition of the rights and dignity of the United States, even amidst the distressing conditions now unhappily obtaining in Mexico.

There can in what we do be no thought of aggression or of selfish aggrandizement. We seek to maintain the dignity and authority of the United States only because we wish always to keep our great influence unimpaired for the uses of liberty, both in the United States and wherever else it may be employed for the benefit of mankind.

[From *Congressional Record,* 63rd Cong., 2d sess., April 20, 1914, vol. 51, pt. 4, p. 6925.]

Document 2. *The Nation* on Mexico

An editorial in *The Nation* questioned whether intervention in Mexico was justified.

The plain facts of the case are these: that the Administration has undertaken hostile operations against a man whom it has refused to recognize as *de-facto* President of Mexico, because he temporized about making reparation to this country for an insult to the flag in the precise form prescribed by international usage. It was not even that an apology had been refused, for it had not. Huerta had made an apology; more, he had undertaken to salute the flag in the manner demanded, the only stipulation being that the salute should be returned and that a protocol to this effect should be put into writing. That was the occasion for the undertaking of an enterprise the end of which no man can foresee, but which has already exacted its price in the lives of Americans and Mexicans. And the reason for the refusal of the protocol? Because it was not in accord with diplomatic usage? But what has diplomatic usage to do with a private individual whose official existence we do not recognize? Or because the mere signing of it might involve that recognition which we have so studiously avoided? So, we may talk to a man through our accredited diplomatic agent in Mexico, but rather than correspond with him we will go to war. It is straining at a gnat and swallowing a camel.

These are the official reasons advanced for our action in Mexico. Nobody pretends that they are the sole reasons. If they were, our justification for the extreme measures that have been taken would appear even more miserably inadequate than it does. Huerta has pursued a policy of pinpricks exceedingly trying to the patience of the Administration, galling to the pride of any but a nation that is truly great and secure in the consciousness of its national honor. The lives and property of American citizens have been in danger in Mexico, and to protect their lives is one of the first duties of a government; but in the part of Mexico controlled by Huerta Americans have enjoyed heretofore a greater security than in those districts which are in the hands of Villa and the rebels. Yet, be it remembered, it is against Huerta, and Huerta alone, not against Villa, not against the Mexican people, Federals or rebels, that all the armed resources of the United States have been arrayed.

These, we think, are the kind of reflections that have been in the minds of many thoughtful Americans during the past week. It is because the majority of the American people realize, perhaps vaguely, the inconsistency which has marked the policy of the Administration, the inadequacy of the grounds on which war has been threatened, that there has been a notable absence of the jingoistic spirit.

[From *The Nation,* 98, no. 2548 (April 30, 1914): 487.]

Document 3. "The President's War"

An essay in *The Independent* sharply attacked President Wilson for starting a war with Mexico.

The war in Mexico is the war of Woodrow Wilson, President of the United States. He was responsible for the policy pursued in dealing with Huerta and Carranza. He was responsible for the diplomacy which failed to assure peace. It was his ultimatum which paved the way to the conflict. It was his seizure of Vera Cruz that brought war.

Granting the President has been actuated by the loftiest sense of patriotism, it must be admitted that his conduct of the war in its first vital stages has been reprehensible in the highest degree. Incredible as it may seem, he ordered American marines and bluejackets to take the custom house at the most important port of the torn republic, believing that General Huerta would not dare to offer resistance. . . .

[T]he President rejected expert advice and planned, in its initial stages, his own war. The result will be a heavy toll in American lives and American treasure.

What justification had the President for the war he has made? In his address to Congress, he based it upon the refusal of General Huerta to salute the Stars and Stripes for the arrest of the American bluejackets by a Mexican Federal officer at Tampico. He spoke also of the arrest of an American mail orderly at Vera Cruz and of the holding up by the official censor of a dispatch address by the Secretary of State to the American chargé d'affaires in Mexico City.

He made no reference to the Americans slain and outraged, to others harassed and insulted, to vast property interests destroyed. He based his action, the action of war; upon the mere matter of ceremony.

The truth of the matter is that the President probably saw that his policy of "watchful waiting" was a failure. It was inspired unquestionably by a purpose to refrain from intervention at all hazards. But he learned almost simultaneously with the occurrence of the Tampico incident that Huerta had negotiated a loan of $60,000,000, which would be sufficient to keep him in office another twelve months. He probably realized that if Huerta should be able to retain power that length of time he (the President) would be made ridiculous. Obsessed as he was by an apparently keen personal hatred of the dictator, he determined upon a step which he believed would assure the elimination of the latter without war.

It is extraordinary that the President from the very beginning has
failed to grasp the true situation in Mexico. When he came into office,
he issued a declaration that he would not recognize a government
founded on force. Idealistic as was this policy it was in flat contra-
vention of the attitude of non-intervention in the domestic concerns of
other and particularly pan-American states which the United States
has observed with one or two exceptions from the time of its foundation.

[From John Callan O'Laughlin, "The President's War," *The Independent,* 78, no. 3413 (May 4, 1914): 194.]

Document 4. The Fourteen Points: Wilson's Address to Congress, January 8, 1918

In his famous address to Congress of January 8, 1918, Wilson explained the war aims of
the United States. His Fourteen Points formed
the basis for the peace negotiations.

Gentlemen of the Congress:

. . . It will be our wish and purpose that the processes of peace,
when they are begun, shall be absolutely open and that they shall
involve and permit henceforth no secret understandings of any kind.
The day of conquest and aggrandizement is gone by; so is also the
day of secret covenants entered into in the interest of particular governments and likely at some unlooked-for moment to upset the peace
of the world. It is this happy fact, now clear to the view of every public man whose thoughts do not still linger in an age that is dead and
gone, which makes it possible for every nation whose purposes are
consistent with justice and the peace of the world to avow now or at
any other time the objects it has in view.

We entered this war because violations of right had occurred which
touched us to the quick and made the life of our own people impossible unless they were corrected and the world secured once for all
against their recurrence. What we demand in this war, therefore, is
nothing peculiar to ourselves. It is that the world be made fit and safe
to live in; and particularly that it be made safe for every, peace-loving
nation which, like our own, wishes to live its own life, determine its
own institutions, be assured of justice and fair dealing by the other
peoples of the world as against force and selfish aggression. All the
peoples of the world are in effect partners in this interest, and for our
own part we see very clearly that unless justice be done to others it
will not be done to us. The program of the world's peace, therefore, is
our program; and that program, the only possible program, as we see
it, is this:

I. Open covenants of peace, openly arrived at, after which there
shall be no private international understandings of any kind but
diplomacy shall proceed always frankly and in the public view.

II. Absolute freedom of navigation upon the seas, outside territorial waters, alike in peace and in war, except as the seas may be closed

in whole or in part by international action for the enforcement of international covenants.

III. The removal, so far as possible, of all economic barriers and the establishment of an equality of trade conditions among all the nations consenting to the peace and associating themselves for its maintenance.

IV. Adequate guarantees given and taken that national armaments will be reduced to the lowest point consistent with domestic safety.

V. A free, open-minded, and absolutely impartial adjustment of all colonial claims, based upon a strict observance of the principle that in determining all such questions of sovereignty the interests of the populations concerned must have equal weight with the equitable claims of the government whose title is to be determined.

VI. The evacuation of all Russian territory and such a settlement of all questions affecting Russia as will secure the best and freest cooperation of the other nations of the world in obtaining for her an unhampered and unembarrassed opportunity for the independent determination of her own political development and national policy and assure her of a sincere welcome into the society of free nations under institutions of her own choosing; and, more than a welcome, assistance also of every kind that she may need and may herself desire. The treatment accorded Russia by her sister nations in the months to come will be the acid test of their good will, of their comprehension of her needs as distinguished from their own interests, and of their intelligent and unselfish sympathy.

VII. Belgium, the whole world will agree, must be evacuated and restored, without any attempt to limit the sovereignty which she enjoys in common with all other free nations. No other single act will serve as this will serve to restore confidence among the nations in the laws which they have themselves set and determined for the government of their relations with one another. Without this healing act the whole structure and validity of international law is forever impaired.

VIII. All French territory should be freed and the invaded portions restored, and the wrong done to France by Prussia in 1871 in the matter of Alsace-Lorraine, which has unsettled the peace of the world for nearly fifty years, should be righted, in order that peace may once more be made secure in the interest of all.

IX. A readjustment of the frontiers of Italy should be effected along clearly recognizable lines of nationality.

X. The peoples of Austria-Hungary, whose place among the nations we wish to see safeguarded and assured, should be accorded the freest opportunity of autonomous development.

XI. Rumania, Serbia, and Montenegro should be evacuated; occupied territories restored; Serbia accorded free and secure access to the sea; and the relations of the several Balkan states to one another determined by friendly counsel along historically established lines of allegiance and nationality; and international guarantees of the political and economic independence and territorial integrity of the several Balkan states should be entered into.

XII. The Turkish portions of the present Ottoman Empire should be assured a secure sovereignty, but the other nationalities which are now under Turkish rule should be assured an undoubted security of life and an absolutely unmolested opportunity of autonomous development, and the Dardanelles should be permanently opened as a free passage to the ships and commerce of all nations under international guarantees.

XIII. An independent Polish state should be erected which should include the territories inhabited by indisputably Polish populations, which should be assured a free and secure access to the sea, and whose political and economic independence and territorial integrity should be guaranteed by international covenant.

XIV. A general association of nations must be formed under specific covenants for the purpose of affording mutual guarantees of political independence and territorial integrity to great and small states alike.

In regard to these essential rectifications of wrong and assertions of right we feel ourselves to be intimate partners of all the governments and peoples associated together against the Imperialists. We cannot be separated in interest or divided in purpose. We stand together until the end.

For such arrangements and covenants we are willing to fight and to continue to fight until they are achieved; but only because we wish the right to prevail and desire a just and stable peace such as can be secured only by removing the chief provocations to war, which this program does not remove. We have no jealousy of German greatness, and there is nothing in this program that impairs it. We grudge her no achievement or distinction of learning or of pacific enterprise such as have made her record very bright and very enviable. We do not wish to injure her or to block in any way her legitimate influence or power. We do not wish to fight her either with arms or with hostile arrangements of trade if she is willing to associate herself with us and the other peace-loving nations of the world in covenants of justice and law and fair dealing. We wish her only to accept a place of equality among the peoples of the world,—the new world in which we now live,—instead of a place of mastery.

Neither do we presume to suggest to her any alteration or modification of her institutions. But it is necessary, we must frankly say, and necessary as a preliminary to any intelligent dealings with her on our part, that we should know whom her spokesmen speak for when they speak to us, whether for the Reichstag majority or for the military party and the men whose creed is imperial domination.

We have spoken now, surely, in terms too concrete to admit of any further doubt or question. An evident principle runs through the whole program I have outlined. It is the principle of justice to all peoples and nationalities, and their right to live on equal terms of liberty and safety with one another, whether they be strong or weak. Unless this principle be made its foundation no part of the structure of international justice can stand. The people of the United States could act upon no other principle; and to the vindication of this principle they are ready to devote their lives, their honor, and everything that they possess. The moral climax of this the culminating and final war for human liberty has come, and they are ready to put their own strength, their own highest purpose, their own integrity and devotion to the test.

[From *A Compilation of the Messages and Papers of the Presidents,* Supplement, 1917–1921, vol. 2 (New York: Bureau of National Literature, 1921), pp. 8421ff.]

Questions for Reflection

How did President Wilson rationalize U.S. military involvement in Mexico? What criticisms of the presidential decision came from *The Nation* and *The Independent?* What were the other reasons for U.S. intervention hinted at by *The Nation?* In your opinion, was U.S. action in Mexico justified?

Compare Wilson's difficulty explaining U.S. action in 1914 against Mexico with his enunciation of the United States' position on entering World War I. On what grounds should the United States intervene militarily in another country? Were Wilson's Fourteen Points a practical program for peace? Explain. Describe the controversy sparked by Point XIV. How would you assess Wilson's role in this controversy? Is the "principle of justice to all peoples and nationalities" a useful basis for foreign policy? Why or why not?

ANSWERS TO MULTIPLE-CHOICE AND TRUE-FALSE QUESTIONS

Multiple-Choice Questions

1-C, 2-B, 3-C, 4-B, 5-D, 6-A, 7-D, 8-A

True-False Questions

1-F, 2-T, 3-F, 4-T, 5-F, 6-T, 7-F, 8-F

26 ✲

THE MODERN TEMPER

CHAPTER OBJECTIVES

*After you complete the reading and study of
this chapter, you should be able to:*

1. Depict and account for the mood of the
   1920s.
2. Describe the nativist reaction in the twenties and the revival of the Ku Klux Klan,
   and their consequences.
3. Trace the emergence of fundamentalism
   and its effects.
4. Account for the experiment in Prohibition
   and its persistence in the face of widespread evasion of the law.
5. Compare the political and social position
   of women and blacks in the twenties.
6. Explain the scientific basis of the moral
   relativism of the decade.
7. Describe the literary flowering of the
   1920s and the contributions of major U.S.
   novelists and poets of the era.

CHAPTER OUTLINE

I. Impact of war
   A. Disillusionment with old values
   B. Emergence of modernism
   C. Political and social radicalism

II. Reactions in the 1920s
   A. Nativism
      1. Sacco and Vanzetti case
      2. Efforts to restrict immigration
      3. Revival of Ku Klux Klan
   B. Fundamentalism
      1. Growth of fundamentalism
      2. Leaders
      3. Scopes trial
   C. Prohibition
      1. Temperance organizations
      2. Eighteenth Amendment
      3. Effects of Prohibition
      4. Links to organized crime
      5. Al Capone
      6. Wickersham Report

III. The Roaring Twenties
   A. A time of cultural conflict
   B. Disdain for rural–small-town values
   C. The Jazz Age
      1. Blend of musical traditions
      2. Movies
   D. The new morality of youth
      1. Emphasis on youth
      2. Loosened taboos
      3. Obsession with sex
         a. Freud
         b. Popular entertainment
      4. The flapper

5. Aspects of persistence into the 1930s
6. Impact on family life
E. The women's movement
   1. The work for women's suffrage
      a. Alice Paul and new tactics
      b. Contributions of Carrie Chapman Catt
      c. Passage and ratification of the amendment
   2. Transformation into the League of Women Voters
   3. Push for an Equal Rights Amendment
   4. Women in the workforce
F. The "New Negro"
   1. The Great Migration north
      a. Demographics
      b. Impact of the move
   2. The Harlem Renaissance
   3. Marcus Garvey and Negro Nationalism
      a. Racial separatism
      b. Racial pride and self-reliance
      c. Fate of Garvey
   4. Development of the NAACP
      a. Emergence of the organization
      b. Role of Du Bois
      c. Effect of legislation
      d. The campaign against lynching
      e. Oscar De Priest: first northern black congressional representative
      f. Defeat of Judge Parker

IV. The culture of modernism
A. Loss of faith in progress
B. Determinism of Freud and Marx

C. Einstein and the theory of relativity
   1. The development of the theory
   2. Its impact on popular thinking
D. Toward the principle of uncertainty
   1. The relationship of mass and energy
   2. Planck's quantum theory
   3. Heisenberg's principle of uncertainty
   4. Ramifications of the uncertainty theory
      a. Denial of absolute values
      b. Assertion of relativism in cultures
E. Modernist literature
   1. Chief features
      a. Exploration of the irrational
      b. Uncertainty seen as desirable
      c. Positive view of conflict
      d. Formal manners discounted for contact with "reality"
   2. Artistic bohemias
   3. The Armory show
   4. Chief U.S. prophets of modernism
      a. Ezra Pound
      b. T. S. Eliot
      c. Gertrude Stein
      d. F. Scott Fitzgerald
      e. Ernest Hemingway
         i. Cult of masculinity
         ii. Terse literary style
F. Southern Literary Renaissance
   1. Reaction to growth of modern world
   2. Fugitive poets
   3. Thomas Wolfe
   4. William Faulkner

KEY ITEMS OF CHRONOLOGY

Einstein's paper on the theory of relativity	1905
Organization of the NAACP	1910
Formation of the new Ku Klux Klan	1915
Ratification of the Eighteenth Amendment (Prohibition)	1919
Ratification of the Nineteenth Amendment (women's suffrage)	1920
Sinclair Lewis's *Babbit*	1922

Scopes trial	1924
Hemingway's *The Sun Also Rises*	1926
Execution of Sacco and Vanzetti	1927
Heisenberg's principle of uncertainty stated	1927
The Jazz Singer	1927
Look Homeward, Angel	1929
The Sound and the Fury	1929
I'll Take My Stand	1930

TERMS TO MASTER

Listed below are some important terms or people with which you should be familiar after you complete the study of this chapter. Explain the significance of each name or term.

1. Sacco and Vanzetti
2. KKK
3. the "Five Points"
4. "monkey trial"
5. Eighteenth Amendment
6. Great Migration
7. Marcus Garvey
8. NAACP
9. theory of relativity
10. principle of uncertainty
11. modernist movement
12. F. Scott Fitzgerald
13. Fugitive poets
14. Thomas Wolfe
15. William Faulkner

VOCABULARY BUILDING

Listed below are some words or phrases used in this chapter. Look up each word in your dictionary unless the meaning is given here.

1. polyglot
2. gratuitous
3. regeneration
4. miscellany
5. heresy
6. disrepute
7. racketeer
8. entourage
9. banality
10. syncopated
11. sublimation
12. lurid
13. melioristic
14. atonal
15. expatriate
16. conduit
17. arbiter
18. blithesome
19. frenetic
20. bohemian

EXERCISES FOR UNDERSTANDING

When you have completed reading the chapter, answer each of the following questions. If you have difficulty, go back and reread the section of the chapter related to the question.

Multiple-Choice Questions

Select the letter of the response that best completes the statement.

1. In the United States, the end of World War I brought
   A. a renewed belief in the old values of glory, honor, and courage.
   B. the optimistic conviction that the world was constantly improving.
   C. disillusionment with modern civilization.
   D. a greater appreciation of diversity and change in U.S. life.
2. In 1921 and 1924 Congress passed immigration laws that
   A. allowed more immigrants from war-torn Europe.
   B. restored immigration to prewar levels.
   C. restricted immigration except for people from southern and eastern Europe.

D. favored immigrants from northern and western Europe.

3. The Scopes trial involved
   A. immigrant anarchists accused of robbery.
   B. teaching evolution in public school.
   C. racketeers and violations of Prohibition.
   D. a challenge to women's suffrage.

4. The Harlem Renaissance, an artistic and literary blossoming, featured the works of
   A. Claude McKay, Langston Hughes, and Countée Cullen.
   B. H. L. Mencken, Eugene O'Neill, and Sinclair Lewis.
   C. Thomas Wolfe, Ernest Hemingway, and the Fugitive poets.
   D. Albert Einstein, Sigmund Freud, and Marcus Garvey.

5. According to the *New York Times* in 1929, "the feminine right to equal representation in smoking, drinking, swearing, petting, and upsetting the community peace" was established by
   A. the Twentieth Amendment.
   B. the flapper.
   C. Sigmund Freud and psychoanalysis.
   D. Prohibition and fundamentalism.

6. Marcus Garvey advocated
   A. an end to racial discrimination and segregation.
   B. membership in the National Association for the Advancement of Colored People.
   C. racial pride and self-reliance for Negroes.
   D. modernist thinking, especially the ideas of Freud.

7. The scientific work of Einstein, Heisenberg, and others
   A. reinforced the traditional faith in reason and order.
   B. increased confidence in our ability to fully understand the world.
   C. was incompatible with the disillusionment and despair of the postwar period.
   D. suggested that there is a limit to our understanding of the universe.

8. In the 1920s, the southern advocates of an agrarian way of life were

A. called Fugitive poets.
B. expatriates in Europe.
C. followers of fundamentalism.
D. Thomas Wolfe and William Faulkner, among others.

True-False Questions

Indicate whether each statement is true or false.

1. Modernism included impressionism in art and Freudianism in psychology.
2. William Jennings Bryan was a fundamentalist.
3. Organized crime began during the Depression.
4. The Eighteenth Amendment gave women the right to vote.
5. The NAACP stressed legal action through the courts to end racial discrimination.
6. Marcus Garvey believed blacks should flee America for Africa.
7. Gertrude Stein wrote "A rose is a rose is a rose is a rose."
8. Proponents of literary and artistic change included T. S. Eliot and Ezra Pound.

Essay Questions

1. What did the KKK, prohibitionists, fundamentalists, and opponents of immigration have in common? How were their attitudes similar?
2. How were women involved in the social and cultural changes of the 1920s?
3. Describe the changes that occurred in black life and culture in the 1920s and 1930s.
4. Explain the contributions of Freud, Marx, Einstein, and Heisenberg to the new mood of the 1920s. What were the chief features of modernist literature? Show how those features were exhibited in the works of one of the authors mentioned in the text.
6. Compare the programs of the NAACP and the UNIA.
7. How did changes in scientific thinking affect social and literary thought?

DOCUMENTS

Document 1. John Dewey on William Jennings Bryan and "The American Intellectual Frontier"

In 1922 the influential philosopher and educator at Columbia University John Dewey commented on William Jennings Bryan's fundamentalist campaign against evolution and found its sources in the powerful forces common in the United States past.

The campaign of William Jennings Bryan against science and in favor of obscurantism and intolerance is worthy of serious study. It demands more than the mingled amusement and irritation which it directly evokes. In its success (and it is meeting with success) it raises fundamental questions about the quality of our democracy. It helps us understand the absence of intellectual radicalism in the United States and the present eclipse of social and political liberalism. It aids, abets and gives comfort to the thoroughgoing critics of any democracy. It gives point to the assertion of our Menckens that democracy by nature puts a premium on mediocrity, the very thing in human nature that least stands in need of any extraneous assistance.

For Mr. Bryan is a typical democratic figure. There is no gainsaying that proposition. Economically and politically he has stood for and with the masses, not radically but "progressively." The most ordinary justice to him demands that his usefulness in revolt against privilege and his role as a leader in the late progressive movement—late in every sense of the word, including deceased—be recognized. His leadership in antagonism to free scientific research and to popular dissemination of its results cannot therefore be laughed away as a personal idiosyncrasy. There is a genuine and effective connection between the political and the doctrinal directions of his activity, and between the popular responses they call out.

What we call the middle classes are for the most part the churchgoing classes, those who have come under the influence of evangelical Christianity. These persons form the backbone of philanthropic social interest, of social reform through political action, of pacifism, of popular education. They embody and express the spirit of kindly goodwill toward classes which are at an economic disadvantage and toward other nations, especially when the latter show any disposition toward a republican form of government. The "Middle West," the prairie country, has been the centre of active social philanthropies and political progressivism because it is the chief home of this folk. Fairly well to do, enough so at least to be ambitious and to be sensitive to restrictions imposed by railway and financial corporations, believing in education and better opportunities for its own children, mildly interested in "culture," it has formed the solid element in our diffuse national life and heterogeneous populations. It has been the element responsive to appeals for the square deal and more nearly equal opportunities for all, as it has understood equality of opportunity. It followed Lincoln in the abolition of slavery, and it followed Roosevelt in his denunciation of "bad" corporations and aggregations of wealth. It also followed Roosevelt or led him in its distinctions between "on the one hand and on the other hand." It has been the middle in every sense of the word and in every movement. Like every mean it has held things together and given unity and stability of movement.

It has never had an interest in ideas as ideas, nor in science and art for what they may do in liberating and elevating the human spirit. Science and art as far as they refine and polish life, afford "culture," mark stations on an upward social road, and have direct useful social applications, yes: but as emancipations, as radical guides to life, no. There is nothing recondite or mysterious or sinister or adverse to a reputable estimate of human nature in the causes of this state of mind. Historians of thought point out the difference between the fortunes of the new ideas of science and philosophy in the eighteenth century in England and France. In the former, they were accommodated, partially absorbed; they permeated far enough to lose their own inherent quality. Institutions were more or less liberalized, but the ideas were lost in the process. In France, the opposition was entrenched in powerful and inelastic institutions. The ideas were clarified and stripped to fighting weight. They had to fight to live, and they became weapons. What happened in England happened in America only on a larger scale and to greater depths. The net result is social and political liberalism combined with intellectual illiberality. Of the result Mr. Bryan is an outstanding symbol.

Mr. Bryan can have at best only a temporary triumph, a succés d'estime, in his efforts to hold back biological inquiry and teaching. It is not in this particular field that he is significant. But his appeals and his endeavors are a symptom and a symbol of the forces which are most powerful in holding down the intellectual level of American life. He does not represent the frontier democracy of Jackson's day. But he represents it toned down and cultivated as it exists in fairly prosperous villages and small towns that have inherited the fear of whatever threatens the security and order of a precariously attained civilization, along with pioneer impulses to neighborliness and decency. Attachment to stability and homogeneity of thought and belief seem essential in the midst of practical heterogeneity, rush and unsettlement. We are not Puritans in our intellectual heritage, but we are evangelical because of our fear of ourselves and of our latent frontier disorderliness. The depressing effect upon the free life of inquiry and criticism is the greater because of the element of soundness in frontier fear, and because of the impulses of goodwill and social aspiration which have become entangled with its creeds. The forces which are embodied in the present crusade would not be so dangerous were they not bound up with so much that is necessary and good. We have been so taught to respect the beliefs of our neighbors that few will respect the beliefs of a neighbor when they depart from forms which have become associated with aspiration for a decent neighborly life. This is the illiberalism which is deep-rooted in our liberalism. No account of the decay of the idealism of the progressive movement in politics or of the failure to develop an intelligent and enduring idealism out of the emotional fervor of the war, is adequate unless it reckons with this fixed limit to thought. No future liberal movement, when active liberalism revives, will be permanent unless it goes deep enough to affect it. Otherwise we shall have in the future what we have had in the past, revivalists like Bryan, Roosevelt and Wilson, movements which embody moral emotions rather than the insight and policy of intelligence.

[John Dewey, "The American Intellectual Frontier," *New Republic* 30, no. 388 (May 10, 1922): 303–5.]

Document 2. Walter Lippmann on the Controversial Issues of the Day

An editorialist with the *New York World* in 1927, Walter Lippmann later became a prize-winning columnist and commentator. Below he explains the issues that really stirred Americans' interests in the 1920s.

The questions which really engage the emotions of the masses of the people are of a quite different order. They manifest themselves in the controversies over prohibition, the Ku Klux Klan, Romanism, Fundamentalism, immigration. These, rather than the tariff, taxation, credit, and corporate control, are the issues which divide the American people. These are the issues men care about. They are just beneath the surface of political discussion. In theory they are not supposed to be issues. The party platforms and the official pronouncements deal with them obliquely, if at all. But they are the issues men talk about privately, and they are, above all, the issues about which men have deep personal feelings.

These questions are diverse, but they all arise out of the same general circumstances. They arise out of the great migration of the last fifty years, out of the growth of cities, and out of the spread of that rationalism and the deepening of that breach with tradition which invariably accompany the development of a metropolitan civilization. Prohibition, the Ku Klux Klan, Fundamentalism, and xenophobia are an extreme but authentic expression of the politics, the social outlook, and the religion of the older American village civilization making its last stand against what looks to it like an alien invasion. The alien invasion is in fact the new America produced by the growth and the prosperity of America.

The evil which the old-fashioned preachers ascribe to the Pope, to Babylon, to atheists, and to the Devil is simply the new urban civilization, with its irresistible economic and scientific and mass power. The Pope, the Devil, jazz, the bootleggers, are a mythology which expresses symbolically the impact of a vast and dreaded social change. The change is real enough. The language in which it is discussed is preposterous only as all mythology is preposterous if you accept it literally. The mythology of the Ku Klux Klan is a kind of primitive science, an animistic and dramatized projection of the fears of a large section of our people who have yet to accommodate themselves to the strange new social order which has arisen in their midst.

This new social order is dominated by metropolitan cities of which New York is the largest and most highly developed. Therefore New York has become the symbol of all that is most wicked and of all that is most alluring in modern America. But New York to-day is only what Chicago, St. Louis, Detroit, Cleveland, Jacksonville, and Miami expect to be to-morrow. It is the seat of a vast population, mixed in its origins, uncertain of its social status, rather vague about the moral code. In these metropolitan centres the ancient social bonds are loosened. The patriarchal family, the well-established social hierarchy, the old roots of belief, and the grooves of custom are all obscured by new human relationships based on a certain kind of personal independence, on individual experiment and adventure, which are yet somehow deeply controlled by fads and fashions and great mass movements.

The campaign in certain localities to forbid the teaching of 'Darwinism' is an attempt to stem the tide of the metropolitan spirit, to erect a spiritual tariff against an alien rationalism which threatens to dissolve the mores of the village civilization. To many of us the effort seems quixotic, as indeed it is, judged by the intellectual standards of metropolitan life. But if we look at the matter objectively, disregarding the petty mannerisms of the movement, there is a pathos about it which always adheres to the last struggle of an authentic type of human living. The anti-evolutionists are usually less alarming than Don Quixote. Perhaps that is because they have not been transfigured by an artist. They are at any rate fighting for the memory of a civilization which in its own heyday, and by its own criteria, was as valid as any other.

The anti-evolution bills are, of course, a comparatively trivial symptom of this profound maladjustment. The overt struggle turns politically on two questions: on the Eighteenth Amendment and on the nomination of Governor Alfred E. Smith. The struggle over these two issues implicates all the antagonisms between the older America and the new. The Eighteenth Amendment is a piece of legislation embodied in the Constitution which attempts to impose the moral ideals of the villages upon the whole nation. The force behind the Eighteenth Amendment is the Anti-Saloon League, which is the political arm of the evangelical churches in the small communities. The financial and political strength of the Anti-Saloon League is derived from the members of these churches, chiefly Methodist and Baptist, with other denominations divided but following these militant sects. And the strength of these sects in the last analysis arises from the spiritual isolation of communities which have not yet been radically invaded by the metropolitan spirit.

The defense of the Eighteenth Amendment has, therefore, become much more than a mere question of regulating the liquor traffic. It involves a test of strength between social orders, and when that test is concluded, and if, as seems probable, the Amendment breaks down, the fall will bring down with it the dominion of the older civilization. The Eighteenth Amendment is the rock on which the evangelical church militant is founded, and with it are involved a whole way of life and an ancient tradition. The overcoming of the Eighteenth Amendment would mean the emergence of the cities as the dominant force in America, dominant politically and socially as they are already dominant economically.

[Walter Lippmann, "The Causes of Political Indifference Today," *Atlantic Monthly* 139, no. 2 (February 1927): 265–67.]

Questions for Reflection

How did Dewey and Lippmann each explain the appeal of fundamentalism, the KKK, and Prohibition? Did they agree entirely? How did they differ in emphasis? Are they persuasive for the 1920s? Are there other explanations that occur to you? Do their analyses have any pertinence today?

ANSWERS TO MULTIPLE-CHOICE AND TRUE-FALSE QUESTIONS

Multiple-Choice Questions

1-C, 2-D, 3-B, 4-A, 5-B, 6-C, 7-D, 8-A

True-False Questions

1-F, 2-T, 3-F, 4-F, 5-T, 6-F, 7-T, 8-T

27

REPUBLICAN RESURGENCE
AND DECLINE

CHAPTER OBJECTIVES

After you complete the reading and study of this chapter, you should be able to:

1. Assess the effects of the Harding presidency on the nation.
2. Explain the new prosperity of the 1920s.
3. Delineate the features of the economy in the New Era decade.
4. Explain Hoover's policies for the nation and indicate their effects.
5. Account for the stock market crash of 1929.
6. Understand the status of farmers during the 1920s.
7. Describe the status of labor unions during the 1920s.

CHAPTER OUTLINE

I. The fate of progressivism in the 1920s
  A. Causes for the dissolution of the progressive coalition in Congress
    1. Disaffection with U.S. entry into the war and with the war's aftermath
    2. Administration's attitude toward labor

    3. Farmers' concerns about wartime price controls
    4. Intellectuals' disillusionment with conservative trends like Prohibition
    5. Middle- class preoccupation with business
  B. Survivals of progressivism in the 1920s
    1. Domination of Congress
    2. Strong pressure at local levels for "good government" and public services
    3. Reform impulse transformed into the drive for moral righteousness

II. Election of 1920
  A. Mood of the country
  B. Republican shift to the right
  C. Democratic nomination contest
  D. The campaign
  E. Results

III. The Harding administration
  A. The Harding appointments
    1. Cabinet
    2. Supreme Court
  B. Harding presidency
  C. Efforts for economy
    1. Tax cut

2. Higher tariff
D. Deemphasis on regulating agencies
E. Corruption in the administration
   1. Veterans' Bureau
   2. Justice Department
   3. Teapot Dome
F. Harding's death
G. Public reaction

IV. The Coolidge years
A. Character of the man
B. Election of 1924
   1. Coolidge's control of the Republican party
   2. Dissension among the Democrats
   3. Emergence of the Progressive party
   4. Results of the election
C. Aspects of the New Era
   1. Absorption of the progressive coalition
   2. Growth of the economy and advertising
   3. Impact of installment buying
   4. Development of the movies
   5. Growth of radio
   6. Growth of aviation
   7. Impact of the automobile
   8. Advent of mass production
D. Hoover's role
   1. His concept of voluntary cooperation
   2. Growth of the Commerce Department
   3. Promotion of trade associations
E. Problems in agriculture
   1. Reasons for the agricultural slump
   2. Mechanization of farms
   3. New farm organizations
      a. Marketing associations
      b. American Farm Bureau Federation
      c. Formation of the Farm Bloc in Congress
   4. Legislation favorable to agriculture
      a. Early acts
      b. The McNary-Haugen scheme

F. Setbacks for unions
   1. Earnings in industry
   2. Development of the "American Plan"
   3. Other efforts to forestall unions
   4. Results of these policies
G. Election of 1928
   1. Republican position
   2. The Democratic choice
   3. Issues of the election
   4. Results

V. The Hoover presidency
A. The prospects for success
B. Hoover's general policies
C. His support for agriculture
   1. Aids for cooperative marketing
   2. Tariff increases
D. The speculative mania
   1. The Florida real estate bubble
   2. Development of the Great Bull Market
   3. Efforts to curb the market
E. The crash
   1. Description of the crash
   2. Immediate effects
   3. Causes for the crash
      a. Imbalance between productivity and purchasing power
      b. Governmental policies
      c. Gold standard
F. Human costs of depression
   1. Unemployment
   2. Hunger
   3. Homelessness
G. Hoover's efforts for recovery
   1. Advocates of laissez-faire
   2. Hoover's exhortations
   3. Public works and credit
   4. Democratic victory in 1930
   5. Hoover's insistence on voluntarism
   6. International complications
H. Congressional initiatives
   1. The RFC and its role
   2. Help for financial institutions
   3. Plans for relief
I. Plight of the farmers
   1. Their problems

2. Means of farmer protest
   a. Farmers' Holiday Association
   b. Revolutionary appeals

   c. The Bonus Expeditionary
     Force
J. Mood of the nation

KEY ITEMS OF CHRONOLOGY

Model T Ford	1908
F. W. Taylor's *Principles of Scientific Management*	1911
Birth of a Nation first presented	1915
Station KDKA began regular broadcasts	November 1920
Fordney-McCumber Tariff	1922
Lindbergh flight	May 1927
McNary-Haugen bills passed Congress	1927, 1928
Stock market crash	October 1929
Smoot-Hawley Tariff	1930
Hoover's moratorium on war-debt payments	1931
Creation of RFC	1932
Attack on the Bonus Expeditionary Force	July 1932

TERMS TO MASTER

Listed below are some important terms or people with which you should be familiar after you complete the study of this chapter. Explain the significance of each name or term.

1. normalcy
2. Andrew Mellon
3. Teapot Dome affair
4. Robert M. La Follette
5. *Birth of a Nation*
6. Charles A. Lindbergh, Jr.
7. Taylorization
8. associationalism
9. Bureau of Standards
10. marketing cooperatives
11. Farm Bureau Federation
12. McNary-Haugen scheme
13. "American Plan"
14. Alfred E. Smith
15. Agricultural Marketing Act
16. margin buying
17. gold standard
18. Reconstruction Finance Corporation
19. Federal Home Loan Bank Act
20. Bonus Expeditionary Force

VOCABULARY BUILDING

Listed below are some words or phrases used in this chapter. Look up each word in your dictionary unless the meaning is given here.

1. equipoise
2. nonentity
3. crony
4. reminiscent
5. behest
6. nullification
7. peculation
8. impropriety
9. barbarous
10. incongruous
11. vindication
12. coercion
13. brokerage
14. foreclose
15. deflationary
16. rummage
17. predicament
18. squalid
19. forlorn
20. melee

EXERCISES FOR UNDERSTANDING

When you have completed reading the chapter, answer each of the following questions. If you have difficulty, go back and reread the section of the chapter related to the question.

Multiple-Choice Questions

Select the letter of the response which best completes the statement.

1. The Democrats hoped the 1920 election would be a "solemn referendum" on
   A. associationalism.
   B. Taylorism.
   C. the Teapot Dome scandal.
   D. the League of Nations.
2. The Harding administration tried to overturn progressive reforms by
   A. appointing conservatives to the Supreme Court.
   B. following pro-business policies.
   C. reducing income taxes and raising tariffs.
   D. all of the above
3. "The chief business of the American people is business," said
   A. Andrew Mellon.
   B. Calvin Coolidge.
   C. Warren Harding.
   D. Henry Ford.
4. The commercial radio industry
   A. received a major boost from Al Jolson's *The Jazz Singer.*
   B. started in 1920.
   C. really grew when Ford put radios in automobiles.
   D. got its start during World War I.
5. As secretary of commerce, Herbert Hoover promoted
   A. keen competition among corporations.
   B. standardization of products (tires, bricks, etc.).
   C. a vigorous trust-busting campaign.
   D. federal ownership of the radio and airline industries.
6. Organized labor in the 1920s was weakened by
   A. the Red Scare.
   B. "yellow dog" contracts.
   C. welfare capitalism.
   D. all the above
7. A precursor of the stock market crash occurred in the speculative mania of the mid-1920s in
   A. Hollywood.
   B. Teapot Dome, Wyoming.
   C. Florida.
   D. Highland Park, Michigan.
8. Hoover's approach to recovery placed an emphasis on
   A. government construction of housing.
   B. voluntary efforts of the people.
   C. assistance to European trade.
   D. government aid to the unemployed.

True-False Questions

Indicate whether each statement is true or false.

1. Coolidge became president when Harding resigned in the midst of the Teapot Dome scandal.
2. Teapot Dome was an oil deposit.
3. The ideology of populism continued in the 1920s with the Farm Bureau.
4. Union membership in the 1920s remained steady.
5. *Real* wages of labor *increased* in the decade of the 1920s.
6. Buying stocks on margin helped restrain speculation in the stock market.
7. Excessively high wages for labor in the 1920s helped cause the stock market crash in 1929.
8. Herbert Hoover's philosophy was "industrial democracy."

Essay Questions

1. What reform efforts continued into the 1920s from the Progressive Era and what new reforms appeared in the decade after World War I?
2. Why was consumption so necessary in the 1920s? Explain its connection to labor,

production, farmers, and government
policies.

3. Which of the three Republican presidents
   in the 1920s was the most successful in
   achieving his goals and which was the
   least effective? Explain.

4. Describe the health of U.S. agriculture in
   the 1920s and evaluate the efforts to help

farmers.

5. What factors contributed to the collapse of
   the U.S. economy at the end of the 1920s?

6. How did Hoover's idea of "rugged individ-
   ualism" and "associationalism" affect his
   policies to deal with the collapse of the
   economy?

DOCUMENT

Document 1. "Keep the Consumer Dissatisfied"

Charles F. Kettering, general director of the
research laboratories at General Motors, discussed one of the major purposes of industrial

research and its relationship to prosperity in the
New Era.

> Not long ago one of the great bankers of the country said to me:
> "The trouble with you fellows is that you are all the time changing
> automobiles and depreciating old cars, and you are doing it at a time
> when people have three or four payments to make on the cars they
> already have.
> "Yesterday I got an engraved invitation from one of your compa-
> nies to see a new model. Out of curiosity I went. I darn near bought
> one. I didn't because you people wouldn't allow me enough money
> for my old car."
> A few weeks later I was again talking with this banker. He
> appeared to be greatly disgruntled.
> "I bought that new model," he barked. "But it was a rotten shame
> that I had to accept so much depreciation on my old car. You are the
> fellow who is to blame. You, with all your changes and refinements,
> made me dissatisfied with the old model."
> He paused, then added, mournfully, "And that old car ran like
> new."
> I told him I thought it was worth what he paid—that is, the differ-
> ence between the old and the new model—to have his mind changed.
> He didn't argue over that but he did say something to the general
> effect that "the only reason for research is to keep your customers rea-
> sonably dissatisfied with what they already have."
> I might observe, here and now, that he was right.
> A few weeks back I was sitting with a group of executives. All
> were admiring a new model.
> "It is absolutely the best automobile that can be made," enthused
> one. I objected to that statement.
> "Let's take this automobile which, you say, is the 'best that can be
> made' and put it into a glass showcase," I said. "Let's put it in there—

seal it so no person can possibly touch it. Just before we seal it in the case let us mark the price in big letters inside the case.

"Let us do that and come back here a year from today. After looking at it and appraising it, we will mark a price on the outside of the glass. It will be a price something less than what we think the car is worth today. Probably $200 less. Then, let's come back once every year for ten years, look through the glass, and mark a new price. At the end of ten years we won't be able to put down enough ciphers to indicate what we think of the car. That is, of course, eliminating its value as junk.

"In those ten years, no one could possibly have touched the car. There could be no lessened value through handling. The paint would be just as good as new; the crank case just as good; the rear axle just as good; and the motor just as good as ever.

"What, then, has happened to this car?

"People's minds will have been changed; improvements will have come in other cars; new styles will have come. What you have here today, a car that you call 'the best that can be made,' will then be useless. So it isn't the best that can be made. It may be the best you have made and, if that is what you meant, I have no quarrel with what you said." . . .

Change, to a research engineer, is improvement. People, though, don't seem to think of it in that manner. When a change is suggested they hold back and say, "What we have is all right—it does the work." Doing the work is important but doing it better is more important. The human family in industry is always looking for a park bench where it can sit down and rest. But the only park benches I know of are right in front of an undertaker's establishment.

There are no places where anyone can sit and rest in an industrial situation. It is a question of change, change, change, all the time—and it is always going to be that way. It must always be that way for the world only goes along one road, the road to progress. Nations and industries that have become satisfied with themselves and their ways of doing things, don't last. While they are sitting back and admiring themselves other nations and other concerns have forgotten the looking-glasses and have been moving ahead. . . .

The younger generation—and by that I mean the generation that is always coming—knows what it wants and it will get what it wants. This is what makes for change. It brings about improvements in old things and developments in new things.

You can't stop people being born. You can't stop the thing we call progress. You can't stop the thing we call change. But you can get in tune with it. Change is never waste—it is improvement, all down the line. Because I have no further need for my automobile doesn't mean that that automobile is destroyed. It goes to someone who has need for it and, to get it, he disposes of something that is unnecessary to his happiness. And so on to the end where the thing that is actually thrown away is of no further use to anyone. By this method living standards, all around, are raised.

We hear people complaining because of new models in automobiles. If it were not for these new models these same people would be paying more for what they have. Recognition of the fact that progress is inevitable forces us to recognize that we must have improvements in motor cars.

We, as manufacturers, must offer those improvements after they have been found to be capable improvements. The public buys and disposes of what it has. The fact that it is able to dispose of what it has enables us, as producers, to put a lower price tag on the new model. The law of economy in mass production enters here. We are permitted to turn out cars in volume because there is a market for them.

If automobile owners could not dispose of their cars to a lower buying strata they would have to wear out their cars with a consequent tremendous cutting in the yearly demand for automobiles, a certain increase in production costs, and the natural passing along of these costs to the buyer.

If every one were satisfied, no one would buy the new thing because no one would want it. The ore wouldn't be mined; timber wouldn't be cut. Almost immediately hard times would be upon us.

You must accept this reasonable dissatisfaction with what you have and buy the new thing, or accept hard times. You can have your choice.

[From Charles F. Kettering, "Keep the Consumer Dissatisfied," *Nation's Business*, 17, no. 1 (January 1929), 30–31, 79.]

Questions for Reflection

The textbook quotes a newspaper editorial from the 1920s as saying that the American's "first importance to his country is no longer that of citizen but that of consumer. Consumption is the new necessity." How does GM's Charles Kettering explain the role of industry in promoting consumption?

ANSWERS TO MULTIPLE-CHOICE AND TRUE-FALSE QUESTIONS

Multiple-Choice Questions

1-D, 2-D, 3-B, 4-B, 5-B, 6-D, 7-C, 8-B

True-False Questions

1-F, 2-T, 3-F, 4-F, 5-T, 6-F, 7-F, 8-F

28

NEW DEAL AMERICA

CHAPTER OBJECTIVES

After you complete the reading and study of this chapter, you should be able to:

1. Depict the character and appeal of FDR.
2. Characterize the sources for New Deal legislation.
3. Explain the New Deal approaches to the problems of recovery in industry and agriculture.
4. Delineate the criticisms made of the New Deal by the left and the right.
5. Describe New Deal efforts to deal with unemployment and welfare.
6. Assess the changes in the United States wrought by the New Deal.
7. Appreciate the cultural changes of the thirties.

CHAPTER OUTLINE

I. Election of 1928
   A. Republican action
   B. Democratic race for the nomination
   C. Roosevelt's background and character
   D. Campaign contrasts
   E. Results of the election

F. "The interregnum of despair"

II. The early New Deal
   A. Inauguration
   B. General policies
      1. Influences on New Deal policies
         a. Wartime experience
         b. Social work background
         c. Pragmatic approach
      2. Competing proposals
         a. Antitrust laws
         b. Collaboration with big business
         c. Expanded welfare and government spending
   C. Initial efforts
      1. Banking and the economy
         a. Bank holiday
         b. Emergency Banking Act
         c. Economy Act
         d. Refinancing farm and home mortgages
         e. Reform of banking and stock markets
            i. Creation of FDIC
            ii. Regulation of stocks and bonds
         f. Abandonment of gold standard
      2. Relief measures

  a. Civilian Conservation Corps
  b. Federal Emergency Relief
     Administration
  c. Civil Works Administration

III. Recovery through regulation
  A. Aid for agriculture
    1. Wide variety of options within
       AAA
    2. Immediate action to prevent
       surpluses
    3. Creation of the Commodity Cred-
       it Corporation
    4. Establishment of marketing quo-
       tas for cotton and tobacco
    5. General effects on farm income
    6. Dust bowl migrants
      a. From cotton-belt communities
      b. To California
      c. Okie subculture
    7. Second AAA
      a. Supreme Court overturns first
         AAA
      b. Soil Conversion Act
  B. Efforts for the recovery of industry
    1. National Industrial Recovery Act
    2. Title II: the Public Works Admin-
       istration (PWA)
    3. The National Recovery Adminis-
       tration (NRA)
      a. Two primary aims
      b. Nature of the NRA operation
      c. Development of the "blanket
         code"
      d. Objections to the NRA codes
      e. Enduring impact of the NRA
  C. Regional planning: Tennessee Valley
     Authority (TVA)
    1. Historical basis for the concept
    2. The legislation
    3. Impact of the TVA
    4. Creation of the Rural Electrifica-
       tion Association (REA)

IV. The Second New Deal
  A. Critics left and right
    1. Increased support for FDR in
       1934
    2. Conservatives launch the Ameri-
       can Liberty League

    3. Thunder on the left
      a. Huey Long's threat
      b. Francis Townsend's program
      c. Father Coughlin's role
      d. Potential threat of the left
    4. Pressure on FDR to restore
       competition
    5. Roadblocks from the Supreme
       Court
  B. Overview of the legislation
  C. The Wagner Act for workers
  D. The Social Security Act
    1. Precedents
    2. Pension program
    3. Unemployment insurance
    4. Grants for public assistance
    5. Flaws and limitations
  E. The Works Progress Administration
     (WPA) for "employables"
  F. Strengthened control of the banking
     system and public utilities
  G. The Wealth Tax Act
  H. Conservative criticisms
  I. Continuing personal impact of
     depression
    1. Effects of unemployment
    2. Family life
  J. Minorities and New Deal
    1. Racial discrimination of some
       programs
    2. Mexican Americans
    3. Native Americans
    4. Supreme Court and blacks
    5. "Black Cabinet"

V. Social effects of the depression
  A. Personal lives and families
    1. Persistent unemployment
    2. Crime, suicide, divorce, desertion
    3. Postponed marriages and children
    4. Effects on children
  B. African Americans
    1. "Black Cabinet"
    2. NAACP activity
    3. Scottsboro case

VI. Second-term developments
  A. The election of 1936
    1. Republicans choose progressive
       Landon

2. The new Roosevelt coalition
3. Results of the election
B. Eleanor Roosevelt
1. Background
2. Marriage to FDR
   a. Contrasts with husband
   b. Sara Roosevelt's effects
   c. Lucy Mercer
   d. New mutual interest
3. As public figure
   a. Presidential adviser
   b. Advocate for women and blacks
   c. Liaison to liberals
C. Stirrings among labor
1. Impetus to unionization
2. Rise of industrial unions
3. Intense conflict with management
   a. Techniques used by management
   b. Action by autoworkers
      i. Sit-down strike
      ii. Walter Reuther
      iii. United Auto Workers
   c. CIO victories
   d. Growing power for organized labor
D. Reaction to a new depression
1. Course of the 1937 slump
2. Administration's reaction
3. The battle over spending
   a. Fear of the unbalanced budget
   b. Keynesian theory
4. Roosevelt's call for spending
5. Reforms of 1937
   a. Housing legislation
   b. Assistance for rural poverty
      i. Farm Tenant Act

ii. Work of the Farm Security Administration
6. The legislation of 1938
   a. Second AAA
   b. Food, Drug and Cosmetic Act
   c. Fair Labor Standards Act
E. Setbacks to the New Deal
1. Emergence of an opposition
   a. Defection of the southerners
   b. Victories of the opposition in 1938
2. Roosevelt's 1938 purge
3. Results of the 1938 elections
4. Limited legislation in 1939

VII. Impact of the New Deal
A. Some enduring changes
B. A course between extremes
C. Creation of the "broker state"

VIII. Culture in the 1930s
A. Renewed social commitment
B. Communist party activity
C. Novelists of social significance
1. John Steinbeck
2. Richard Wright
D. Documentary expression
1. Federal Writers' Project
2. Photographers
E. Popular culture
1. Radio
   a. Soap operas
   b. Children's programs
2. Movies
   a. Gangster films
   b. Musicals
   c. Comedies
   d. *Gone with the Wind*

KEY ITEMS OF CHRONOLOGY

FDR contracts polio	1921
Scottsboro case begins	1931
Bonus Army March	1932
Roosevelt's administrations	March 4, 1933–April 12, 1945
The Hundred Days	March 4–June 16, 1933

Tennessee Valley Authority created	May 1933
Indian Reorganization Act passed	1934
Second New Deal initiatives	1935
Wagner Act passed	July 1935
Social Security started	August 1935
AFL expelled CIO	1936
Court-packing plan presented	1937
The Grapes of Wrath	1939
Gone with the Wind	1939

TERMS TO MASTER

Listed below are some important terms or people with which you should be familiar after you complete the study of this chapter. Explain the significance of each name or term.

1. brain trust
2. Twentieth Amendment
3. the Hundred Days
4. Securities and Exchange Commission
5. CCC
6. Okies
7. *US.* v. *Butler*
8. National Recovery Administration
9. Tennessee Valley Authority
10. Huey P. Long
11. "sick chicken" case
12. National Labor Relations Act
13. Social Security Act
14. Indian Reorganization Act
15. "Black Cabinet"
16. court-packing plan
17. CIO
18. sit-down strike
19. Walter Reuther
20. John Maynard Keynes
21. Fair Labor Standards Act
22. broker state
23. popular front
24. John Steinbeck
25. Federal Writers' Project
26. *Let Us Now Praise Famous Men*

VOCABULARY BUILDING

Listed below are some words or phrases used in this chapter. Look up each word in your dictionary unless the meaning is given here.

1. ebullient
2. affinity
3. penchant
4. affable
5. interregnum
6. privation
7. vacillate
8. rampant
9. nostrums
10. consummate
11. imprudent
12. regressive
13. impede
14. repatriation
15. indomitable
16. senility
17. veneration
18. decimate
19. grandiloquent
20. disgruntled

EXERCISES FOR UNDERSTANDING

When you have completed reading the chapter, answer each of the following questions. If you have difficulty, go back and reread the section of the chapter related to the question.

Multiple-Choice Questions

Select the letter of the response that best completes the statement.

1. The Agricultural Adjustment Act of 1933
   A. wanted farmers to increase production.
   B. sought parity for farm prices.
   C. helped tenants keep their jobs.
   D. all the above

2. The National Industrial Recovery Act provided for
   A. $3.3 billion in spending through the PWA.
   B. codes of fair practice for industries.
   C. the right of workers to form unions.
   D. all the above

3. The New Deal's "cornerstone" and "supreme achievement," according to FDR, was
   A. Social Security.
   B. the Wagner Labor Relations Act.
   C. the Tennessee Valley Authority.
   D. the PWA and WPA.

4. Under John Collier, the New Deal program for Native Americans sought
   A. to extend the Dawes Act's Americanization of Indians.
   B. to convert Indians to Christianity.
   C. to restore their cultural traditions.
   D. to eliminate the Bureau of Indian Affairs.

5. Eleanor Roosevelt helped the president by
   A. shielding him from labor and women activists.
   B. providing a happy and serene home life.
   C. taking political risks he could not take.
   D. all the above

6. The Supreme Court packing plan was defeated in part because of
   A. Democratic losses in 1936.
   B. its violation of the Constitution.
   C. a change in the Court's direction in rulings on key measures.
   D. all the above

7. Walter Reuther was a leader in
   A. the early motion picture industry.
   B. organizing automobile workers.
   C. the Federal Writers' Project.
   D. opposing FDR's court-packing plan.

8. The most popular form of entertainment in the 1930s was
   A. radio.
   B. vaudeville.
   C. movies.
   D. television.

True-False Questions

Indicate whether each statement is true or false.

1. An early New Deal program called for slaughtering six million pigs.
2. Codes of fair competitive practice were established by the NRA.
3. *The Grapes of Wrath* depicted dust bowl immigrants to California.
4. Only the New Deal agricultural programs did not discriminate against blacks.
5. FDR's cabinet had several African-American members; it was therefore called the "Black Cabinet."
6. Perhaps the most enduring voting change brought by FDR was the shift of the farm vote to the Democratic party.
7. Keynesianism involves reducing government spending in times of severe unemployment.
8. The leading black novelist in the depression was Richard Wright.

Essay Questions

1. Which of the three competing solutions presented by FDR's advisers for easing depression had the greatest effects on the American economy?
2. What role did the Supreme Court play in the 1930s?
3. Compare and contrast the New Deal's policies toward labor and industry.
4. How did the Great Depression affect the lives of ordinary U.S. citizens?
5. What were the major accomplishments of FDR and the New Deal?
6. What was the impact of the depression on U.S. writers?
7. What changes occurred in American popular culture in the thirties despite the depression?

A Match of New Deal Agencies

The New Deal period witnessed the creation of a plethora of new government agencies which became known as the alphabet agencies because they were referred to by their initials. To help you focus on major agencies and to test *your grasp of the material, match the description or statement in the right column on the following page with the agencies or act in the left. Some of the agencies or acts may match with more than one description. Answers are at the end of this chapter.*

Agency or Act	Description
1. FDIC	a. created a regional rehabilitation of a river basin
2. FERA	b. investigated the concentration of economic power in the United States
3. Economy Act	c. set minimum wages and maximum hours for certain industries in interstate commerce
4. First AAA	d. provided a variety of methods for increasing farm income
5. Civilian Conservation Corps	e. provided insurance for bank deposits
6. PWA	f. $3.3 billion for jobs on major building projects
7. TVA	g. a stopgap plan for aiding the unemployed in 1933–1935
8. NRA	h. loans to rural cooperatives to run electrical lines to remote farms
9. REA	i. a plan to cut wages of veterans and federal employees
10. Wagner Act	j. jobs for young men in the nation's parks
11. Social Security Act	k. an agency to regulate the sale of stocks and bonds
12. Wealth Tax Act	l. allowed industries to collaborate together to limit production of goods and raise wages
13. SEC	m. provided farmers payments to conserve soil by not planting crops
14. TNEC	n. created a committee to oversee elections for unions
15. Farm Security Administration	o. established the welfare system for mothers and dependent children
16. Soil Conservation Act	p. greatly increased income taxes
17. Fair Labor Standards Act	q. provided a tax on incomes to ensure retirement benefits
18. WPA	r. placed a tax on farm products when first processed for market
	s. provided loans to help farm tenants buy their land
	t. a long-term federal program to provide jobs, including symphony, artistic, and theater projects
	u. provided states aid for work projects as well as a dole
	v. built dams to produce and sell electricity
	w. a counterpart to NRA, this agency provided jobs on major construction projects

DOCUMENTS

Document 1. Broke at Fifty-five

The Great Depression struck the once comfortable professionals as well as the workers and labors in American society. In 1931, an unemployed editor described the acutely personal effects of economic hardship during the depression.

I've done a good deal of thinking in the past year, largely because I haven't had anything else to do. Prior to that, for twenty-five years, I wrote editorials, without thinking—sort of caught ideas out of the air, mechanically, as a riveter catches red-hot bolts.

Most of the editorials were intended to comfort the poor and downtrodden. I didn't know the poor and downtrodden personally. But they existed in large numbers, and subscribed to the paper for which I wrote. It was a farm paper, one dollar a year. . . .

There was good money in it, for publisher and editor both. . . . It looked as though the condition and the position were permanent. It really wasn't a bad job, as jobs go, telling the farmer how poor he was, for $200 a week, with an annual bonus if advertising remained good. . . .

. . . One Monday morning I brought in the newspaper early, and found myself out of a job. The paper I had worked for as second in command for twenty years had been sold the day before, on Sunday.

A few weeks later a national bank in which I had invested the residue of what had seemed a small salary, until I lost it, found it advisable to merge with a larger bank. Before that, stock which had cost $250 a share went so low that it made a fellow wake up in the middle of the night, all hot and scared, and hearing every board in the house creak, he was so sure the morning mail would bring the notice of a double assessment on the poor innocent stockholders.

There's the picture: broke at fifty-five, and four hungry people still demanding three meals a day. . . .

A man's egotism is an anaesthetic allaying the first pains. He works fifteen, twenty, twenty-five years, no matter how many. He is either good or he becomes acclimated and the boss lets him stay on, like an old piece of furniture hardly worth carrying away. He loses his job. He says to himself, "Well, I've worked hard and faithfully a good many years. The last three years I didn't take my regular office vacation, at full pay. Sorry now that I didn't, but a rest won't hurt me. In fact, it will do me good. I was getting in a rut. And while I'm resting other firms or plants or factories will hear that I'm out, and I'll choose from among the good offers they make me."

"Well, you're fixed all right; no need for you to worry; you'll get along fine. You can always get a good job, anywhere." So the home folks said, as they stopped me on the street and then hurried on, remembering I was no longer in the newspaper business and therefore no longer useful to them, and their children's parties, with layout, on the Sunday society page.

"It seems to be the tendency of the times; reducing overhead expenses." This from a few editors, still permanently located and pretty sure of a few years more.

As for the offers, they never came at all. It was weeks before I could figure it out. The little notice about me in the home-town paper had been hidden away between a patent-medicine advertisement and the notice of a concern passing its dividend. Maybe I'd better send out a few letters to prominent publishers and editors to let them know my address. I had opened up an office in one f the bedrooms at home and was typing, "Now is the time for all god men to come to the ad of the party," hour after hour, in order to make the neighbors think I was still writing—for a living.

I have a large number of very splendid endorsements which I shall be glad to loan to anyone prepaying the postage. The name can easily be changed. So many of those to whom I wrote giving them first chance at my services would have grabbed me off just a little while before, but "recent additions to our staff make it impossible," "we have built up a stalwart organization which we hesitate," and so on. "Surprised to hear that *you* should have been let out." No more surprised than I was, and the italics are not mine, either. You can't even get credit for them at the cash-and-carry grocery stores.

The trusting hopefulness of the first few weeks turned to bitterness. "A fine fellow, when he had a paper back of him; quite a dub without one." "Pretty cocky, wasn't he? Sort of held himself aloof from the gang. Oh, well, roll out another money ball and let the ancient and noble game of Kelly pool continue." I was sore for a while; then I laughed it off. No doubt I had done the same many a time. Nobody every considers anything until it comes right home. I've often wondered if Longfellow wrote "There is no death" with his fingers crossed. He sure slipped it over on them that day.

First, indifference; next, reassuring faith; third, galling bitterness; fourth, morbidity. And the last is what hurts and causes folks to fall out of ten-story windows, accidentally. "Nothing wrong with his accounts; happily married," say the newspapers. How about the rapidly dwindling bank balance; the determination that the loved ones, who were in no way to blame for the bad luck, shall go on having the things they were accustomed to having; the stiff upper lip the grand old Scotch mother used to talk about, before you ever had a penny of your own and were too young to go out in the world and work?

Around fifty a man loses nerve—I don't mean the nerve it takes to accompany Wilkins under the ice to the North Pole, or to fly with Byrd and moving-picture men over the South Pole. I mean the nerve it takes to ask a stranger for a job, when you've turned down thousands of men yourself without batting an eye; to tell a friend how good you are, and watch his face continue blank; to approach the banker whom you puffed in your paper for years and who was only too glad to lend you whatever you wanted at 6 per cent, and not even take the interest out in advance. This time he suggests that the wife sign the note, too, and makes it 7 per cent, in advance, and asks for a credit statement.

You have just as much ability as ever. You've got a book half started—a whale of a plot never used before, good dialogue, nice, clean, moral sort of a book. You'll sell it soon and then you'll be all right. Maybe you'll make $10,000 out of it. But the home folks know you've lost your $200 a week, and that's ever so much bigger. And nowadays if you're counting on a $10,000 book, the home folks are right; the $200 check is much bigger—and surer.

Finally, in course of time, you begin to feel toward yourself as you imagine other folks are feeling toward you. I've never cared a rap for money. I never carried much, however far from home I went. I could always get it somehow, from somebody. There would be whole days at home when there wasn't even a penny in the pockets of any of the two suits. Now that I'm broke I always carry a few silver dollars, so I can jingle them and not feel so downcast. It has the effect on listeners, too.

Have you read Stevenson's "The Amateur Emigrant"? If you have, read it again. He tells of coming over on a steamer, second cabin, when that was different from what it is now, while the class of people with whom he was wont to associate were traveling first class. They ignored him. "I'm my normal circumstances," he says, "it appeared every young lady must have paid some tribute of a glance, and though I had not often detected it when it was given, I was well aware of its absence when it was withheld." He reflects a bit and concludes, "I wish someone . . . would find out exactly at what stage of toilet a man becomes invisible to the well-regulated female eye."

I have a similar problem. I should like to find out at what stage of your poverty other people realize or sense it, and pass you by as one no longer interesting or useful to them. You wear the same suit, more carefully brushed and pressed than ever before to conceal your poverty. You walk just as cockily. You know as much; you know a lot more, in fact—things you didn't suspect or believe before. I guess, after all, it's the droop in the shoulders, the look in your eyes—furtive, expectant, resentful.

The nights are the worse; the time when all you can see is the unseen. You've done everything humanly possible to avert the inevitable. You've gone over your life-insurance policies, to be sure they are all incontestable after the first year. You've taken out additional accident insurance. You realize that for the first time in your rather carefree, indifferent life you are worth more dead than alive—a good deal more.

The boards in the house creak. Your heart gives a jump. Will it be the last one? Perhaps it's a burglar. Your last chance to be a hero. To have the papers, which you pretend to scorn, use you as first-page copy. X marks the spot where the burglar was killed. Don't laugh! It's all terribly real; no make-believe. But it's a grand joke on the burglar—robbing the house of a man who is broke, at fifty-five. Poor devil!

Another board creaks. You hear Andy figuring his income tax. "Five million." "Seven million." You go over, in your head, the dwindling bank balance. "Three hundred and two." "Two hundred and eighty." "Two hundred and forty-nine."

You're wide awake now. The perspiration runs from you. It's only the ring of the window shade hitting the glass this time. The birds are beginning to sing. Pretty little things. They don't have tow work on a salary. They don't take men's words, and find them salty in the mouth. A little light in the east window. Everybody else is sleeping. You've stopped all the clocks. You can't stand them any more. Every tick is one of the few remaining dollars gone.

Another day. Nobody knows, but yourself. And you're getting terribly close-mouthed about things lately.

[Frank G. Moorhead, "Broke at Fifty-Five," from *The Nation* 132, no. 3436 (May 13, 1931): 528–30]

Document 2. Excerpts from the Federal Writers' Project Interviews with Depression Victims

Through the efforts of New Deal Agencies Americans learned much about themselves in the 1930s. The Federal Writers' Project, for instance, published poignant accounts of the lives of people in some southern states. The excerpts below come from those accounts.

From the Account of a White Brick-Plant Worker and His Washer-Woman Wife

"Hub's hired solid time and has been for two years. He works every day from six in the morning till six at night in Mr. Hunter's brick plant across the tracks. Some days more'n that—twenty-four hours on a stretch. That's over-time, but it don't mean no extra pay. It's forty dollars a month straight, no matter what."

Rena Murray—small, stooped, hollow-chested—put her whole ninety pounds behind the heavy flatiron. Collar and cuffs came from under the heat, stiff and slick. She lifted the shirt from the board for final inspection.

"Hub fires the boiler most of the time. Then when they're drying bricks, he has to run the fan for twenty-four hours. They couldn't make out in that kiln unless Hub was there.

"He ought to git more for the work he puts out. Forty dollars a month just ain't enough for us to live on. Me and Hub and the three children. We have to pay four dollars out every month for this shack. Mr. Hunter makes the hands live close by the plant. And he gits ahold of that four dollars for rent before we ever see a cent of Hub's wages. This shack ain't worth four dollars a month, neither. Mr. Hunter won't do nothing toward fixing it up. If a window pane's broke, we do the putting in. Leak done ruins the paper and it's up to us to see to new paper."

Rena stooped to the tub of sprinkled clothes. She shook out a rolled-up bundle and slipped another shirt over the narrow end of the home-made ironing board. She settled the board again between the center table and the lard bucket set in a backless kitchen chair.

"I take in washing or do what I can to help out."

"We ain't been to church for years. I was taught working on Sunday was wrong. Folks that holds out against working on Sunday don't have to hire others to work for 'em if they don't show up. Hub had to pay a dollar and a quarter yesterday to git a man to turn the fan so's he could see after his sister. She's about to die. Dirty shame for a man to have to pay to go see his own die. I sure wish he could find hisself a better job."

"What he aims to do is to turn over every stone he can to git back on the WPA. We got along a lot better on the WPA. We had our check regular and had good warm clothes for the girls. And they give Hub clothes, too, because his work kept him in the open. I didn't git none but I could manage all right when the others was gifting all they did. Whenever one of us would git down, the WPA would send a doctor and medicine. They give us food, too. Things that are supposed to be healthy for eating such as prunes and raisins. We can't buy 'em now."

"Burial insurance is a good thing. I wish I had a policy on me and every one of the children. That's just wishing. It pinches us plumb to death to keep Hub's going. We was always behind in dues till he got put on solid time. I couldn't git no insurance noways on account of my bad health. I've had the pneumonia since we've been here. Down three months. There wasn't a Hunter had feeling enough to set foot in this shack. Mrs. Hunter has spoke to me times since, but Mr. Hunter don't trouble about speaking to them that slaves for him. My mammy taught me a dog was good enough to be nice to."

From the Account of a Young Shoe-Factory Worker

"My work is hard all right. It's hard on me because I ain't but only seventeen and ain't got my full growth yet. It's work down in the steam room which they call it that because it's always full of steam which sometimes when you go in it you can't hardly see. You steam leather down there and that steam soaks you clean to the skin. It makes me keep a cold most of the time because when I go out doors I'm sopping wet. Another thing that's hard about it is having so much standing up to do. My hours is from seven o'clock in the morning till four in the evening. And it's stand on my feet the whole time. When noon time comes and I'm off an hour, why I just find me somewheres to set and I sure set there. You couldn't pay me to stand up during lunch time.

"I'm on piecework now and I can't seem to get my production up to where I make just a whole lot. You get paid by the production hour and it takes fifty pair of shoes to make that hour. You get forty-two cents for the hour. Highest I ever made in one week was eleven dollars and the lowest was seven dollars and forty-two cents. I usually hit in between and make eight or nine dollars.

"Now and then somebody will say, 'We ought to have us a union here of some sort.' That kind of talk just makes me mad all over. Mr. Pugh is a Christian man. He brought his factory here to give us some work which we didn't have any before. We do pretty well, I think, to just stay away from that kind of talk. All but the sore-heads and trouble-makers is satisfied and glad to have work.

"I don't blame Mr. Pugh a bit the way he feels about the unions. The plant manager knows Mr. Pugh mighty well and he told my foreman what Mr. Pugh said. Mr. Pugh said, 'If the union ever comes in here and I have to operate my plant under a union, why I'll just close the plant down and move it away from Hancock so quick it'll make your head swim.' That's his word on it and I don't blame him none. I'd hate to see a union try here. No plant and no jobs for anybody. They just operate these unions out of Wall Street, anyhow, trying to ruin people like Mr. Pugh. . . .

"My money has to go a long way. I've got to pay eight dollars a month rent and I have to buy coal and stove wood. I got to buy clothes for the family and something to eat for them. Then twice a month there's that five dollar ambulance bill which it's to take my brother that's got the T.B. to the City Hospital in Memphis where they take and drain his lungs. Sure charge you for an ambulance, don't they? Now, some people say if you just take one trip in an ambulance, the undertaker won't ask a cent for it. Figures he'll get your custom if you pass on. But they sure charge me for my brother.

"Well, I'm always glad when it's quitting time. I like to work there, but you can't help getting tired. I go on home. I walk four blocks and I'm there. Usually I have to wait a while for supper so I just set at the window. I like to watch and see if maybe something will come along the street and I can watch it. Sometimes there's a new funny paper there and I will look it over—specially if it's Tarzan. That's the best thing in a funny paper, the Tarzan part. Nobody ever gets it over old Tarzan, do they? Most times, though, I like to just set there and watch."

"I work steady but I'm most always financially in need of money. It takes a lot to keep a family going. My little sister needs glasses but they cost too much. All of my family has weak eyes but we can't afford to wear glasses.

"So I haven't the money for running around. I wouldn't if I had the money, either. The Bible is against running around and playing cards and seeing the moving pictures. People should study their Bible more and we'd have more Christian men like Mr. Pugh and more jobs. So me and a young lady I know of go to church and Sunday School instead of running around. My family belongs to the Baptist Church, but this certain young lady is a Nazarene and that's where we go.

"You know, when you're blue and down at the mouth and don't see any use anyhow, a good sermon just lifts you up. You haven't got a thing to lose by living a Christian life. Take Mr. Pugh. He lives it and look where he is now. And if you don't make out that way, if you're poor all your life, then you get a high place in the Kingdom. Just do the best you know how and the Lord will take care of you either here or hereafter. It sure is a comfort."

[From *These Are Our Lives* (1939), as told to and written by members of the Federal Writers' Project of the WPA (New York: Norton, 1975), pp. 224–28, 231–35]

Questions for Reflection

How did the economic crisis of the 1930s affect people, both those unaccustomed to great financial distress and the working poor? Did one suffer more or differently than the other? What were the psychological ramifications of unemployment for them? What would be the long-term implications of such widespread unemployment? How do these accounts differ form the Boston women workers in Chapter 21?

ANSWERS TO MULTIPLE-CHOICE, TRUE-FALSE, AND MATCHING QUESTIONS

Multiple-Choice Questions

1-B, 2-D, 3-A, 4-C, 5-C, 6-C, 7-B, 8-C

True-False Questions

1-T, 2-T, 3-T, 4-F, 5-F, 6-F, 7-F, 8-T

Matching Questions

1-e, 2-q,u, 3-i, 4-d,r, 5-j, 6-f,w, 7-a,v, 8-l, 9-h, 10-n, 11-o,q, 12-p, 13-k, 14-b, 15-s, 16-m, 17-c, 18-t

29 ∽

FROM ISOLATION TO GLOBAL WAR

CHAPTER OBJECTIVES

After you complete the reading and study of this chapter, you should be able to:

1. Recount the foreign policy pursued by the United States in the interwar period.
2. Outline the aggressions of Japan, Italy, and Germany in the decade of the 1930s.
3. Account for U.S. efforts at neutrality in the face of aggression and assess its effectiveness in preventing war.
4. Describe the election of 1940.
5. Tell why and how the United States supported Britain and Russia prior to its entry into the war.
6. Explain the effectiveness of the attack on Pearl Harbor.

CHAPTER OUTLINE

I. Postwar isolationism
   A. Evidences of isolationist sentiment
   B. Counteractions of world involvement
   C. Relations with the League
      1. Gradual involvement with social issues after 1924
      2. Repeated rejection of the World Court
   D. War-debt tangle

1. Level of Allied war debts
2. Problems with repayment of debt.
3. Linkage of debts to reparations
4. Depression and debt cancellation
   E. Efforts toward disarmament
      1. Substitute for League membership
      2. Strained Japanese-American relationships
      3. Washington Armaments Conference
         a. Hughes's initiative
         b. Agreements made at the conference
         c. Effects of the treaties
      4. The movement to outlaw war
         a. Origins of the movement
         b. Development of the Kellogg-Briand Pact
   F. The Good-Neighbor Policy
      1. Early efforts to improve relations with Latin America
      2. Protection of U.S. rights in Mexico
      3. Hoover's moves to improve policy
         a. Ending *de jure* recognition
         b. Clark Memorandum on the Monroe Doctrine
      4. Further improvements under FDR

II. War clouds

A. Japanese incursion in China
  1. Japanese occupation of Manchuria
  2. Reactions to occupation
     a. The Stimson Doctrine
     b. League condemnation
     c. Japan's withdrawal from the League
B. Mussolini's rise to power
C. Hitler's rise to power
  1. Events leading to his control
  2. Reactions to his provocations
D. U.S. actions
  1. Roosevelt's refusal to support the London Economic Conference
  2. Hull's Reciprocal Trade Agreements
  3. Recognition of the Soviet Union
E. Aggression in Asia and Europe
  1. Italian invasion of Ethiopia, 1935
  2. Hitler's occupation of the Rhineland, 1936
  3. Spanish Civil War, 1936
  4. Japanese invasion of China, 1937
  5. Hitler's *Anschluss* with Austria, 1938
  6. The Munich Agreement, 1938
  7. War began over Poland, 1939

III. U.S. efforts for neutrality
  A. Impact of the Nye Committee investigations
  B. Walter Millis's popular view
  C. Congressional effort to avoid World War I
  D. The first Neutrality Act, 1935
     1. Forbade sale of arms to belligerents
     2. Travel discouraged on belligerent ships
  E. Reaction to the invasion of Ethiopia
  F. The second Neutrality Act forbade loans to belligerents
  G. Extension of the Neutrality Act to cover civil wars
  H. Further neutrality provisions
  I. Reactions to Japanese action in China
     1. Lack of use of neutrality laws
     2. Quarantine speech

  3. *Panay* incident
  4. Ludlow Amendment
  J. Reactions to war in Europe
     1. Change to cash-and-carry arms sales
     2. Extension of war zone
     3. Actions in the Western Hemisphere

IV. The storm in Europe
  A. Hitler's *Blitzkrieg*
  B. U.S. aid to embattled Britain
     1. Growth of U.S. defense effort
     2. Sales of arms to Britain
  C. Other defense measures
  D. The destroyer-bases deal
  E. Peacetime conscription
  F. Polarization of public opinion
     1. Committee to Defend America
     2. America First Committee

V. The election of 1940
  A. The choice of Willkie
  B. The choice of FDR
  C. The campaign
  D. Results of the election

VI. The arsenal of democracy
  A. The Lend-Lease program
  B. Further Axis gains
  C. Reaction to the invasion of the Soviet Union
  D. The Atlantic Charter
  E. Conflict with the Germans in the Atlantic

VII. The storm in the Pacific
  A. Japanese aggression in Southeast Asia
  B. Effect of Germany's invasion of Russia
  C. Negotiations between Japan and the United States
  D. Warlords gain control in Japan
  E. Attack on Pearl Harbor
     1. Extent of U.S. foreknowledge
     2. Errors in warning
     3. Damage from the attack
     4. Other Japanese aggression in the Pacific
  F. Declaration of war

KEY ITEMS OF CHRONOLOGY

Washington Disarmament Conference	1921–1922
Mussolini took power in Italy	1925
Kellogg-Briand Pact	1928
Japanese invasion of Manchuria	1931
Hitler took power in Germany	1933
London Economic Conference	1933
Nye Committee	1934–1937
Italy's invasion of Ethiopia	1935
Japan's invasion of China	1937
Quarantine Speech	1937
World War II began	September 1, 1939
First peacetime draft	1940
Fall of France	June 1940
Lend-Lease program began	1941
Germany's invasion of Russia	June 1941
Japanese extend protectorate over Indochina	July 1941
Attack on Pearl Harbor	December 7, 1941

TERMS TO MASTER

Listed below are some important terms or people with which you should be familiar after you complete the study of this chapter. Explain the significance of each name or term.

1. World Court
2. Washington Armaments Conference
3. reparations
4. Five-Power Treaty
5. Kellogg-Briand Pact
6. Good Neighbor Policy
7. Stimson Doctrine
8. London Naval Conference
9. Cordell Hull
10. Reciprocal Trade Agreements
11. Nye Committee
12. Neutrality Acts
13. cash and carry
14. Ludlow Amendment
15. *Blitzkrieg*
16. Committee to Defend America by Aiding the Allies
17. America First Committee
18. Wendell Willkie
19. Lend-Lease program
20. Atlantic Charter

VOCABULARY BUILDING

Listed below are some words or phrases used in this chapter. Look up each word in your dictionary unless the meaning is given here.

1. aloof
2. extranational
3. default
4. hiatus
5. pious
6. ploy
7. tacitly
8. allay
9. enmity
10. abrogate
11. incursion
12. cadre
13. pretext
14. hybrid
15. dissension
16. ludicrous
17. avail
18. inhibition
19. flank (v.)
20. conscription

EXERCISES FOR UNDERSTANDING

When you have completed reading the chapter, answer each of the following questions. If you have difficulty, go back and reread the section of the chapter related to the question.

Multiple-Choice Questions

Select the letter of the response that best completes the statement.

1. In the 1930s, a major cause of isolationism in the United States was
   A. business and investment interests overseas.
   B. possessions in the Pacific.
   C. involvements with the League of Nations and World Court.
   D. problems with the Allies' payments of debts from World War I.
2. European payments of war debts after World War I were tied to
   A. rates of immigration to the United States.
   B. American tariff barriers.
   C. Germany's reparations payments.
   D. the success of disarmament efforts.
3. The "good neighbor policy" involved
   A. FDR and Latin America.
   B. Hoover and postwar Europe.
   C. Mussolini and Ethiopia.
   D. the United States and Canada.
4. The Nye Committee investigations seemed to prove that
   A. the United States entered World War I to permit the munitions manufacturers to make greater profits.
   B. the United States should back down from its dispute with Japan over China.
   C. the only way to end the war was with a treaty.
   D. the United States was not responsible for the success of the attack by Japan.
5. The Neutrality Act of 1939
   A. prohibited all trade with belligerents.
   B. allowed trade with only one side in a war.
   C. kept U.S. ships from war zones but

approved cash-and-carry trade even for arms.
   D. permitted nonmilitary trade in U.S. ships only.
6. FDR no longer pretended to be neutral in the European war after
   A. his re-election in 1940.
   B. Germany occupied Czechoslovakia.
   C. the sinking of the *Panay.*
   D. Italy conquered Ethiopia.
7. In the summer of 1940
   A. the United States and Britain swapped destroyers for naval and air bases.
   B. Congress appropriated $4 billion for a two-ocean navy.
   C. the first peacetime draft became law.
   D. all the above
8. Before the attack on Pearl Harbor, Japan had
   A. not expanded outside its national boundaries.
   B. conquered all China.
   C. captured all southeast Asia.
   D. control of Manchuria, Shanghai, and French Indochina.

True-False Questions

Indicate whether each statement is true or false.

1. "You just don't want a surrender of the United States," said FDR in reference to opposition to the League of Nations.
2. Charles Evans Hughes believed in 1921 that "the way to disarm is to disarm."
3. In 1933, President Roosevelt advocated joining the League of Nations.
4. In 1935, Hitler began Germany's conquest of Ethiopia.
5. The United States gave diplomatic recognition to the Soviet Union in 1933.
6. The *Panay* incident increased U.S. dislike for Japan.
7. The Kellogg-Briand Pact called for a national referendum for a declaration of war.
8. The United States's declaration of war in 1941 passed the Congress unanimously.

Essay Questions

1. In what ways did the U.S. follow a foreign policy of isolationism in the 1920s? In what ways did it not?
2. What efforts did America make to achieve peace and disarmament during the 1920s?
3. Compare U.S. relations with Japan and with Latin America.
4. How did the mounting hostilities in Asia resemble the increasing conflicts in Europe in the late 1930s?
5. Why did the United States seek to remain neutral in the 1930s?
6. How did the Great Depression affect U.S. foreign policy?
7. Account for the attack on Pearl Harbor in 1941 and assess its consequences.
8. How did the U.S. move from neutrality in the mid-1930s to a declaration of war in 1941?

DOCUMENTS

Document 1. Roosevelt's Quarantine Speech, 1937

In the wake of the rearmament of Germany, the Italian invasion of Ethiopia, the Spanish Civil War, and finally the Japanese invasion of China, Roosevelt visited Chicago, the heart of isolationist sentiment in the United States, on October 5, 1937, to make what has generally been dubbed his Quarantine Speech. Look carefully in the following excerpts for the promises or pledges that the president sought to exact on the issues of peace and war.

> Without a declaration of war and without warning or justification of any kind, civilians, including women and children, are being ruthlessly murdered with bombs from the air. In times of so-called peace ships are being attacked and sunk by submarines without cause or notice. Nations are fomenting and taking sides in civil warfare in nations that have never done them any harm. Nations claiming freedom for themselves deny it to others. . . .
>
> The peace-loving nations must make a concerted effort in opposition to those violations of treaties and those ignorings of humane instincts which today are creating a state of international anarchy and instability from which there is no escape through mere isolation or neutrality. . . .
>
> There is a solidarity and interdependence about the modern world, both technically and morally, which makes it impossible for any nation completely to isolate itself from economic and political upheavals in the rest of the world, specially when such upheavals appear to be spreading and not declining.
>
> It seems to be unfortunately true that the epidemic of world lawlessness is spreading.
>
> When an epidemic of physical disease starts to spread, the community approves and joins in a quarantine of the patients in order to protect the health of the community against the spread of the disease.
>
> War is a contagion, whether it be declared or undeclared. It can engulf states and peoples remote from the original scene of hostilities.

. . . We are adopting such measures as will minimize our risk of involvement, but we cannot have complete protection in a world of disorder in which confidence and security have broken down.

If civilization is to survive the principles of the Prince of Peace must be restored. Shattered trust between nations must be revived.

Most important of all, the will for peace on the part of peace-loving nations must express itself to the end that nations that may be tempted to violate their agreements and the rights of others will desist from such a cause. There must be positive endeavors to preserve peace.

America hates war. America hopes for peace. Therefore, America actively engages in the search for peace.

[U.S. Department of State, *Peace and War: United States Foreign Policy, 1931–1941* (Washington, D.C.: U.S. Government Printing Office, 1943), pp. 384–87.]

Document 2. Roosevelt's "Four Freedoms" Speech, 1941

The "Four Freedoms," formulated in Roosevelt's annual message to Congress on January 6, 1941, have come to be accepted as the most succinct statement of the things for which the U.S. people were prepared to fight.

To the Congress of the United States:

I address you, the Members of the Seventy-Seventh Congress, at a moment unprecedented in the history of the Union. I use the word "unprecedented," because at no previous time has American security been as seriously threatened from without as it is today. . . .

It is true that prior to 1914 the United States often had been disturbed by events in other Continents. We had even engaged in two wars with European nations and in a number of undeclared wars in the West Indies, in the Mediterranean and in the Pacific for the maintenance of American rights and for the principles of peaceful commerce. In no case, however, had a serious threat been raised against our national safety or our independence.

What I seek to convey is the historic truth that the United States as a nation has at all times maintained opposition to any attempt to lock us in behind an ancient Chinese wall while the procession of civilization went past. Today, thinking of our children and their children, we oppose enforced isolation for ourselves or for any part of the Americas.

Even when the World War broke out in 1914, it seemed to contain only small threat of danger to our own American future. But, as time went on, the American people began to visualize what the downfall of democratic nations might mean to our own democracy.

We need not over-emphasize imperfections in the Peace of Versailles. We need not harp on failure of the democracies to deal with problems of world deconstruction. We should remember that the Peace of 1919 was far less unjust than the kind of "pacification" which began even before Munich, and which is being carried on under the new order of tyranny that seeks to spread over every continent today. The American people have unalterably set their faces against that tyranny.

Every realist knows that the democratic way of life is at this moment being directly assailed in every part of the world—assailed either by arms, or by secret spreading of poisonous propaganda by those who seek to destroy unity and promote discord in nations still at peace. During sixteen months this assault has blotted out the whole pattern of democratic life in an appalling number of independent nations, great and small. The assailants are still on the march, threatening other nations, great and small.

Therefore, as your President, performing my constitutional duty to "give to the Congress information of the state of the Union," I find it necessary to report that the future and the safety of our country and of our democracy are overwhelmingly involved in events far beyond our borders.

Armed defense of democratic existence is now being gallantly waged in four continents. If that defense fails, all the population and all the resources of Europe, Asia, Africa and Australasia will be dominated by the conquerors. The total of those populations and their resources greatly exceeds the sum total of the population and resources of the whole of the Western Hemisphere—many times over.

In times like these it is immature—and incidentally untrue—for anybody to brag that an unprepared America, single-handed, and with one hand tied behind its back, can hold off the whole world.

No realistic American can expect from a dictator's peace international generosity, or return of true independence, or world disarmament, or freedom of expression, or freedom of religion—or even good business. Such a peace would bring no security for us or for our neighbors. "Those, who would give up essential liberty to purchase a little temporary safety, deserve neither liberty nor safety." As a nation we may take pride in the fact that we are soft-hearted; but we cannot afford to be soft-hearted. We must always be wary of those who with sounding brass and a tinkling cymbal preach the "ism" of appeasement. We must especially beware of that small group of selfish men who would clip the wings of the American eagle in order to feather their own nests.

I have recently pointed out how quickly the tempo of modern warfare could bring into our very midst the physical attack which we must expect if the dictator nations win this war.

There is much loose talk of our immunity from immediate and direct invasion from across the seas. Obviously, as long as the British Navy retains its power, no such danger exists. Even if there were no British Navy, it is not probable that any enemy would be stupid enough to attack us by landing troops in the United States from across thousands of miles of ocean, until it had acquired strategic bases from which to operate. But we learn much from the lessons of the past years in Europe—particularly the lesson of Norway, whose essential seaports were captured by treachery and surprise built up over a series of years. The first phase of the invasion of this Hemisphere would not be the landing of regular troops. The necessary strategic points would be occupied by secret agents and their dupes—and great numbers of them are already here, and in Latin America.

As long as the aggressor nations maintain the offensive, they—not we—will choose the time and the place and the method of their attack. That is why the future of all American Republics is today in serious danger. That is why this Annual Message to the Congress is unique in our history. That is why every member of the Executive branch of the government and every member of the Congress face great responsibility—and great accountability.

The need of the moment is that our actions and our policy should be devoted primarily—almost exclusively—to meeting this foreign peril. For all our domestic problems are now a part of the great emergency. Just as our national policy in internal affairs has been based upon a decent respect for the rights and dignity of all our fellowmen within our gates, so our national policy in foreign affairs has been based on a decent respect for the rights and dignity of all nations, large and small. And the justice of morality must and will win in the end.

Our national policy is this.

First, by an impressive expression of the public will and without regard to partisanship, we are committed to all-inclusive national defense.

Second, by an impressive expression of the public will and without regard to partisanship, we are committed to full support of all those resolute peoples, everywhere, who are resisting aggression and are thereby keeping war away from our Hemisphere. By this support, we express our determination that the democratic cause shall prevail; and we strengthen the defense and security of our own nation.

Third, by an impressive expression of the public will and without regard to partisanship, we are committed to the proposition that principles of morality and considerations for our own security will never permit us to acquiesce in a peace dictated by aggressors and sponsored by appeasers. We know that enduring peace cannot be bought at the cost of other people's freedom.

In the recent national election there was no substantial difference between the two great parties in respect to that national policy. No issue was fought out on this line before the American electorate. Today, it is abundantly evident that American citizens everywhere are demanding and supporting speedy and complete action in recognition of obvious danger. Therefore, the immediate need is a swift and driving increase in our armament production. . . .

Our most useful and immediate role is to act as an arsenal for them as well as for ourselves. They do not need man power. They do need billions of dollars worth of the weapons of defense. . . .

Let us say to the democracies: "We Americans are vitally concerned in your defense of freedom. We are putting forth our energies, our resources and our organizing powers to give you the strength to regain and maintain a free world. We shall send you, in ever-increasing numbers, ships, planes, tanks, guns. This is our purpose and our pledge." In fulfillment of this purpose we will not be intimidated by the threats of dictators that they will regard as a breach of international law and as an act of war our aid to the democracies which dare to resist their aggression. Such aid is not an act of war, even if a dictator should unilaterally proclaim it so to be. When the dictators are ready to make war upon us, they will not wait for an act of war on our part. They did not wait for Norway or Belgium or the Netherlands to commit an act of war. Their only interest is in a new one-way international law, which lacks mutuality in its observance, and, therefore, becomes an instrument of oppression.

The happiness of future generations of Americans may well depend upon how effective and how immediate we can make our aid felt. No one can tell the exact character of the emergency situations that we may be called upon to meet. The Nation's hands must not be tied when the Nation's life is in danger. We must all prepare to make the sacrifices that the emergency—as serious as war itself—demands. Whatever stands in the way of speed and efficiency in defense preparations must give way to the national need.

A free nation has the right to expect full cooperation from all groups. A free nation has the right to look to the leaders of business, of labor, and of agriculture to take the lead in stimulating effort, not among other groups but within their own groups. The best way of dealing with the few slackers or trouble makers in our midst is, first, to shame them by patriotic example, and, if that fails, to use the sovereignty of government to save government.

As men do not live by bread alone, they do not fight by armaments alone. Those who man our defenses, and those behind them who build our defenses, must have the stamina and courage which come from an unshakable belief in the manner of life which they are defending. The mighty action which we are calling for cannot be based on a disregard of all things worth fighting for.

The Nation takes great satisfaction and much strength from the things which have been done to make its people conscious of their individual stake in the preservation of democratic life in America. Those things have toughened the fibre of our people, have renewed their faith and strengthened their devotion to the institutions we make ready to protect. Certainly this is no time to stop thinking about the social and economic problems which are the root cause of the social revolution which is today a supreme factor in the world.

There is nothing mysterious about the foundations of a healthy and strong democracy. The basic things expected by our people of their political and economic systems are simple. They are: equality of opportunity for youth and for others; jobs for those who can work; security for those who need it; the ending of special privilege for the few; the preservation of civil liberties for all; the enjoyment of the fruits of scientific progress in a wider and constantly rising standard of living.

These are the simple and basic things that must never be lost sight of in the turmoil and unbelievable complexity of our modern world. The inner and abiding strength of our economic and political systems is dependent upon the degree to which they fulfill these expectations.

Many subjects connected with our social economy call for immediate improvement. As examples: We should bring more citizens under the coverage of old age pensions and unemployment insurance. We should widen the opportunities for adequate medical care. We should plan a better system by which persons deserving or needing gainful employment may obtain it.

I have called for personal sacrifice. I am assured of the willingness of almost all Americans to respond to that call. . . .

In the future days, which we seek to make secure, we look forward to a world founded upon four essential human freedoms.

The first is freedom of speech and expression—everywhere in the world.

The second is freedom of every person to worship God in his own way—everywhere in the world.

The third is freedom from want—which, translated into world terms, means economic understandings which will secure to every nation a healthy peace time life for its inhabitants—everywhere in the world.

The fourth is freedom from fear—which, translated into world terms, means a worldwide reduction of armaments to such a point and in such a thorough fashion that no nation will be in a position to commit an act of physical aggression against any neighbor— anywhere in the world.

That is no vision of a distant millennium. It is a definite basis for a kind of world attainable in our own time and generation. That kind of world is the very antithesis of the so-called new order of tyranny which the dictators seek to create with the crash of a bomb.

To that new order we oppose the greater conception—the moral order. A good society is able to face schemes of world domination and foreign revolutions alike without fear.

Since the beginning of our American history we have been engaged in change—in a perpetual peaceful revolution—a revolution which goes on steadily, quietly adjusting itself to changing conditions—without the concentration camp or the quick-lime in the ditch. The world order which we seek is the cooperation of free countries, working together in a friendly, civilized society.

This nation has placed its destiny in the hands and heads and hearts of its millions of free men and women; and its faith in freedom under the guidance of God. Freedom means the supremacy of human rights everywhere. Our support goes to those who struggle to gain those rights or keep them. Our strength is in our unity of purpose.

To that high concept there can be no end save victory.

[From *The Public Papers and Addresses of Franklin D. Roosevelt*, vol. 9 (New York: Macmillan Co., 1940), pp. 663ff.]

Questions for Reflection

What actions did Roosevelt ask of the United States or other powers in his 1937 Quarantine Speech? What actions *seemed* to be *implied?* Why do you think this speech caused a great outcry of opposition from those groups who did not want the United States to become involved in the affairs of other countries?

What, specifically, did Roosevelt propose the United States do in his 1941 speech? Was Roosevelt able to stake out a position between isolation and intervention? How would you assess his leadership in this crisis?

ANSWERS TO MULTIPLE-CHOICE AND TRUE-FALSE QUESTIONS

Multiple-Choice Questions

1-D, 2-C, 3-A, 4-A, 5-C, 6-B, 7-D, 8-D

True-False Questions

1-F, 2-T, 3-F, 4-F, 5-T, 6-T, 7-F, 8-F

30

THE SECOND WORLD WAR

CHAPTER OBJECTIVES

After you complete the reading and study of this chapter, you should be able to:

1. Describe the major military strategies in both the European and Pacific Theaters.
2. Explain the problems relating to mobilization for, and finance of, the war.
3. Describe the impact of the war on the economy.
4. Assess the impact of the war on women, African Americans, Native Americans, Japanese Americans, and the West.
5. Explain the decisions made at the Yalta Conference.
6. Account for the decision to use the atomic bomb and discuss its consequences.

CHAPTER OUTLINE

I. United States's early battles
 A. Retreat in the Pacific
  1. Collapse along the Pacific
  2. Surrender of the Philippines
  3. Japanese strategy
  4. U.S. harassment
  5. Battle of the Coral Sea, May 1942
 B. Midway: a turning point

C. Early setbacks in the Atlantic
 1. Devastation from German submarines
 2. Strategy of small patrol vessels
II. Mobilization at home
 A. Mobilization of the armed forces
 B. Economic conversion to war
  1. Prewar planning
  2. War Production Board
  3. Role of the Reconstruction Finance Corporation
  4. Methods of supplying strategic materials
 C. Financing the war
  1. Roosevelt's effort to raise taxes
  2. Congressional reaction to taxation
  3. Sale of bonds
 D. Impact of the war on the economy
  1. Impact on personal incomes
  2. Efforts to control prices
  3. Efforts to control wages and farm prices
  4. Seizure of industries
 E. Development of the West
  1. Defense contracts
  2. Population growth
  3. Problems
   a. Housing shortages
   b. Rural labor shortages

    c. "Zoot suit" riots
  F. Domestic conservatism
    1. Congressional elections of 1942
    2. Abolition of New Deal agencies
    3. Antilabor actions

III. Social effects of the war
  A. Women
    1. In the civilian workforce and the military
    2. Changing attitudes toward sex roles
  B. Blacks
    1. Segregation in the armed forces
    2. In war industries
      a. March on Washington Movement
      b. Black militancy
    3. Challenges to other discrimination
    4. Militant white reaction
  C. Native Americans
    1. Jobs in military and industry
    2. Reasons for service
    3. "Code talkers"
  D. Japanese Americans
    1. Civil liberties
    2. Internment of the Nisei
  E. Mexican Americans

IV. The war in Europe
  A. Basis for moving against Germany first
  B. Aspects of joint conduct of the war
  C. The formulation of the decision for the North African invasion
  D. North African campaign
    1. Eisenhower's landing
    2. German surrender
  E. Agreements at Casablanca
  F. The battle of the Atlantic
    1. Techniques for fighting submarines
    2. Impact on the battle
  G. Sicily and Italy
    1. Invasion of Sicily
    2. Italian surrender
    3. German control of northern Italy
    4. The battle for Rome
  H. Strategic bombing of Europe
    1. British and U.S. cooperation

    2. Impact of the bombing
  I. Decisions of the Teheran Conference
  J. D Day Invasion
    1. Allied planning
    2. German preparations
    3. Invasion
      a. Size of force
      b. Threats to success
      c. Losses
    4. German reaction
    5. Invasion of French Mediterranean coast
    6. Slow drive on Germany

V. The war in the Pacific
  A. Guadalcanal offensive
  B. MacArthur's sweep up the West Pacific
    1. Approval for the MacArthur plan
    2. The technique of "leapfrogging"
    3. The MacArthur sweep
  C. Nimitz's moves in the Central Pacific
  D. The naval battle of Leyte Gulf

VI. The election of 1944
  A. Republican strategy
  B. Democratic vice-presidential choice
  C. Campaign and results

VII. The end of the war
  A. Closing on Germany
    1. The German counteroffensive
    2. Final Russian offensive
    3. Allied moves
  B. The Yalta Conference
    1. Decisions
    2. Call for a United Nations
    3. Occupation of Germany
    4. Eastern Europe
    5. Assessment of decisions
  C. Collapse of the Third Reich
    1. FDR's death
    2. Fall of Germany
    3. Discovery of Nazi Holocaust
  D. The grinding war in the Pacific
    1. Japanese resistance in the Pacific
    2. Occupation of Iwo Jima and Okinawa
    3. Impact of successes on conduct of war

E. The atomic bomb
  1. Its development
  2. The decision to use it
    a. Truman's opinion
    b. Costs of invasion
    c. Military practices
    d. Conditions in Japan
  3. Effects of two bombs
  4. Negotiations for surrender
F. Final ledger on the war

1. Death and destruction
2. Impact on United States
  a. Prosperity
  b. Catalyst to civil rights and women's movements
  c. Solidification of Democratic power
  d. Growth of government
  e. Global responsibilities

KEY ITEMS OF CHRONOLOGY

Battle of Midway	June 1942
U.S. troops invade North Africa	November 1942
Imposition of payroll tax deduction	1943
Casablanca Conference	January 1943
Teheran Conference	November–December 1943
D Day Invasion	June 6, 1944
Yalta Conference	February 1945
Roosevelt's death and Truman's accession	April 12, 1945
V E Day	May 8, 1945
Potsdam Conference	July 1945
Atomic bomb dropped on Hiroshima	August 6, 1945
Japan's surrender	September 2, 1945

TERMS TO MASTER

Listed below are some important terms or people with which you should be familiar after you complete the study of this chapter. Explain the significance of each name or term.

1. Battle of Midway
2. War Production Board
3. Office of Price Administration
4. rationing
5. Revenue Act of 1942
6. Rosie the Riveter
7. "Double V" slogan
8. War Relocation Camps
9. second front
10. unconditional surrender
11. General Dwight D. Eisenhower
12. Operation "Overlord"
13. "leapfrogging"
14. General Douglas MacArthur
15. Battle of Leyte Gulf
16. Yalta Conference
17. Nazi Holocaust
18. Hiroshima

VOCABULARY BUILDING

Listed below are some words or phrases used in this chapter. Look up each word in your dictionary unless the meaning is given here.

1. surreal
2. genocide
3. dismember
4. impregnable
5. repulse
6. havoc
7. ominous

8. conjure
9. chafe
10. watershed
11. mete
12. valor
13. eviscerate
14. motley
15. brunt
16. dictum
17. jettison
18. galvanize
19. inadvertent
20. pincers

EXERCISES FOR UNDERSTANDING

When you have completed reading the chapter, answer each of the following questions. If you have difficulty, go back and reread the section of the chapter related to the question.

Multiple-Choice Questions

Select the letter of the response that best completes the statement.

1. U.S. military forces halted Japanese advances at the battles of
   A. Corregidor and Iwo Jima.
   B. Coral Sea and Midway.
   C. Okinawa and Guadalcanal.
   D. Solomons and New Guinea.
2. During World War II,
   A. the government controlled farm prices.
   B. sales of cars soared.
   C. coffee and sugar were rationed.
   D. all the above
3. The "Double V" campaign called for
   A. victories over the Germans and the Russians.
   B. defeating the Italians and the Japanese.
   C. victory at home over discrimination and abroad against the enemy.
   D. Republicans to defeat FDR and regain control of Congress in the 1940 elections.

4. Germany took priority in the fighting because
   A. Nazi forces posed a greater threat to the western hemisphere.
   B. German science had greater potential for devising a devastating weapon.
   C. the Atlantic was crucial to victory.
   D. all of the above
5. One reason Operation Overlord succeeded was
   A. the Allies attacked at the narrowest point in the English Channel.
   B. the Germans were completely unprepared for an invasion.
   C. perfect weather—clear skies and calm seas.
   D. Eisenhower surprised the Germans by attacking at Normandy.
6. "Leapfrogging" was
   A. random attacks against the Japanese on the islands of the Pacific.
   B. using air and sea power, not combat troops, to neutralize enemy positions.
   C. long-range bombing of Japan.
   D. the United States's biggest strategic mistake of the war.
7. The decisions made at the Yalta Conference did *not* include agreement that
   A. Russia would have three votes in the U.N. General Assembly.
   B. Russia would have an occupation zone in the nonindustrialized area of East Germany as well as in part of Berlin.
   C. both the Soviet Union and the United States would reduce their armaments by half after the war ended.
   D. free elections would be held in Poland to select a government.
8. U.S. officials were slow to aid Jewish refugees because
   A. they feared anti-Semitism in the United States.
   B. experience with wartime propaganda created doubts about reports of the Holocaust.
   C. reported evidence of genocide seemed beyond belief.
   D. all the above

True-False Questions

Indicate whether each statement is true or false.

1. The Battle of Leyte Gulf was the turning point in the war in the Pacific.
2. To finance the war, FDR preferred taxes to borrowing.
3. Native Americans were segregated in the military.
4. During World War II, Congress readily renewed and extended such New Deal programs as the National Youth Administration.
5. The invasion of Sicily came only six weeks after the Normandy invasion.
6. The largest naval engagement in history occurred in the Battle of Leyte Gulf.
7. The War Refugee Board was amazingly successful at rescuing Jews from Europe.
8. The Manhattan Project developed the atomic bomb.

Essay Questions

1. How effective was the wartime alliance between Great Britain and the United States? How well did the Soviet Union fit in the alliance?
2. Compare the European and Pacific strategies followed by the United States.
3. What happened at the Yalta Conference, and why was it important?
4. Did the war affect minorities in the United States? Explain.
5. What impact did the war have on American government and society?
6. What role did the atomic bomb play in the war?

DOCUMENTS

Document 1. Executive Order 9066 Authorizing the Secretary of War to Prescribe Military Areas

On February 19, 1942, President Roosevelt issued an executive order that would later be used as the authority to remove Japanese Americans from the West coast to areas in the interior of the nation. Another executive order one month later (no. 9102) established the War Relocation Authority to carry out the removal program.

> Whereas the successful prosecution of the war requires every possible protection against espionage and against sabotage to national-defense material, national-defense premises, and national defense utilities. . . .
>
> Now, therefore, by virtue of the authority vested in me as President of the United States, and Commander in Chief of the Army and Navy, I hereby authorize and direct the Secretary of War, and the Military Commanders whom he may from time to time designate, whenever he or any designated commander deems such action necessary or desirable, to prescribe military areas in such places and of such extent as he or the appropriate Military Commander may determine, from which any or all persons may be excluded, and with respect to which, the right of any person to enter, remain in, or leave shall be subject to whatever restrictions the Secretary of War or the appropriate Military Commander may impose in his discretion. The Secretary of War is

hereby authorized to provide for residents of any such area who are excluded therefrom, such transportation, food, shelter, and other accommodations as may be necessary, in the judgment of the Secretary of War or the said Military Commander, and until other arrangements are made, to accomplish the purpose of this order. . . .

I hereby further authorize and direct the Secretary of War and the said Military Commanders to take such other steps as he or the appropriate Military Commander may deem advisable to enforce compliance with the restrictions applicable to each Military area herein-above authorized to be designated, including the use of Federal troops and other Federal Agencies with authority to accept assistance of state and local agencies.

I hereby further authorize and direct all Executive Departments, independent establishments and other Federal Agencies, to assist the Secretary of War or the said Military Commanders in carrying out this Executive Order, including the furnishing of medical aid, hospitalization, food, clothing, transportation, use of land, shelter, and other supplies, equipment, utilities, facilities, and services.

[From Federal Register, vol. 7, no. 38 (February 25, 1942), p. 1407.]

Document 2. *Korematsu* v. *United States*, 1944

In a case challenging the forced relocation of Japanese-Americans during the war, the Supreme Court upheld as constitutional the work of the War Relocation Authority as necessary for military reasons. It followed by two years the Court's endorsement in *Hirabayshi* v. *United States* (320 U. S. 81) of a curfew for Japanese-Americans on the West Coast.

The petitioner, an American citizen of Japanese descent, was convicted in a federal district court for remaining in San Leandro, California, a "Military Area," contrary to Civilian Exclusion Order No. 34, of the Commanding General of the Western Command, U.S. Army, which directed that after May 9, 1942, all persons of Japanese ancestry should be excluded from that area. No question was raised as to petitioner's loyalty to the United States. The Circuit Court of Appeals affirmed, and the importance of the constitutional question involved caused us to grant certiorari.

It should be noted, to begin with, that all legal restrictions which curtail the civil rights of a single racial group are immediately suspect. That is not to say that all such restrictions are unconstitutional. It is to say that courts must subject them to the most rigid scrutiny. Pressing public necessity may sometimes justify the existence of such restrictions; racial antagonism never can. . . .

Exclusion Order No. 34, which the petitioner knowingly and admittedly violated, was one of a number of military orders and proclamations, all of which were substantially based upon Executive Order No. 9066, 7 Fed. Reg. 1407. . . .

[W]e are unable to conclude that it was beyond the war power of Congress and the Executive to exclude those of Japanese ancestry from the West Coast war area at the time they did. True, exclusion from the area in which one's home is located is a far greater deprivation than constant confinement to the home from 8 P.M. to 6 A.M. Nothing short of apprehension by the proper military authorities of the gravest imminent danger to the public safety can constitutionally justify either. But exclusion from a threatened area, no less than curfew, has a definite and close relationship to the prevention of espionage and sabotage. The military authorities, charged with the primary responsibility of defending our shores, concluded that curfew provided inadequate protection and ordered exclusion. They did so . . . in accordance with Congressional authority to the military to say who should, and who should not, remain in the threatened areas.

In this case the petitioner challenges the assumptions upon which we rested our conclusions in the *Hirabayashi* case. He also urges that by May 1912, when Order No. 31 was promulgated, all danger of Japanese invasion of the West Coast had disappeared. After careful consideration of these contentions we are compelled to reject them. . . .

[E]xclusion of those of Japanese origin was deemed necessary because of the presence of an unascertained number of disloyal members of the group, most of whom we have no doubt were loyal to this country. It was because we could not reject the finding of the military authorities that it was impossible to bring about an immediate segregation of the disloyal from the loyal that we sustained the validity of the curfew order as applying to the whole group. In the instant case, temporary exclusion of the entire group was rested by the military on the same ground. The judgment that exclusion of the whole group was for the same reason a military imperative answers the contention that the exclusion was in the nature of group punishment based on antagonism to those of Japanese origin. That there were members of the group who retained loyalties to Japan has been confirmed by investigations made subsequent to the exclusion. Approximately five thousand American citizens of Japanese ancestry refused to swear unqualified allegiance to the United States and to renounce allegiance to the Japanese Emperor, and several thousand evacuees requested repatriation to Japan.

We uphold the exclusion order as of the time it was made and when the petitioner violated it. . . . In doing so, we are not unmindful of the hardships imposed by it upon a large group of American citizens. . . . But hardships are part of war, and war is an aggregation of hardships. All citizens alike, both in and out of uniform, feel the impact of war in greater or lesser measure. Citizenship has its responsibilities as well as its privileges, and in time of war the burden is always heavier. Compulsory exclusion of large groups of citizens from their homes, except under circumstances of direst emergency and peril, is inconsistent with our basic governmental institutions. But when under conditions of modern warfare our shores are threatened by hostile forces, the power to protect must be commensurate with the threatened danger. . . .

After May 3, 1942, the date of Exclusion Order No. 34, Korematsu was under compulsion to leave the area not as he would choose but via an Assembly Center. The Assembly Center was conceived as a part of the machinery for group evacuation. The power to exclude includes the power to do it by force if necessary. And any forcible measure must necessarily entail some degree of detention or restraint whatever method of removal is selected. But whichever view is taken, it results in holding that the order under which petitioner was convicted was valid.

It is said that we are dealing here with the case of imprisonment of a citizen in a concentration camp solely because of his ancestry, without evidence or inquiry concerning his loyalty and good disposition towards the United States. Our task would be simple, our duty clear, were this a case involving the imprisonment of a loyal citizen in a concentration camp because of racial prejudice. Regardless of the true nature of the assembly and relocation centers—and we deem it unjustifiable to call them concentration camps with all the ugly connotations that term implies—we are dealing specifically: with nothing but an exclusion order. To cast this case into outlines of racial prejudice, without reference to the real military dangers which were presented, merely confuses the issue. Korematsu was not excluded from the Military Area because of hostility to him or his race. He *was* excluded because we are at war with the Japanese Empire, because the properly constituted military authorities feared an invasion of our West Coast and felt constrained to take proper security measures, because they decided that the military urgency of the situation demanded that all citizens of Japanese ancestry be segregated from the West Coast temporarily and finally, because Congress, reposing its confidence in this time of war in our military leaders—as inevitably it must—determined that they should have the power to do just this. There was evidence of disloyalty on the part of some, the military authorities considered that the need for action was great and time was short. We cannot—by availing ourselves of the calm perspective of hindsight—now say that at that time these actions were unjustified.

[From 323 U.S. 214 (1944).]

Document 3. Public Law 100-383, 1988

More than forty years after the internment of Japanese Americans during World War II, Congress apologized for the violation of their civil liberties.

SECTION 1. PURPOSES.

The purposes of this Act are to—

(1) acknowledge the fundamental injustice of the evacuation, relocation, and internment of United States citizens and permanent resident aliens of Japanese ancestry during World War II;

(2) apologize on behalf of the people of the United States for the

evacuation, relocation, and internment of such citizens and permanent resident aliens;

(3) provide for a public education fund to finance efforts to inform the public about the internment of such individuals so as to prevent the recurrence of any similar event;

(4) make restitution to those individuals of Japanese ancestry who were interned; . . .

(6) discourage the occurrence of similar injustices and violations of civil liberties in the future; and

(7) make more credible and sincere any declaration of concern by the United States over violations of human rights committed by other nations.

SEC. 2. STATEMENT OF THE CONGRESS.

(a) WITH REGARD TO INDIVIDUALS OF JAPANESE ANCESTRY.—The Congress recognizes that, as described by the Commission on Wartime Relocation and Internment of Civilians, a grave injustice was done to both citizens and permanent resident aliens of Japanese ancestry by the evacuation, relocation, and internment of civilians during World War II. As the Commission documents, these actions were carried out without adequate security reasons and without any acts of espionage or sabotage documented by the Commission, and were motivated largely by racial prejudice, wartime hysteria, and a failure of political leadership. The excluded individuals of Japanese ancestry suffered enormous damages, both material and intangible, and there were incalculable losses in education and job training, all of which resulted in significant human suffering for which appropriate compensation has not been made. For these fundamental violations of the basic civil liberties and constitutional rights of these individuals of Japanese ancestry, the Congress apologizes on behalf of the Nation. . . .

[From *U.S. Statutes at Large* 102 (1988): 903–4.]

Questions for Reflection

How did the federal government justify the relocation of the Japanese-Americans during World War II? Would you have supported the wartime action? Why did the Congress in 1988 apologize for the internment? In the interven-ing years, how and why had attitudes toward civil liberties and the rights of minorities changed? Would such an action by the govern-ment be permitted today?

ANSWERS TO MULTIPLE-CHOICE AND TRUE-FALSE QUESTIONS

Multiple-Choice Questions

1-B, 2-C, 3-C, 4-D, 5-D, 6-B, 7-C, 8-D

True-False Questions

1-F, 2-T, 3-F, 4-F, 5-F, 6-T, 7-F, 8-T

31

THE FAIR DEAL AND CONTAINMENT

CHAPTER OBJECTIVES

After you complete the reading and study of this chapter, you should be able to:

1. Analyze the problems of demobilization and conversion to peacetime production.
2. Account for Truman's troubles with Congress and evaluate his accomplishments.
3. Explain the policy of containment and trace its development to 1950.
4. Describe Truman's reelection in 1948.
5. Appraise the strength of McCarthyism in the United States.
6. Explain the origins of the Korean War and trace its major developments.

CHAPTER OUTLINE

I. Demobilization under Truman
   A. The Truman style
      1. Truman's background and character
      2. Domestic proposals of 1945
      3. Relations with Congress
   B. Demobilization
      1. Rapid reduction of armed forces
      2. Escalation of birthrate
      3. Efforts for economic stabilization

C. Efforts to control inflation
   1. Demands for wage increases
   2. A wave of strikes
   3. Truman's response to strikes
   4. Efforts to control prices
   5. End of controls
D. Significant legislative achievements
   1. Employment Act of 1946
   2. Control of atomic energy
E. Congressional elections of 1946
F. Relations with Congress
   1. Taft-Hartley Act
   2. Taxes
   3. National Security Act

II. Development of the cold war
   A. Creating the United Nations
      1. Background of the United Nations
      2. Scheme of its operations
      3. U.S. ratification of U.N. membership
   B. Trials for war criminals
      1. Nature of the trials
      2. Debate over the justice of the trials
   C. Differences with the Soviets
      1. Conflicting interpretations
      2. Problems relating to eastern Europe

3. Development of the peace treaties
4. Proposals to control atomic energy
D. Development of the containment policy
   1. Kennan's theory
   2. Problems in Iran, Turkey, and Greece
   3. The Truman Doctrine
   4. Greek-Turkish Aid
   5. The Marshall Plan
      a. The proposal
      b. European response
      c. Work of the ERP
   6. Division of Germany
      a. Merger of Allied zones
      b. Berlin Blockade
      c. Berlin Airlift
      d. Creation of West and East Germany
   7. Development of NATO
   8. Establishment of Israel

III. Domestic affairs
   A. Civil rights
      1. Truman administration
         a. Effect of foreign relations
         b. Truman's views
         c. Recommendations of Committee on Civil Rights
         d. Employment and the military
      2. Baseball and Jackie Robinson
   B. Democratic divisions
   C. Truman's game plan
   D. The 1948 election
      1. The Republican position
      2. Democratic battle over civil rights
      3. Creation of the Dixiecrats

4. Wallace's Progressive party
5. Nature of the campaign
6. Election results
7. Assessment of the results
E. The fate of the Fair Deal

IV. The cold war heats up
   A. Point Four Program
   B. China's fall to communism
      1. History of the movement in China
      2. Assessment of the Communist victory
   C. Soviet atomic bomb
   D. Work on the hydrogen bomb
   E. NSC-68

V. The Korean War
   A. Background to the conflict
   B. Response to the invasion
   C. Military developments
      1. Rout of the U.N. forces
      2. Counterattack
      3. The decision to invade the North
      4. Entry of the Chinese Communists
   D. The dismissal of MacArthur
      1. Reasons for the action
      2. Reactions to the firing
   E. Negotiations for peace

VI. Another Red Scare
   A. Evidences of espionage
   B. The Truman loyalty program
   C. The Alger Hiss case
   D. Conviction of spies
   E. Joseph McCarthy's witch-hunt
      1. The emergence of Senator McCarthy
      2. Assessment of his tactics
   F. McCarran Internal Security Act

KEY ITEMS OF CHRONOLOGY

FDR dies	April 1945
Employment Act	1946
Truman Doctrine	1947
Marshall Plan launched	1947
Jackie Robinson joins the Dodgers	1947
Berlin Blockade and Berlin Airlift	June 1948–May 1949
Creation of Israel	1948

Executive order desegregating the military	1948
Hiss case	1948–1950
Establishment of NATO	April 1949
China becomes Communist	1949
Senator McCarthy's speech in Wheeling, W.Va., citing Communists in the State Department	February 1950
Korean War	June 1950–July 1953
MacArthur dismissed	April 1951

TERMS TO MASTER

Listed below are some important terms or people with which you should be familiar after you complete the study of this chapter. Explain the significance of each name or term.

1. baby-boom generation
2. GI Bill of Rights
3. inflation
4. Employment Act of 1946
5. Atomic Energy Commission
6. closed shop
7. Taft-Hartley Act
8. National Security Act of 1947
9. United Nations
10. Nuremberg trials
11. *ex post facto*
12. George F. Kennan
13. containment
14. iron curtain
15. Truman Doctrine
16. Marshall Plan
17. Berlin Blockade
18. NATO
19. Jackie Robinson
20. Dixiecrats
21. Fair Deal
22. Nationalist Chinese
23. Douglas MacArthur
24. Alger Hiss
25. Joseph McCarthy
26. McCarran Internal Security Act

VOCABULARY BUILDING

Listed below are some words or phrases used in this chapter. Look up each word in your dictionary unless the meaning is given here.

1. congenial
2. tribunal
3. pillage
4. collaborate
5. compliant
6. ensconce
7. consign
8. wrangle
9. brandish
10. opt
11. intermittent
12. virulent
13. deprecate
14. preclude
15. intractable
16. transliteration
17. glean
18. brazen
19. colossus
20. refute

EXERCISES FOR UNDERSTANDING

When you have completed reading the chapter, answer each of the following questions. If you have difficulty, go back and reread the section of the chapter related to the question.

Multiple-Choice Questions

Select the letter of the response which best completes the statement.

1. To deal with labor strikes after World War II, Truman

    A. supported the Taft-Hartley Act.
    B. backed wage increases.
    C. nationalized the railroads.
    D. drafted strikers into the army.
2. The Employment Act of 1946
    A. guaranteed every citizen a job.
    B. provided for unemployment insurance.
    C. established the Council of Economic Advisers.
    D. all the above
3. The Taft-Hartley Act
    A. banned the closed shop and permitted the union shop.
    B. created the Central Intelligence Agency.
    C. provided educational and vocational benefits for veterans.
    D. gave a civilian commission control of atomic energy.
4. Postwar disagreements between the United States and the Soviet Union especially concerned
    A. the formation of the United Nations.
    B. governments in Eastern Europe.
    C. the reconstruction of Japan.
    D. the Nuremberg trials.
5. The creator of the concept of containment was
    A. Douglas MacArthur.
    B. Harry Truman.
    C. George Kennan.
    D. Joseph McCarthy.
6. In response to Truman's Fair Deal proposals, the Democratic Congress
    A. enlarged many New Deal programs.
    B. enacted major civil rights legislation.
    C. repealed the Taft-Hartley Act.
    D. provided for national health insurance.
7. General Douglas MacArthur said,
    A. "there is no substitute for victory."
    B. "once war is forced upon us, there is no alternative than to apply every available means to bring it to a swift end."
    C. "old soldiers never die, they just fade away."
    D. all of the above

8. The Korean War
    A. occurred after McCarthy's campaign against Communists in government.
    B. came at the height of the Red Scare.
    C. had no connection to anti-communism.
    D. caused the outbreak of the Red Scare.

True-False Questions

Indicate whether each statement is true or false.

1. The GI Bill guaranteed every former soldier a job.
2. President Truman vetoed the Taft-Hartley bill.
3. Japanese were tried at Nuremberg for war crimes.
4. The Yalta agreements succeeded in establishing free governments in Eastern Europe
5. In 1948, Truman banned racial discrimination in federal employment.
6. Branch Rickey was the first Negro baseball player in the American league.
7. The Communists gained control of China, the Soviets exploded an atomic device, and the Korean War started—all in 1949.
8. More than a dozen countries sent troops to fight in Korea.

Essay Questions

1. How did the Truman administration deal with the postwar economic problems facing the United States?
2. What were the causes of the cold war?
3. Who were the candidates and what were the issues in the 1948 presidential election? Was it a particularly crucial election?
4. What was the Fair Deal and how important was it?
5. Explain the United States's involvement in the Korean War.
6. What were the issues involved in the clash between Truman and MacArthur? Who was right?
7. How did U.S. foreign policy and domestic affairs interact in the postwar years?

READINGS

Reading 1. Arthur Schlesinger Explains the Origins of the Cold War

The origin of the cold war is one of the more complex and controversial historiographical problems current today. The issues involve which side was responsible for the hostility that developed after World War II between the United States and the Soviet Union. In the article excerpted here, Arthur M. Schlesinger, Jr., a prominent historian and adviser to President Kennedy, takes a position somewhat more centrist than that of the revisionists who place the blame for the cold war on the United States. Writing in 1967 just after he had broken with the Johnson administration over the Vietnam War, Schlesinger here attempts to show just how complex the development of the cold war was.

The orthodox American view, as originally set forth by the American government and as reaffirmed until recently by most American scholars, has been that the Cold War was the brave and essential response of free men to communist aggression. Some have gone back well before the Second World War to lay open the sources of Russian expansionism. Geopoliticians traced the Cold War to imperial Russian strategic ambitions which in the nineteenth century led to the Crimean War, to Russian penetration of the Balkans and the Middle East and to Russian pressure on Britain's "lifeline" to India. Ideologists traced it to the Communist Manifesto of 1848 ("the violent overthrow of the bourgeoisie lays the foundation for the sway of the proletariat"). Thoughtful observers (a phrase meant to exclude those who speak in Dullese about the unlimited evil of godless, atheistic, militant communism) concluded that classical Russian imperialism and Pan-Slavism, compounded after 1917 by Leninist messianism, confronted the West at the end of the Second World War with an inexorable drive for domination.

The revisionist thesis is very different. In its extreme form, it is that, after the death of Franklin Roosevelt and the end of the Second World War, the United States deliberately abandoned the wartime policy of collaboration and, exhilarated by the possession of the atomic bomb, undertook a course of aggression of its own designed to expel all Russian influence from Eastern Europe and to establish democratic-capitalist states on the very border of the Soviet Union. As the revisionists see it, this radically new American policy—or rather this resumption by Truman of the pre-Roosevelt policy of insensate anti-communism—left Moscow no alternative but to take measures in defense of its own borders. The result was the Cold War.

. . .

. . . Any honest reappraisal of the origins of the Cold War requires the imaginative leap—which should in any case be as instinctive for the historian as it is prudent for the statesman—into the adversary's viewpoint. We must strive to see how, given Soviet perspectives, the Russians might conceivably have misread our signals, as we must reconsider how intelligently we read theirs.

Nor can the historian forget the conditions under which decisions are made, especially in a time like the Second World War. These were tired, overworked, aging men: in 1945, Churchill was 71 years old, Stalin had governed his country for 17 exacting years, Roosevelt his for 12 years nearly as exacting. . . . All—even Stalin, behind his screen of ideology—had become addicts of improvisation, relying on authority and virtuosity to conceal the fact that they were constantly surprised by developments. . . . None showed great tactical consistency, or cared much about it; all employed a certain ambiguity to preserve their power to decide big issues; and it is hard to know how to interpret anything any one of them said on any specific occasion. . . .

Peacemaking after the Second World War was not so much a tapestry as it was a hopelessly raveled and knotted mess of yarn. Yet, for purposes of clarity, it is essential to follow certain threads. One theme indispensable to an understanding of the Cold War is the contrast between two clashing views of world order: the "universalist" view, by which all nations shared a common interest in all the affairs of the world, and the "sphere-of-influence" view, by which each great power would be assured by the other great powers of an acknowledged predominance in its own area of special interest. The universalist view assumed that national security would be guaranteed by an international organization. The sphere-of-interest view assumed that national security would be guaranteed by the balance of power. While in practice these views have by no means been incompatible (indeed, our shaky peace has been based on a combination of the two), in the abstract they involved sharp contradictions.

The tradition of American thought in these matters was universalist. . . .

The Kremlin, on the other hand, thought *only* of spheres of interest; above all, the Russians were determined to protect their frontiers, and especially their border to the west, crossed so often and so bloodily in the dark course of their history. . . .

It is now pertinent to inquire why the United States rejected the idea of stabilizing the world by division into spheres of influence and insisted on an East European strategy. . . .

The first reason is that they regarded this solution as containing within itself the seeds of a third world war. The balance-of-power idea seemed inherently unstable. . . .

. . . the second objection: that the sphere-of-influence approach would, in the words of the State Department in 1945, "militate against the establishment and effective functioning of a broader system of general security in which all countries will have their part." The United Nations, in short, was seen as the alternative to the balance of power. . . .

Third, the universalists feared that the sphere-of-interest approach would be what Hull termed "a haven for the isolationists," who would advocate America's participation in Western Hemisphere affairs on condition that it did not participate in European or Asian affairs. . . .

Fourth, the sphere-of-interest solution meant the betrayal of the principles for which the Second World War was being fought—the Atlantic Charter, the Four Freedoms, the Declaration of the United Nations. . . .

Fifth, the sphere-of-influence solution would create difficult domestic problems in American politics. Roosevelt was aware of the six million or more Polish votes in the 1944 election. . . .

Sixth, if the Russians were allowed to overrun Eastern Europe without argument, would that satisfy them? . . .

But the great omission of the revisionists—and also the fundamental explanation of the speed with which the Cold War escalated—lies precisely in the fact that the Soviet Union was not a traditional national state. The Soviet Union was a phenomenon very different from America or Britain: it was a totalitarian state, endowed with an all-explanatory, all-consuming ideology, committed to the infallibility of government and party, still in a somewhat messianic mood, equating dissent with treason, and ruled by a dictator who, for all his quite extraordinary abilities, had his paranoid moments.

Marxism-Leninism gave the Russian leaders a view of the world according to which all societies were inexorably destined to proceed along appointed roads by appointed stages until they achieved the classless nirvana. . . .

A revisionist fallacy has been to treat Stalin as just another Real-politik statesman, as Second World War revisionists see Hitler as just another Stresemann or Bismarck. But the record makes it clear that in the end nothing could satisfy Stalin's paranoia. His own associates failed. Why does anyone suppose that any conceivable American policy would have succeeded?

The difference between America and Russia in 1945 was that some Americans fundamentally believed that, over a long run, a modus vivendi with Russia was possible; while the Russians, so far as one can tell, believed in no more than a short-run modus vivendi with the United States.

In retrospect, if it is impossible to see the Cold War as a case of American aggression and Russian response, it is also hard to see it as a pure case of Russian aggression and American response. . . .

The Cold War could have been avoided only if the Soviet Union had not been possessed by convictions both of the infallibility of the communist word and of the inevitability of a communist world. These convictions turned an impasse between national states into a religious war, a tragedy of ability into one of necessity. One might wish that America had preserved the poise and proportion of the first years of the Cold War and had not succumbed to its own forms of self-righteousness. But the most rational American policies could hardly have averted the Cold War. Only if Russia began to recede from its messianic mission and to accept, in fact if not yet in principle, the permanence of the world of diversity, only then did the hope flicker that this long, dreary, costly contest may at last be taking forms less dramatic, less obsessive and less dangerous to the future kind.

[From Arthur M. Schlesinger, Jr., "Origins of the Cold War," *Foreign Affairs* 46 (October 1967): 22–52.]

Reading 2. Barton Bernstein Presents a Revisionist View

Barton Bernstein has been one of the leading revisionists in the controversy over the origins of the cold war. The excerpt below will introduce the reader to the essentials of that view.

Despite some dissents, most American scholars have reached a general consensus on the origins of the Cold War. As confirmed internationalists who believe that Russia constituted a threat to America and its European allies after World War II, they have endorsed their nation's acceptance of its obligations as a world power in the forties and its desire to establish a world order of peace and prosperity. Convinced that only American efforts prevented the Soviet Union from expanding past Eastern Europe, they have generally praised the containment policies of the Truman Doctrine, the Marshall Plan, and NATO as evidence of America's acceptance of world responsibility. While chiding or condemning those on the right who opposed international involvement (or had even urged preventive war), they have also been deeply critical of those on the left who have believed that the Cold War could have been avoided, or that the United States shared substantial responsibility for the Cold War.

Despite the widespread acceptance of this interpretation, there has long been substantial evidence (and more recently a body of scholarship) which suggests that American policy was neither so innocent nor so nonideological; that American leaders sought to promote their conceptions of national interest and their values even at the conscious risk of provoking Russia's fears about her security. In 1945 these leaders apparently believed that American power would be adequate for the task of reshaping much of the world according to America's needs and standards.

By overextending policy and power and refusing to accept Soviet interests, American policy-makers contributed to the Cold War. There was little understanding of any need to restrain American political efforts and desires. Though it cannot be proved that the United States could have achieved a *modus vivendi* with the Soviet Union in these years there is evidence that Russian policies were reasonably cautious and conservative, and that there was at least a basis for accommodation. But this possibility slowly slipped away as President Harry S. Truman reversed Roosevelt's tactics of accommodation. As American demands for democratic governments in Eastern Europe became more vigorous, as the new administration delayed in providing economic assistance to Russia and in seeking international control of atomic energy, policy-makers met with increasing Soviet suspicion and antagonism. Concluding that Soviet-American cooperation was impossible, they came to believe that the Soviet state could be halted only by force or the threat of force. . . .

. . . It is clear that Truman was either incapable or unwilling to reexamine his earlier assumption (or decision) of using the bomb. Under the tutelage of Byrnes and Stimson, Truman had come to assume by July that the bomb should be used, and perhaps he was incapable of reconsidering this strategy because he found no compelling reason not to use the bomb. Or he may have consciously rejected the options because he wanted to use the bomb. Perhaps he was vindictive and wished to retaliate for Pearl Harbor and other atrocities. (In justifying the use of the bomb against the Japanese, he wrote a few days after Nagasaki, "The only language they seem to understand is the one we have been using to bombard them. When you have to deal with a beast you have to treat him as a beast.") Or, most likely, Truman agreed with Byrnes that using the bomb would advance other American policies: It would end the war before the Russians could gain a hold in Manchuria, it would permit the United States to exclude Russia from the occupation government of Japan, and it would make the Soviets more manageable in Eastern Europe. It would enable the United States to shape the peace according to its own standards.

At minimum, then, the use of the bomb reveals the moral insensitivity of the President—whether he used it because the moral implications did not compel a reexamination of assumptions, or because he sought retribution, or because he sought to keep Russia out of Manchuria and the occupation government of Japan, and to make her more manageable in Eastern Europe. In 1945 American foreign policy was not innocent, nor was it unconcerned about Russian power, nor did it assume that the United States lacked the power to impose its will on the Russian state, nor was it characterized by high moral purpose or consistent dedication to humanitarian principles.

While the Soviet Union would not generally permit in Eastern Europe conditions that conformed to Western ideals, Stalin was pursuing a cautious policy and seeking accommodation with the West. He was willing to allow capitalism but was suspicious of American efforts at economic penetration which could lead to political dominance. Though by the autumn of 1945 the governments in Russia's general area of influence were subservient in foreign policy, they varied in form and in degree of independence. Democracy in Czechoslovakia (the only country in this area with a democratic tradition), free elections and the overthrow of the Communist party in Hungary, a Communist-formed coalition government in Bulgaria, a broadly based but Communist-dominated government in Poland, and a Soviet-imposed government in Rumania (the most anti-Russian of these nations). In all of these countries Communists controlled the ministries of interior (the police) and were able to suppress anti-Soviet groups, including anti-communist democrats.

Those who have attributed to Russia a policy of inexorable expansion have often neglected this immediate postwar period, or they have interpreted it simply as a necessary preliminary (a cunning strategy to allay American suspicions until the American Army demobilized and left the continent) to the consolidation and extension of power in east-central Europe. From this perspective, however, much of Stalin's behavior becomes strangely contradictory and potentially self-defeating. If he had planned to create puppets rather than an area of "friendly governments," why (as Isaac Deutscher asks) did Stalin "so stubbornly refuse to make any concessions to the Poles over their eastern frontiers"? Certainly, also, his demand for reparations from Hungary, Rumania, and Bulgaria would have been unnecessary if he had planned to take over these countries. (America's insistence upon using a loan to Russia to achieve political goals, and nearly twenty-month delay after Russia first submitted a specific proposal for assistance, led Harriman to suggest in November that the loan policy "may have contributed to their [the Soviet's] avaricious policies in the countries occupied or liberated by the Red Army.")

Russian sources are closed, so it is not possible to prove that Soviet intentions were conservative; nor for the same reason is it possible for those who adhered to the thesis of inexorable Soviet expansion to prove their theory. But the available evidence better supports the thesis that these years should be viewed not as a cunning preliminary to the harshness of 1947 and afterward, but as an attempt to establish a *modus vivendi* with the West and to protect "socialism in one country." This interpretation explains more adequately why the Russians delayed nearly three years before ending dissent and hardening policies in the countries behind their own military lines. It would also explain why the Communist parties in France and Italy were cooperating with the coalition governments until these parties were forced out of the coalitions in 1947. . . .

If the Russian policy was conservative and sought accommodation (as now seems likely), then its failure must be explained by looking beyond Russian actions. Historians must reexamine this period and reconsider American policies. Were they directed toward compromise? Can they be judged as having sought adjustment? Or did they demand acquiescence to the American world view, thus thwarting real negotiations?

There is considerable evidence that American actions clearly changed after Roosevelt's death. Slowly abandoning the tactics of accommodation, they became even more vigorous after Hiroshima. The insistence upon rolling back Soviet influence in Eastern Europe, the reluctance to grant a loan for Russian reconstruction, the inability to reach an agreement on Germany, the maintenance of the nuclear monopoly—all of these could have contributed to the sense of Russian insecurity. The point, then, is that in 1945 and 1946 there may still have been possibilities for negotiations and settlements, for accommodations and adjustments, if the United States had been willing to recognize Soviet fears, to accept Soviet power in her areas of influence, and to ease anxieties.

[From Barton J. Bernstein, "American Foreign Policy and the Origins of the Cold War," in Barton J. Bernstein, ed., *Politics and Policies of the Truman Administration* (Chicago: Quadrangle Books, 1970), pp. 15–49.]

Questions for Reflection

After reading both excerpts and answering the questions below, attempt to write in a few paragraphs your own view of the origins of the cold war.

What is the orthodox view of the origins of the cold war? The revisionist view? What special considerations should be taken into account in attempting to explain the cold war? What important theme does Schlesinger want the reader to consider in explaining the development of cold war events? What does he think the revisionists have omitted in their analysis of the cold war?

How does Bernstein's initial description of the consensus view of cold war origins compare with Schlesinger's view above? Needless use of the atomic bomb is one of the central themes of revisionist history. How does Bernstein deal with this matter? How does he argue that the United States acted incorrectly in eastern Europe? How do we know the Soviet Union's motives after World War II? What limitation does that place on historians?

ANSWERS TO MULTIPLE-CHOICE AND TRUE-FALSE QUESTIONS

Multiple-Choice Questions

1-B, 2-C, 3-A, 4-B, 5-C, 6-A, 7-D, 8-B

True-False Questions

1-F, 2-T, 3-F, 4-F, 5-T, 6-F, 7-F, 8-T

32

THROUGH THE PICTURE WINDOW:
SOCIETY AND CULTURE, 1945–1960

CHAPTER OBJECTIVES

After you complete the reading and study of this chapter, you should be able to:

1. Account for the emergence of a consumer culture in the prosperous postwar era.
2. Discuss the relationships among the baby boom, the growth of suburbs, the youth culture, and consumerism in the 1950s.
3. Describe the growth of suburbs in the United States after World War II.
4. Illustrate the widespread conformity in U.S. culture in the 1950s.
5. Understand the ideas of the major critics of conformity.
6. Explain the artistic and literary dissent beginning in the 1950s.

CHAPTER OUTLINE

I. Postwar economy
  A. Growth and prosperity
    1. Military spending
    2. International trade dominance
    3. Technological innovation
    4. Baby boom and consumer demand
  B. GI Bill of Rights

    1. Economic measure
    2. Veterans Administration
    3. Benefits and effects
    4. Participants
  C. Consumer culture
    1. Television
      a. Popularity
      b. "Electronic hearth"
    2. Dispersion of affluence
      a. Labor and blacks
      b. Exceptions
    3. Marketing and packaging
    4. Credit cards
  D. Youth culture
    1. Consumerism at shopping malls
    2. Permissive parents
    3. Juvenile delinquency
    4. Mobility
  E. Rock 'n' roll
    1. Origins
    2. Bridge between white and black music
    3. Elvis Presley
    4. Vehicle for youth revolt
    5. Controversial
  F. Growth of suburbs
    1. Rural-to-urban migration
    2. Levittowns
    3. Automobiles and roads

4. "White flight"
G. African-American migration
   1. Reasons for moving
   2. Effects on northern cities

II. Postwar conformity
  A. Corporate life
    1. White-collar jobs
    2. Large corporations
  B. Women and the cult of domesticity
  C. Religion
    1. Growth in church membership
      a. Religious revival
      b. Patriotism
      c. Marketing of religion
    2. Religion on television
      a. Bishop Fulton J. Sheen
      b. Reverend Billy Graham
    3. Reverend Norman Vincent Peale and positive thinking
    4. Neo-orthodoxy
      a. Critical of religiosity
      b. Reinhold Niebuhr
  D. Social critics of conformity
    1. John Kenneth Galbraith's *The Affluent Society*
    2. *The Crack in the Picture Window*
    3. David Riesman and *The Lonely Crowd*
    4. *White Collar* by C. Wright Mills

III. Alienation and liberation in the arts
  A. Drama

1. Oppressiveness of mass culture
2. Arthur Miller's *Death of a Salesman*
3. Tennessee Williams and Edward Albee
B. The novel
   1. The individual's struggle for survival
   2. J. D. Salinger's *Catcher in the Rye*
   3. *From Here to Eternity* by James Jones
C. Painting
   1. Edward Hopper and desolate loneliness
   2. Abstract expressionism
     a. Violent and chaotic modern society
     b. Jackson Pollock
     c. William de Kooning, Mark Rothko, et al.
D. The Beats
   1. Liberation of self-expression
   2. Greenwich Village background
   3. William Burroughs's *Naked Lunch*
   4. *Howl* by Allen Ginsberg
   5. Jack Kerouac's *On the Road*
   6. Influences
     a. Mort Sahl
     b. Lenny Bruce
     c. Bob Dylan

KEY ITEMS OF CHRONOLOGY

Benjamin Spock's *Baby and Child Care*	1946
The first Levittown in New York	1947
Arthur Miller's *Death of a Salesman*	1949
David Riesman's *The Lonely Crowd*	1950
J. D. Salinger's *Catcher in the Rye*	1951
"One Nation under God" added to the Pledge of Allegiance	1954
The Blackboard Jungle	1955
Allen Ginsburg's *Howl*	1956
Jack Kerouac's *On the Road*	1967
John Kenneth Galbraith's *The Affluent Society*	1958

TERMS TO MASTER

Listed below are some important terms or people with which you should be familiar after you complete the study of this chapter. Explain the significance of each name or term.

1. baby boom
2. silent generation
3. rock 'n' roll
4. Elvis Presley
5. sunbelt
6. suburbs
7. William Levitt
8. "white flight"
9. white collar
10. cult of domesticity
11. "in God we trust"
12. Norman Vincent Peale
13. neo-orthodoxy
14. Reinhold Niebuhr
15. "other directed"
16. *Death of a Salesman*
17. Holden Caulfield
18. Saul Bellow
19. abstract expressionism
20. Jackson Pollock
21. the Beats

VOCABULARY BUILDING

Listed below are some words or phrases used in this chapter. Look up each word in your dictionary unless the meaning is given here.

1. deprivation
2. ubiquitous
3. dispersion
4. obsolescence
5. adept
6. bask
7. corrosive
8. fester
9. disproportionate
10. cavort
11. surmount
12. confiscate
13. pagan
14. burgeoning
15. corridor
16. quell
17. castigate
18. harangue
19. lambast
20. regiment (v.)

EXERCISES FOR UNDERSTANDING

When you have completed reading the chapter, answer each of the following questions. If you have difficulty, go back and reread the section of the chapter related to the question.

Multiple-Choice Questions

Select the letter of the response that best completes the statement.

1. One likely casue of juvenile deliquency during the 1950s was the
   A. greater mobility provided by cars.
   B. large baby boom generations.
   C. wide dispersion of television.
   D. rapid growth of surburban communities.
2. After World War II, a significant migration occurred from
   A. cities to suburbs.
   B. the rural South to the rural North and Midwest by southern African Americans.
   C. the South, Southwest, and West to the Northeast.
   D. rural areas to central cities.
3. In the postwar era, big business grew because
   A. labor union contracts favored large companies.
   B. government contracts during wartime had favored big business concentration.
   C. members of "the lonely crowd" preferred to work for large corporations.
   D. all of the above
4. The ideal for middle-class women in the 1950s was to be
   A. an independent white-collar professional.
   B. a wife and mother.

C. employed outside the home.

D. like Rosie the Riveter.

5. The religious revival of the 1950s was spurred by

A. the cold war.

B. television.

C. a mobile population's need for community.

D. all the above

6. Norman Vincent Peale was a leading exponent of

A. modern art.

B. neo-orthodox religion.

C. domesticity for women.

D. positive thinking.

7. John Keats's *The Crack in the Picture Window* attacked

A. the new television culture.

B. neo-orthodox religion.

C. suburbia.

D. rock 'n' roll and the youth culture.

8. A "pack of oddballs who celebrate booze, dope, sex, and despair" was *Time*'s description of

A. C. Wright Mills, John Kenneth Galbraith, and John Keats.

B. the Beat writers, poets, painters, and musicians.

C. abstract expressionists.

D. white-collar residents of suburbs.

True-False Questions

Indicate whether each statement is true or false.

1. Defense spending was the most important contributor to economic growth after World War II.

2. The gap between average incomes of whites and blacks narrowed during the prosperous 1950s.

3. Elvis Presley coined the term "rock 'n' roll."

4. The suburban boom was stimulated by favorable government mortgage policies.

5. "One nation under God" was added to all U.S. currency in 1955.

6. According to David Riesman, the inner-directed person lived according to a set of basic values similar to the Protestant work ethic.

7. In the 1950s most major novels celebrated American life and had happy endings.

8. Bob Dylan first recorded "Howl" and "On the Road" in 1959.

Essay Questions

1. What factors contributed to the economic growth and prosperity of the postwar period?

2. How was the growth of suburbs a key to other changes in postwar American society?

3. What was the "youth culture" of the 1950s and how did it resemble or differ from the larger culture?

4. In what ways did conformity characterize the postwar American? Was it a characteristic peculiar to the period?

5. What happened in U.S. religious life after World War II?

6. Who were the important contemporary critics of life in the 1950s and what were their criticisms?

DOCUMENTS

Document 1. "I Believe in Television"

An unsigned commentary in a journal published in 1950 by a New York Catholic society expressed optimism about the future of television while it also recognized many possible pitfalls facing the new medium.

The telecast of President Truman's Inaugural was the high point in the history of news reporting. Ten million "gawks," to use Lippmann's phrase, saw more of the spectacle than did the bystanders on Pennsylvania Avenue. That was the day when the magic screen first emerged from its chrysalis in the taverns and definitely challenged the primacy of press and radio. Here at long last was the latest news reported instantaneously to your eyes and ears in your own living room.

There are incredible and unpredictable wonders in the horoscope of this infant industry. . . . An alert and informed public can make the best of it, can make it a useful instrument for the public good. . . .

Some critics look on television as a fearful calamity. Reinhold Niebuhr, for instance, says it will further vulgarize our culture and "much of what is still wholesome in our life will perish under the impact of the new visual aid." Others claim that this little box will make us a nation of illiterates or perhaps "a chair-bound, myopic and speechless race."

Harsh words, those! But is the television lens really such an evil eye? In itself, television is good: it is a visual aid and the eye is capable of absorbing more information than the ear. It can be misused, certainly, but what is there on God's green earth that cannot be misused? . . .

Properly controlled, television will exert a tremendous and beneficial influence on our way of life. . . . It will be the largest factor in shaping American thought and conduct. It ought to revolutionize politics, for instance. It was TV that revealed to American people generally the antics of the Democratic and Republican Conventions. It is safe to say that the delegates to these conventions in 1952 will behave in a more civilized fashion: less bombast and circus-parading and more of the dignity of serious men meeting for a serious purpose. TV also made the ordinary voter aware of the bargainings and machinations in the smoke-filled rooms.

Television will be more successful than was radio in presenting so-called "high-brow" programs. The CBS feature "Invitation to Learning" has not been popular: the CBS publicity department once referred to it as "the sixty-ninth most popular program on CBS." But interest in such a program will rise when the audience can actually see the speakers. . . .

An official of the American Broadcasting Company, writing in *The Atlantic Monthly,* says that television may bring comfort and inspiration as a handmaiden of religion "not alone to the sick and old but to vast numbers to whom religion is either a new or a forgotten experience." The apostolic possibilities of television for Catholic Church are unique. In the jargon of the profession, the Catholic Church is telegenic. Its colorful rites and ceremonies are the answer to a telecaster's prayer. . . .

If organizations and individuals who love the things of the spirit get behind television, it can become an immense force for good. But if we abandon it to the low tastes of advertisers and entertainers, it

will become a vulgarizing force. As for the Church, how long, O
Lord, how long shall we neglect this amazing medium for preaching
Christ in the living rooms of America?

[From "I Believe in Television," *The Catholic World,* March 1950,
pp. 401–5.]

Document 2. A Vast Wasteland

A decade after the positive forecast in Document 1, the new chairman of the Federal Com-
munications Commission, Newton N. Minow, made some sharp criticisms of television in a
bold address to the convention of the National
Association of Broadcasters.

. . . I want you to know that you have my admiration and respect.
Yours is a most honorable profession. Anyone who is in the broadcasting business has a tough row to hoe. You earn your bread by using
public property. When you work in broadcasting you volunteer for
public service, public pressure, and public regulation. You must com-
pete with other attractions and other investments, and the only way
you can do it is to prove to us every three years that you should have
been in business in the first place.

I can think of easier ways to make a living.

But I cannot think of more satisfying ways.

I admire your courage—but that doesn't mean I would make life
any easier for you. . . .

I have confidence in your [financial] health.

But not in your product.

It is with this and much more in mind that I come before you today.

. . .

. . . In a time of peril and opportunity, the old complacent, unbalanced fare of Action-Adventure and Situation Comedies is simply not
good enough.

Your industry possesses the most powerful voice in America. It has
an inescapable duty to make that voice ring with intelligence and with
leadership. In a few years, this exciting industry has grown from a
novelty to an instrument of overwhelming impact on the American
people. It should be making ready for the kind of leadership that
newspapers and magazines assumed years ago, to make our people
aware of their world.

Ours has been called the jet age, the atomic age, the space age. It is
also, I submit, the television age. And just as history will decide
whether the leaders of today's world employed the atom to destroy
the world or rebuild it for mankind's benefit, so will history decide
whether today's broadcasters employed their powerful voice to enrich
the people or debase them.

If I seem today to address myself chiefly to the problems of television, I don't want any of you radio broadcasters to think we've gone
to sleep at your switch—we haven't. We still listen. But in recent

years most of the controversies and cross-currents in broadcast programming have swirled around television. And so my subject today is the television industry and the public interest.

Like everybody, I wear more than one hat. I am the Chairman of the FCC. I am also a television viewer and the husband and father of other television viewers. I have seen a great many television programs that seemed to me eminently worthwhile, and I am not talking about the much bemoaned good old days of Playhouse 90 and Studio One.

I am talking about this past season. Some were wonderfully entertaining, such as The Fabulous Fifties, the Fred Astaire Show, and the Bing Crosby Special; some were dramatic and moving, such as Conrad's Victory and Twilight Zone; some were marvelously informative, such as The Nation's Future, CBS Reports, and The Valiant Years. I could list many more—programs that I am sure everyone here felt enriched his own life and that of his family. When television is good, nothing—not the theatre, not the magazines or newspapers—nothing is better.

But when television is bad, nothing is worse. I invite you to sit down in front of your television set when your station goes on the air and stay there without a book, magazine, newspaper, profit and loss sheet or rating book to distract you—and keep your eyes glued to that set until the station signs off. I can assure you that you will observe a vast wasteland.

You will see a procession of game shows, violence, audience participation shows, formula comedies about totally unbelievable families, blood and thunder, mayhem, violence, sadism, murder, western badmen, western good men, private eyes, gangsters, more violence, and cartoons. And, endlessly, commercials—many screaming, cajoling, and offending. And most of all, boredom. True, you will see a few things you will enjoy. But they will be very, very few. And if you think I exaggerate, try it.

Is there one person in this room claims that broadcasting can't do better?

Well, a glance at next season's proposed programming can give us little heart. Of 73 1/2 hours of prime evening time, the networks have tentatively scheduled 59 hours to categories of "action-adventure," situation comedy, variety, quiz, and movies.

Is there one network president in this room who claims he can't do better?

Well, is there at least one network president who believes that the other networks can't do better?

Gentlemen, your trust accounting with your beneficiaries is overdue.

Never have so few owed so much to so many.

Why is so much of television so bad? I have heard many answers: demands of your advertisers; competition for ever higher ratings; the need always to attract a mass audience; the high cost of television programs; the insatiable appetite for programming material—these are some of them. Unquestionably, these are tough problems not susceptible to easy answers.

But I am not convinced that you have tried hard enough to solve them.

I do not accept the idea that the present over-all programming is aimed accurately at the public taste. The ratings tell us only that some people have their television sets turned on and of that number, so many are tuned to one channel and so many to another. They don't tell us what the public might watch if they were offered half a dozen additional choices. A rating, at best, is an indication of how many people saw what you gave them. Unfortunately, it does not reveal the depth of the penetration, or the intensity of reaction, and it never reveals what the acceptance would have been if what you gave them had been better—if all the forces of art and creativity and daring and imagination had been unleashed. I believe in the people's good sense and good taste, and I am not convinced that the people's taste is as low as some of you assume.

My concern with the rating services is not with their accuracy. Perhaps they are accurate. I really don't know. What, then, is wrong with the ratings? It's not been their accuracy—it's been their use.

Certainly, I hope you will agree that ratings should have little influence where children are concerned. The best estimates indicate that during the hours of 5 to 6 p.m. 60% of your audience is composed of children under 12. And most young children today, believe it or not, spend as much time watching television as they do in the schoolroom. I repeat—let that sink in—most young children today spend as much time watching television as they do in the schoolroom. I used to be said that there were three great influences on a child: home, school, and church. Today, there is a fourth great influence, and you ladies and gentlemen control it.

If parents, teachers, and ministers conducted their responsibilities by following the ratings, children would have a steady diet of ice cream, school holidays, and no Sunday School. What about your responsibilities? Is there no room on television to teach, to inform, to uplift, to stretch, to enlarge the capacities of our children? Is there no room for programs deepening their understanding of children in other lands? Is there no room for a children's news show explaining something about the world to them at their level of understanding? Is there no room for reading the great literature of the past, teaching them the great traditions of freedom? There are some fine children's shows, but they are drowned out in the massive doses of cartoons, violence, and ore violence. Must these be your trademarks? Search your consciences and see if you cannot offer more to your young beneficiaries whose future you guide so many hours each and every day.

What about adult programming and ratings? You know, newspaper publishers take popularity ratings too. The answers are pretty clear: it is almost always the comics, followed by the advice to the lovelorn columns. But, ladies and gentlemen, the news is still on the front page of all newspapers, the editorials are not replaced by more comics, the newspapers have not become one long collection of advice to the lovelorn. Yet newspapers do not need a license from the government to be in business—they do not use public property. But in television—where your responsibilities as public trustees are so plain, the moment that the ratings indicate that westerns are popular there are new imitations of westerns on the air faster than the old coaxial cable could take us from Hollywood to New York. Broadcasting cannot continue to live by the numbers. Ratings ought to be the slave of the broadcaster, not his master. And you and I both know that the rating services themselves would agree. . . .

. . . Your obligations are not satisfied if you look only to popularity as a test of what to broadcast. You are not only in show business; you are free to communicate ideas as well as relaxation. You must provide a wider range of choices, more diversity, more alternatives. It is not enough to cater to the nation's whims—you must also serve the nation's needs.

And I would add this—that if some of you persist in a relentless search for the highest rating and the lowest common denominator, you may very well lose your audience. Because to paraphrase a great American who was recently my law partner, the people are wise, wiser than some of the broadcasters—and politicians—think. . . .

Tell your sponsors to be less concerned with costs per thousand and more concerned with understanding per millions. And remind your stockholders that an investment in broadcasting is buying a share in public responsibility.

The networks can start this industry on the road to freedom from the dictatorship of numbers. . . .

What you gentlemen broadcast through the people's air affects the people's taste, their knowledge, their opinions, their understanding of themselves and of their world, and their future.

The power of instantaneous sight and sound is without precedent in mankind's history. This is an awesome power. It has limitless capabilities for good—and for evil. And it carries with it awesome responsibilities, responsibilities which you and I cannot escape.

In his stirring Inaugural Address our President said, "And so, my fellow Americans: ask not what your country can do for you—ask what you can do for your country."

Ladies and Gentlemen:

Ask not what broadcasting can do for you. Ask what you can do for broadcasting.

I urge you to put the people's airwaves to the service of the people and the cause of freedom. You must help prepare a generation for great decisions. You must help a great nation fulfill its future.

[From Newton N. Minow, "Program Control: The Broadcasters Are Public Trustees," *Vital Speeches of the Day,* June 15, 1961, pp. 533–37.]

Document 3. Television and the Pursuit of Excellence

Two weeks after Minow's indictment, Louis Hausman, an industry spokesman, presented a more positive view of television in a speech to the American Council for Better Broadcasting.

. . . In a very real sense, you of the American Council for Better Broadcasts have identified yourselves with the search for excellence in one area of American life: television.

You have said, in effect: Television has made available to people of even the most modest means and in remote places a spectrum of information, entertainment and cultural experience which 15 years ago was restricted to the most affluent residents of the largest metropolitan areas.

Recognizing this, you have attempted to encourage the viewing of those portions of the program schedule that contribute to greater awareness—not only of the world as it exists today but also of the traditions that have contributed to our civilization.

Your goal is to encourage viewers to partake more fully of programs of this nature.

This is a constructive approach to the question of improving television within its present context. And it is as constructive as it is rare.

A far more popular approach is to indulge in "television baiting"— to concentrate exclusively on what is wrong with television: to decry the extent of formula programming and the lack of style and imagination in the program schedule. . . .

Television contains considerable programming designed for other than maximum audiences. Much of this programming is supported by the broadcasters—as sustaining programs. Increasingly, it is being supported by advertisers who sponsor such programs.

Perhaps there isn't enough. How much special-interest programming there should be is not an easy problem to solve. But, I urge you to remember that television was able to attract six million people to Walter Lippmann chiefly because 40 million viewers watch *Gunsmoke* week after week. It can attract five million to a performance of Don Giovanni because seven or eight times that number come to it regularly for Perry Como. . . .

. . . Over the long haul, *the surest way to get programming of higher quality and taste is to have audiences with better taste.*

To achieve this, however, is an exceedingly difficult assignment in a democratic society.

I happen to think that it is very good that it is difficult. Because even more than I fear ignorance, I fear the superimposition by a relatively small group of people of their tastes and their standards of morality or excellence upon a total society.

This is what obtains in totalitarian countries. In these countries not only the communications media, but the schools, the social activities, and all the other aspects of the society are guided by a monolithic set of standards handed down from above.

This is an efficient way to influence tastes and attitudes. But I question whether any of us would trade our more cumbersome methods for efficiency in this area.

Standards and tastes in a democratic society must come from something comprehending a consensus of the people. It must come from churches, from the families, from the play of interpersonal relationships, from the schools, and from the media to which the people turn for information and entertainment.

None of these influences operates in a vacuum. Each interlocks with and supports the others in the drive to stimulate a greater public tolerance for greater excellence.

I happen to think such a tolerance for excellence is growing in this country, and that the mass media, including television, have played a part in this advancement.

There are some who disagree. But, much as these may scorn the quality of certain of today's best sellers, I think that by any standards, *Marjorie Morningstar* is a better book than Eleanor Glyn's *90 Days,* or *Pollyanna* by Eleanor Porter—best sellers of forty years back. I'm sure even these people would consider *Time* to be more informative than the *Literary Digest.* I happen to think *It Started in Naples* with Sophia Loren and Clark Gable is a better movie than *The Sheik* with Rudolph Valentino; that a *Gunsmoke* is a better western than any in which William S. Hart performed.

Granted that some of these are formula productions, I think the formulae are better than they were fifty years ago. I think the furniture in people's homes and the homes in which most people live, in general, show better, or at least more sophisticated, taste than they did fifty or seventy-five years ago.

A serious challenge exists to raise popular taste so that the bread-and-butter entertainment portion of the television schedule can have greater excellence.

It is the broadcaster's responsibility to be a part of this effort. It is, to an even greater degree, the task of our society. . . .

First, there is no essential conflict between the aspirations of those who seek greater usefulness for television and the objectives of all thoughtful broadcasters.

Each seeks more excellence. Each aims to have television better serve a total society made up of many interests—to serve by better informing and by widening the cultural experience of the huge television audience.

There is, needless to say, considerable disagreement as to means. This disagreement exists between broadcasters and critics, and among critics, themselves.

Second, we have looked briefly at two approaches taken by the critics. One group of critics confines itself, in general, to denouncing what it finds unacceptable. this approach serves as a goad to better performance. It strengthens broadcasters' adherence to self-imposed standards such as are exemplified by the Code of Good Practice of the National Association of Broadcasters.

The other approach—the one you have taken—seems to me to be

the more effective. It lies in encouraging more people to partake of what you consider excellent within the program schedule as it exists. Through this encouragement, and through greater acceptance of such programs, there will—eventually—be more of them.

Third, we have speculated about the real breakthrough that will come when all of those who shape the tastes and values of the generation growing up will have succeeded in elevating these tastes and inculcating higher standards.

In your roles as parents and teachers, as churchmen and churchgoers, as citizens and voters, you can contribute immeasurably to this effort. Television shares this effort with you. It can be effective to the extent that any medium can be effective.

Television can and does help teaching, but it cannot be a teacher. Television can help our citizens to mature legislative judgments, but it cannot be a legislator. It can help parents in shaping attitudes, but it is not a parent. . . .

You have demonstrated your belief that exposure to the existing riches of our heritage, to the world of ideas and of the arts, can lead the American people to share patterns of culture formerly enjoyed by a tiny enclave of the privileged. And you hold to the faith that this is good.

Perhaps this is a naive point of view—a point of view which went out with the beginning of World War I. Perhaps mankind is not perfectible. Perhaps only the base and the meretricious will survive.

I don't think there is persuasive evidence to support the view of those who contemplate with alarm and despair the state of our society.

No nation that supports more symphony orchestras than the rest of the world put together, where the attendance at the New York Metropolitan Museum of Art is twice as large as that of the Louvre in Paris, is a nation in which mass media can be accused of taste degradation. . . .

[From Louis Hausman, "Television and the Pursuit of Excellence: Influencing Tastes and Attitudes," *Vital Speeches of the Day,* July 1, 1961, pp. 568–71.]

Questions for Reflection

In what ways does the debate over television resemble the paradoxes of life in the 1950s? How does the first essay anticipate many of the arguments made a decade later by Minow and Hausman? What had happened in television in the interval? What are the major points of disagreement between Minow and Hausman? Which seems the more accurate assessment of television? Do many of the same arguments about TV persist today? What effects have satellite transmission and cable television had on television programming?

ANSWERS TO MULTIPLE-CHOICE AND TRUE-FALSE QUESTIONS

Multiple-Choice Questions

1-A, 2-A, 3-B, 4-B, 5-D, 6-D, 7-C, 8-B

True-False Questions

1-T, 2-F, 3-F, 4-T, 5-F, 6-T, 7-F, 8-F

33

CONFLICT AND DEADLOCK:
THE EISENHOWER YEARS

CHAPTER OBJECTIVES

After you complete the reading and study of this chapter, you should be able to:

1. Describe the Eisenhower style and his approach to the nation's problems.
2. Assess the nature of modern Republicanism in relation to New Deal liberalism, focusing especially on Eisenhower's stance on key domestic legislation.
3. Evaluate the early performance of Dulles's diplomacy, especially as compared to the policy of containment.
4. Understand the origins of the Indochina War and judge Eisenhower's response to it.
5. Describe the developments in civil rights in the Eisenhower era and assess his responses to them.
6. Explain the Suez Crisis and the Hungarian Revolt, their interrelations and their consequences.
7. Assess the impact of Sputnik.

CHAPTER OUTLINE

I. Election of 1952
  A. Liabilities of the Truman administration

B. Republicans' choice
  1. Taft's position
  2. Eisenhower's appeal
C. Democratic draft of Stevenson
D. The campaign
E. Results

II. Eisenhower's early leadership in domestic affairs
  A. Eisenhower's background and style
    1. Earlier career
    2. Preference for staff administrative organization
    3. Impact of the style
    4. More recent assessment of his actions
  B. The Eisenhower appointments
  C. Assessment of his conservative direction
  D. Efforts to repeal Democratic policies
    1. Tidelands to the states
    2. Abolition of Reconstruction Finance Corporation
    3. Cutting the budget
  E. Extension of New Deal programs
    1. Social Security benefits
    2. Minimum-wage increases
    3. Low-income housing
    4. Farm programs
      a. REA

2. U.S. responses

VI. Stirrings in civil rights
   A. Eisenhower's views of civil rights
   B. Court decisions
      1. Decisions preliminary to *Brown*
      2. The *Brown* decision
      3. Reactions to *Brown*
         a. Ike's reluctance
         b. Token integration
         c. Massive resistance
            i. Citizens' Councils
            ii. Southern Manifesto

C. Montgomery bus boycott
      1. Causes for action
      2. Role of Martin Luther King, Jr.
      3. Results
D. Civil rights legislation
E. Little Rock
      1. Court order
      2. Governor Faubus
      3. Federal intervention

VII. Assessing the Eisenhower years
   A. Accomplishments
   B. The farewell address

KEY ITEMS OF CHRONOLOGY

Fall of Dien Bien Phu	May 1954
Brown v. *Board of Education*	May 1954
Geneva Accords signed	July 1954
SEATO created	September 1954
McCarthy condemned by the Senate	December 1954
Montgomery bus boycott	December 1955– December 1956
Suez crisis (and Hungarian revolt)	October 1956
Little Rock High School crisis	September 1957
Sputnik launched	October 1957
U-2 incident	May 1960

TERMS TO MASTER

Listed below are some important terms or people with which you should be familiar after you complete the study of this chapter. Explain the significance of each name or term.

1. moderate Republicanism
2. Adlai Stevenson
3. dynamic conservatism
4. St. Lawrence Seaway
5. Interstate Highway System
6. Earl Warren
7. liberation
8. massive retaliation
9. Ho Chi Minh
10. Dien Bien Phu
11. Geneva Accords
12. SEATO
13. Quemoy and Matsu
14. de-Stalinization
15. *Brown* v. *Board of Education*
16. massive resistance
17. Martin Luther King, Jr.
18. Suez Crisis
19. Sputnik
20. U-2 incident

VOCABULARY BUILDING

Listed below are some words or phrases used in this chapter. Look up each word in your dictionary unless the meaning is given here.

1. linger
2. potent
3. tenuous
4. covet
5. lackluster

6. incumbent
7. apathetic
8. novice
9. genial
10. renege
11. hobnob
12. dismal
13. rapier
14. skulk
15. dour
16. indiscretion
17. lexicon
18. quandry
19. illusory
20. disarray

EXERCISES FOR UNDERSTANDING

When you have completed reading the chapter, answer each of the following questions. If you have difficulty, go back and reread the section of the chapter related to the question.

Multiple-Choice Questions

Select the letter of the response that best completes the statement.

1. The election of 1952 was a turning point in politics because
   A. Republicans gained control of Congress.
   B. Democrats won the presidency.
   C. Eisenhower won several southern states.
   D. all of the above
2. Eisenhower said that the "biggest damnfool mistake I ever made" was
   A. running for political office.
   B. appointing Earl Warren chief justice of the Supreme Court.
   C. deciding not to use atomic weapons against the Communists in Korea.
   D. helping Senator Joseph McCarthy.
3. Khrushchev's policy of "de-Stalinization" contributed to
   A. conflict in 1956 over the Suez Canal.
   B. an uprising in Hungary in 1956.
   C. an end to the Korean War.
   D. the emergence of Ho Chi Minh in Vietnam.
4. The Geneva Accords involving Southeast Asia
   A. were signed by the United States.
   B. neutralized Vietnam.
   C. divided Laos and Cambodia at the 38th Parallel.
   D. called for elections to unify Vietnam.
5. In *Brown* v. *Board of Education,* the Supreme Court ruled that
   A. racial segregation was constitutional.
   B. "separate but equal" in public education was unconstitutional.
   C. all children under the age of eighteen had to attend school.
   D. Kansas must provide free education for Indian children.
6. The Reverend Martin Luther King, Jr., came to national prominence in the
   A. *Brown* school desegregation case.
   B. Little Rock integration crisis.
   C. Montgomery bus boycott.
   D. Greensboro sit-ins.
7. In 1956
   A. Eisenhower won reelection.
   B. war broke out in the Middle East.
   C. the Soviets sent troops into Hungary.
   D. all the above
8. Eisenhower's farewell address dealt with
   A. the need for greater military spending.
   B. the dangers of a military-industrial complex.
   C. how to solve problems of civil rights.
   D. the need for a better highway system.

True-False Questions

Indicate whether each statement is true or false.

1. "Dynamic conservatism" meant being conservative about money but liberal about people.
2. Eisenhower reduced the number of people covered by Social Security.
3. Eisenhower's secretary of state was John Foster Dulles.

4. The first post–World War II summit conference was held on Quemoy and Matsu.
5. Eisenhower sent federal troops to Little Rock during the school integration crisis.
6. Challenges to the separate-but-equal doctrine were led by the NAACP.
7. Eisenhower had the good fortune to work with Republican-controlled Congresses.
8. The Landrum-Griffin Act of 1959 provided money for the space program.

Essay Questions

1. What were the major domestic accomplishments of the Eisenhower administration?

2. Why did the Geneva Accords not resolve the conflict in Southeast Asia the way negotiations concluded the Korean War?
3. What were the chief characteristics of U.S. foreign policy under Eisenhower and Dulles?
4. Trace the United States's involvement in Southeast Asia from 1945 to 1960.
5. What were the major events in the civil rights movement in the 1950s and what role did the Eisenhower administration play in them?
6. How did the United States respond to the major foreign policy crises of 1956? What determined the responses?
7. Was Eisenhower a successful president? Explain and defend your answer.

DOCUMENTS

Document 1. U.S. Supreme Court Decision in *Brown* v. *Board of Education*, 1954

In a landmark decision in 1954, the Supreme Court ruled school segregation unconstitutional. Speaking for a unanimous court, Chief Justice Earl Warren delivered the opinion, an excerpt of which follows.

These cases come to us from the States of Kansas, South Carolina, Virginia, and Delaware. They are premised on different facts and different local conditions, but a common legal question justifies their consideration together in this consolidated opinion.

In each of the cases, minors of the Negro race, through their legal representatives, seek the aid of the courts in obtaining admission to the public schools of their community on a nonsegregated basis. In each instance, they have been denied admission to schools attended by white children under laws requiring or permitting segregation according to race. This segregation was alleged to deprive the plaintiffs of the equal protection of the laws under the Fourteenth Amendment. In each of the cases other than the Delaware case, a three judge federal district court denied relief to the plaintiffs on the so-called "separate but equal" doctrine announced by this Court in *Plessy v. Ferguson*, 163 U.S. 537. Under that doctrine, equality of treatment is accorded when the races are provided substantially equal facilities, even though these facilities be separate. In the Delaware case, the Supreme Court of Delaware adhered to that doctrine, but ordered that the plaintiffs be admitted to the white schools because of their superiority to the Negro schools.

The plaintiffs contend that segregated public schools are not "equal" and cannot be made "equal," and that hence they are deprived of the equal protection of the laws. . . .

In the instant cases, there are findings below that the Negro and white schools involved have been equalized, or are being equalized, with respect to buildings, curricula, qualifications and salaries of teachers, and other "tangible" factors. Our decision, therefore, cannot turn on merely a comparison of these tangible factors in the Negro and white schools involved in each of the cases. We must look instead to the effect of segregation itself on public education.

In approaching this problem, we cannot turn the clock back to 1868 when the Amendment was adopted, or even to 1896 when *Plessy* v. *Ferguson* was written. We must consider public education in the light of its full development and its present place in American life throughout the Nation. Only in this way can it be determined if segregation in public schools deprives these plaintiffs of the equal protection of the laws.

Today, education is perhaps the most important function of state and local governments. Compulsory school attendance laws and the great expenditures for education both demonstrate our recognition of the importance of education to our democratic society. It is required in the performance of our most basic public responsibilities, even service in the armed forces. It is the very foundation of good citizenship. Today it is a principal instrument in awakening the child to cultural values, in preparing him for later professional training, and in helping him to adjust normally to his environment. In these days, it is doubtful that any child may reasonably be expected to succeed in life if he is denied the opportunity of an education. Such an opportunity, where the state has undertaken to provide it, is a right which must be made available to all on equal terms.

We come then to the question presented: Does segregation of children in public schools solely on the basis of race, even though the physical facilities and other "tangible" factors may be equal, deprive the children of the minority group of equal educational opportunities? We believe that it does.

. . . children in grade and high schools. To separate them from others of similar age and qualifications solely because of their race generates a feeling of inferiority as to their status in the community that may affect their hearts and minds in a way unlikely ever to be undone. The effect of this separation on their educational opportunities was well stated by a finding in the Kansas case by a court which nevertheless felt compelled to rule against the Negro plaintiffs:

"Segregation of white and colored children in public schools has a detrimental effect upon the colored children. The impact is greater when it has the sanction of the law; for the policy of separating the races is usually interpreted as denoting the inferiority of the Negro group. A sense of inferiority affects the motivation of a child to learn. Segregation with the sanction of law, therefore, has a tendency to retard the educational and mental development of Negro children and to deprive them of some of the benefits they would receive in a racially integrated school system." Whatever may have been the extent of psychological knowledge at the time of *Plessy* v. *Ferguson,* this finding is amply supported by modern authority. Any language in *Plessy* v. *Ferguson* contrary to this finding is rejected.

We conclude that in the field of public education the doctrine of "separate but equal" has no place. Separate educational facilities are inherently unequal. Therefore, we hold that the plaintiffs and others similarly situated for whom the actions have been brought are, by reason of the segregation complained of, deprived of the equal protection of the laws guaranteed by the Fourteenth Amendment.

[From *Brown* v. *Board of Education of Topeka,* 347 U.S. 483.]

Document 2. Declaration of Constitutional Principles, 1956

In March 1956, more than one hundred southern congressmen and senators signed the Declaration of Constitutional Principles. Also known as the Southern Manifesto, it presents the objections of many white southerners to the *Brown* decision.

The unwarranted decision of the Supreme Court in the public school cases is now bearing the fruit always produced when men substitute naked power for established law.

The Founding Fathers gave us a Constitution of checks and balances because they realized the inescapable lesson of history that no man or group of men can be safely entrusted with unlimited power. They framed this Constitution with its provisions for change by amendment in order to secure the fundamentals of government against the dangers of temporary popular passion or the personal predilections of public officeholders.

We regard the decision of the Supreme Court in the school cases as a clear abuse of judicial power. It climaxes a trend in the Federal Judiciary undertaking to legislate, in derogation of the authority of Congress, and to encroach upon the reserved rights of the States and the people.

The original Constitution does not mention education. Neither does the 14th amendment nor any other amendment. The debates preceding the submission of the 14th amendment clearly show that there was no intent that it should affect the system of education maintained by the States. . . .

In the case of *Plessy* v. *Ferguson* in 1896 the Supreme Court expressly declared that under the 14th amendment no person was denied any of his rights if the States provided separate but equal public facilities. This decision has been followed in many other cases. It is notable that the Supreme Court, speaking through Chief Justice Taft, a former President of the United States, unanimously declared in 1927 in *Lum* v. *Rice* that the "separate but equal" principle is "within the discretion of the State in regulating its public schools and does not conflict with the 14th amendment."

This interpretation, restated time and again, became a part of the life of the people of many of the States and confirmed their habits, customs, traditions, and way of life. It is founded on elemental humanity and commonsense, for parents should not be deprived by Government of the right to direct the lives and education of their own children.

Though there has been no constitutional amendment or act of Congress changing this established legal principle almost a century old, the Supreme Court of the United States, with no legal basis for such action, undertook to exercise their naked judicial power and substituted their personal political and social ideas for the established law of the land.

This unwarranted exercise of power by the Court, contrary to the Constitution, is creating chaos and confusion in the States principally affected. It is destroying the amicable relations between the white and Negro races that have been created through 90 years of patient effort by the good people of both races. It has planted hatred and suspicion where there has been heretofore friendship and understanding.

Without regard to the consent of the governed, outside agitators are threatening immediate and revolutionary changes in our public-school systems. If done, this is certain to destroy the system of public education in some of the States.

With the gravest concern for the explosive and dangerous condition created by this decision and inflamed by outside meddlers:

We reaffirm our reliance on the Constitution as the fundamental law of the land.

We decry the Supreme Court's encroachments on rights reserved to the States and to the people, contrary to established law, and to the Constitution.

We commend the motives of those States which have declared the intention to resist forced integration by any lawful means.

We appeal to the States and people who are not directly affected by these decisions to consider the constitutional principles involved against the time when they too, on issues vital to them, may be the victims of judicial encroachment.

Even though we constitute a minority in the present Congress, we have full faith that a majority of the American people believe in the dual system of government which has enabled us to achieve our greatness and will in time demand that the reserved rights of the States and of the people be made secure against judicial usurpation.

We pledge ourselves to use all lawful means to bring about a reversal of this decision which is contrary to the Constitution and to prevent the use of force in its implementation.

In this trying period, as we all seek to right this wrong, we appeal to our people not to be provoked by the agitators and troublemakers invading our States and to scrupulously refrain from disorder and lawless acts.

[From *Congressional Record*, 84th Cong., 2d sess., 12 March 1956, pp. 4460–61.]

Questions for Reflection

On what grounds did the Supreme Court overturn the "separate but equal" doctrine? Why did white southerners object to the decision? Did the Southern Manifesto claim to speak for southern African Americans? How could the nation reconcile "public education in the light of its full development and its present place in American life" and the "habits, customs, traditions, and way of life" of the white South? What is the role of the federal courts in bringing about change and in protecting the status quo?

ANSWERS TO MULTIPLE-CHOICE AND TRUE-FALSE QUESTIONS

Multiple-Choice Questions

1-C, 2-B, 3-B, 4-D, 5-B, 6-C, 7-D, 8-B

True-False Questions

1-T, 2-F, 3-T, 4-F, 5-T, 6-T, 7-F, 8-F

34

NEW FRONTIERS: POLITICS
AND SOCIAL CHANGE IN THE 1960s

CHAPTER OBJECTIVES

After you complete the reading and study of this chapter, you should be able to:

1. Describe Kennedy's style and compare it with those of his predecessor and successor.
2. Assess Kennedy's domestic legislative achievements.
3. Assess the Kennedy record in foreign affairs.
4. Describe and account for LBJ's legislative accomplishments.
5. Explain why the Vietnam War became a quagmire for the United States and why LBJ changed his policy there in 1968.
6. Trace the transformation of the civil rights movement into the black power movement.

CHAPTER OUTLINE

I. Kennedy's New Frontier
  A. Election of 1960
    1. Nixon as politician
    2. Kennedy's background
    3. The campaign
      a. Neutralization of religion
      b. Television debates
    4. Results

  B. Kennedy's administration
    1. Caliber of appointments
    2. Kennedy style
  C. Domestic record
    1. Congressional conservatism
    2. The tax-cut proposal
    3. Legislative successes
      a. Foreign aid
      b. Peace Corps
      c. Trade expansion
      d. Housing assistance
      e. Increased minimum wage
      f. Area development
      g. Space race
  D. The Warren Court
    1. School prayer
    2. Criminal justice
  E. Growing movement for civil rights
    1. Kennedy's position
    2. Sit-ins
      a. Mass movement
      b. Student participants
      c. Formation of SNCC
      d. Importance of music
    3. Freedom rides
    4. Federal intervention
      a. Integration of "Ole Miss"
      b. Birmingham demonstrations
        i. *Letter from Birmingham Jail*

        ii. King's shift in strategy
     c. JFK's changing position
     d. Confrontation with George
       Wallace
    5. March on Washington
  F. Foreign frontiers
    1. Bay of Pigs disaster
    2. Vienna Summit
    3. Berlin Wall
    4. Cuban Missile Crisis
     a. The crisis
     b. Kennedy's action
     c. Resolution of the crisis
     d. Aftereffects
       i. Lowered tension
       ii. Sale of wheat
       iii. Washington-Moscow hot-
         line
       iv. Removal of obsolete mis-
         siles
       v. Nuclear test ban treaty
    5. Neutrality for Laos
    6. Vietnam
     a. Diem's failure to reform or
       gain popular support
     b. Kennedy's reluctance to
       escalate
     c. Heightened opposition to
       Diem
     d. Overthrow of Diem
  G. The Kennedy assassination

II. Lyndon Johnson and the Great Society
  A. Johnson's background and style
    1. Paradoxical personality
    2. Political experience
    3. Congressional leadership
    4. "Johnson treatment"
  B. Early legislative achievements
    1. The tax cut
    2. The War on Poverty
  C. The election of 1964
    1. Republicans seek a "choice"
    2. Goldwater's positions
    3. Johnson's appeal to consensus
    4. The Johnson landslide
  D. Landmark legislation
    1. Health insurance
    2. Aid to education
    3. Appalachian redevelopment

    4. Housing and urban development
    5. Immigration Act of 1965
  E. Civil rights movement
    1. Civil Rights Act of 1964
    2. Voting rights
     a. Selma march
     b. LBJ's support
     c. Voting Rights Act of 1965
  F. The development of black power
    1. The riots of 1965 and 1966
    2. Assessment of the urban black
      condition
    3. The focus on black power
     a. Stokely Carmichael
     b. The Black Panthers
     c. Malcolm X
     d. Assessment of black power

III. The tragedy of Vietnam
  A. U.S. involvement
    1. General policies
    2. Costs of war
  B. The Tonkin Gulf Resolution
    1. Basis for the request
    2. Provisions of the resolution
  C. Escalation in 1965
    1. Attack on Pleiku
    2. "Operation Rolling Thunder"
    3. Combat troops
  D. The context for policy
    1. Consistency with earlier foreign
      policy goals
    2. Warnings from advisers
    3. The goal of United States
      involvement
    4. The erosion of support
  E. The turning point of the war
    1. The Tet Offensive
    2. The presidential primaries
    3. Johnson's decision to move out

IV. The crescendo of the sixties
  A. The tragedies of 1968
    1. Martin Luther King, Jr.
    2. Robert Kennedy
  B. Convergence on the election of 1968
    1. Chicago demonstrations
    2. The contrast of Miami
    3. The Wallace campaign
    4. The results

KEY ITEMS OF CHRONOLOGY

Bay of Pigs invasion	April 1961
freedom rides	May 1961
Cuban Missile Crisis	October 1963
Overthrow of Ngo Dinh Diem	November 1963
Kennedy assassination	November 1963
Civil Rights Act (public accommodations)	July 1964
Gulf of Tonkin Resolution	August 1964
Voting Rights Act	1965
Tet Offensive	January–February 1968

TERMS TO MASTER

Listed below are some important terms or people with which you should be familiar after you complete the study of this chapter. Explain the significance of each name or term.

1. New Frontier
2. Robert McNamara
3. Peace Corps
4. sit-in
5. Bay of Pigs invasion
6. Berlin Wall
7. Cuban Missile Crisis
8. Nuclear Test Ban Treaty
9. Ngo Dinh Diem
10. Great Society
11. *The Other America*
12. Medicare and Medicaid
13. Barry Goldwater
14. Martin Luther King, Jr.
15. SNCC
16. freedom rides
17. Watts riot
18. black power
19. Malcolm X
20. Tonkin Gulf Resolution
21. Vietcong
22. Tet Offensive
23. Eugene McCarthy
24. Robert Kennedy

VOCABULARY BUILDING

Listed below are some words or phrases used in this chapter. Look up each word in your dictionary unless the meaning is given here.

1. trauma
2. chameleon
3. tycoon
4. prelate
5. haggard
6. credence
7. sublime
8. lament
9. auspicious
10. debacle
11. demoralize
12. euphemism
13. outmoded
14. hardscrabble
15. recalcitrant
16. impervious
17. fatalistic
18. nihilistic
19. hyperbole
20. fatuous

EXERCISES FOR UNDERSTANDING

When you have completed the reading of the chapter, answer each of the following questions. If you have difficulty, go back and reread the section of the chapter related to the question.

Multiple-Choice Questions

Select the letter of the response that best completes the statement.

1. One of Kennedy's major legislative accomplishments was
   A. the 1962 Trade Expansion Act that cut tariffs with Europe.
   B. the national program of Medicare under Social Security.
   C. federal aid to secondary education.
   D. strong legislation to protect the right of blacks to vote.

2. In the Birmingham campaign in 1962, Martin Luther King, Jr., signaled a change strategy from
   A. educating whites about racism to using violence to achieve change.
   B. seeking federal enforcement and new laws to massive civil disobedience.
   C. massive civil disobedience to using violence to achieve change.
   D. changing southern white attitudes to obtaining federal enforcement and new laws.

3. In the Cuban Missile Crisis, President Kennedy ordered
   A. surgical air strikes of Cuba.
   B. a quarantine of Cuba.
   C. the Bay of Pigs invasion.
   D. removal of U.S. missiles from Turkey.

4. Michael Harrington's *The Other America* influenced the
   A. Alliance for Progress.
   B. War on Poverty.
   C. Civil Rights Act of 1964.
   D. Supreme Court's decision on criminal justice.

5. The Jobs Corps, Head Start, and VISTA were all part of
   A. Martin Luther King, Jr.'s proposals for Birmingham.
   B. the War on Poverty.
   C. Kennedy's New Frontier.
   D. Barry Goldwater's platform in 1964.

6. "I would remind you that in the defense of liberty extremism is no vice," said
   A. Martin Luther King, Jr.
   B. John F. Kennedy.
   C. Barry Goldwater.
   D. Lyndon Johnson.

7. Discrimination in hotels and restaurants was outlawed by
   A. the Supreme Court's *Brown* decision in 1954.
   B. Martin Luther King, Jr.'s "I Have a Dream" speech.
   C. presidential order of Kennedy.
   D. the Civil Rights Act of 1964.

8. Johnson sought to deescalate the Vietnam War because
   A. the Tet Offensive showed that the United States could not win.
   B. political challengers showed the high level of public opposition to the war.
   C. key national leaders called on him to end the war.
   D. all the above

True-False Questions

Indicate whether each statement is true or false.

1. Allegations of JFK's sexual misconduct played a significant role in the 1960 election.

2. The sit-ins in 1960 ignited the first mass movement in African-American history.

3. By the end of 1963, the United States had only 2,000 military advisers in Vietnam.

4. The effects of the 1964 tax cut helped finance the war on poverty.

5. Malcolm X was a leader in the Black Muslim movement.

6. *De jure* segregation resulted from residential patterns.

7. The Immigration Act of 1965 favored immigrants from Western Europe,

8. The Tet Offensive had a great effect on U.S. public opinion.

Essay Questions

1. What was the significance of the Kennedy administration?

2. Was Lyndon Johnson more effective in domestic or foreign policy? Why?

3. Trace U.S. involvement in Vietnam from 1961 to 1986.
4. Discuss the changes in the civil rights movement from 1960 to 1968.

5. Contrast the ideas and strategies of Martin Luther King, Jr., and Malcolm X.
6. Of the presidential elections in 1960, 1964, and 1968, which was the most important?

DOCUMENTS

Document 1. Johnson's Speech on Vietnam, 1965

The speech that follows, given at Johns Hopkins University on April 7, 1965, contains President Johnson's rationale for a critical buildup of U.S. forces in South Vietnam. That year, 1965, proved to be a fateful year for U.S. involvement in Vietnam.

. . . Over this war, and all Asia, is the deepening shadow of Communist China. The rulers in Hanoi are urged on by Peking. This is a regime which has destroyed freedom in Tibet, attacked India, and been condemned by the United Nations for aggression in Korea. It is a nation which is helping the forces of violence in almost every continent. The contest in Vietnam is part of a wider pattern of aggressive purpose.

Why are these realities our concern? Why are we in South Vietnam? We are there because we have a promise to keep. Since 1954 every American President has offered support to the people of South Vietnam. We have helped to build, and we have helped to defend. Thus, over many years, we have made a national pledge to help South Vietnam defend its independence. And I intend to keep our promise.

To dishonor that pledge, to abandon this small and brave nation to its enemy, and to the terror that must follow, would be an unforgivable wrong.

We are also there to strengthen world order. Around the globe, from Berlin to Thailand, are people whose well-being rests, in part, on the belief that they can count on us if they are attacked. To leave Vietnam to its fate would shake the confidence of all these people in the value of American commitment, the value of America's word. The result would be increased unrest and instability, and even wider war.

We are also there because there are great stakes in the balance. Let no one think for a moment that retreat from Vietnam would bring an end to conflict. The battle would be renewed in one country and then another. The central lesson of our time is that the appetite of aggression is never satisfied. To withdraw from one battlefield means only to prepare for the next. We must say in Southeast Asia, as we did in Europe, in the words of the Bible: "Hitherto shalt thou come, but no further."

There are those who say that all our effort there will be futile, that China's power is such it is bound to dominate all Southeast Asia. But there is no end to that argument until all the nations of Asia are swallowed up.

There are those who wonder why we have a responsibility there. We have it for the same reason we have a responsibility for the defense of freedom in Europe. World War II was fought in both Europe and Asia, and when it ended we found ourselves with continued responsibility for the defense of freedom.

Our objective is the independence of South Vietnam, and its freedom from attack. We want nothing for ourselves, only that the people of South Vietnam be allowed to guide their own country in their own way.

We will do everything necessary to reach that objective. And we will do only what is absolutely necessary.

In recent months, attacks on South Vietnam were stepped up. Thus it became necessary to increase our response and to make attacks by air. This is not a change of purpose. It is a change in what we believe that purpose requires.

We do this in order to slow down aggression.

We do this to increase the confidence of the brave people of South Vietnam who have bravely borne this brutal battle for so many years and with so many casualties.

And we do this to convince the leaders of North Vietnam, and all who seek to share their conquest, of a very simple fact:

We will not be defeated.

We will not grow tired.

We will not withdraw, either openly or under the cloak of a meaningless agreement. . . .

Once this is clear, then it should also be clear that the only path for reasonable men is the path of peaceful settlement.

Such peace demands an independent South Vietnam securely guaranteed and able to shape its own relationships to all others, free from outside interference, tied to no alliance, a military base for no other country.

These are the essentials of any final settlement.

We will never be second in the search for such a peaceful settlement in Vietnam.

There may be many ways to this kind of peace: in discussion or negotiation with the governments concerned; in large groups or in small ones; in the reaffirmation of old agreements or their strengthening with new ones.

We have stated this position over and over again fifty times and more, to friend and foe alike. And we remain ready, with this purpose, for unconditional discussions.

And until that bright and necessary day of peace we will try to keep conflict from spreading. We have no desire to see thousands die in battle, Asians or Americans. We have no desire to devastate that which the people of North Vietnam have built with toil and sacrifice. We will use our power with restraint and with all the wisdom we can command. But we will use it. . . .

We will always oppose the effort of one nation to conquer another nation.

We will do this because our own security is at stake.

But there is more to it than that. For our generation has a dream. It is a very old dream. But we have the power and now we have the opportunity to make it come true.

For centuries, nations have struggled among each other. But we dream of a world where disputes are settled by law and reason. And we will try to make it so.

For most of history men have hated and killed one another in battle. But we dream of an end to war. And we will try to make it so.

For all existence most men have lived in poverty, threatened by hunger. But we dream of a world where all are fed and charged with hope. And we will help to make it so.

The ordinary men and women of North Vietnam and South Vietnam—of China and India—of Russia and America—are brave people. They are filled with the same proportions of hate and fear, of love and hope. Most of them want the same things for themselves and their families. Most of them do not want their sons ever to die in battle, or see the homes of others destroyed. . . .

Every night before I turn out the lights to sleep, I ask myself this question: Have I done everything that I can do to unite this country? Have I done everything I can to help unite the world, to try to bring peace and hope to all the peoples of the world? Have I done enough?

Ask yourselves that question in your homes and in this hall tonight. Have we done all we could? Have we done enough? . . .

[From *Department of State Bulletin,* April 26, 1965 (Washington, D.C.: U.S. Government Printing Office, 1940–).]

Document 2. Senator J. William Fulbright on American Foreign Policy in Vietnam

In 1966 Senator J. William Fulbright, chairman of the Senate Foreign Relations Committee and a critic of U.S. policy in Vietnam, also spoke at Johns Hopkins University. He raised serious questions about U.S. foreign policy generally and how it was developed in Vietnam specifically. An excerpt of his remarks as they appeared in the *New York Times Magazine* follows.

We are an extraordinary nation, endowed with rich and productive land and a talented and energetic population. Surely a nation so favored is capable of extraordinary achievement, not only in the area of producing and enjoying great wealth—where our achievements have indeed been extraordinary—but also in the area of human and international relations—in which area, it seems to me, our achievements have fallen short of our capacity and promise. The question that I find intriguing is whether a nation so extraordinarily endowed as the United States can overcome that arrogance of power which has afflicted, weakened and, in some cases, destroyed great nations in the past.

The causes of the malady are a mystery but its recurrence is one of the uniformities of history: Power tends to confuse itself with virtue and a great nation is particularly susceptible to the idea that its power is a sign of God's favor, conferring upon it a special responsibility for other nations—to make them richer and happier and wiser, to remake them, that is, in its own shining image.

Power also tends to take itself for omnipotence. Once imbued with the idea of a mission, a great nation easily assumes that it has the means as well as the duty to do God's work. The Lord, after all, surely would not choose you as His agent and then deny you the sword with which to work His will.

There is a kind of voodoo about American foreign policy. Certain drums have to be beaten regularly to ward off evil spirits—for example, the maledictions which are regularly uttered against North Vietnamese aggression, the "wild men" in Peking, Communism in general. . . . Certain pledges must be repeated every day lest the whole free world go to rack and ruin—for example, we will never go back on a commitment no matter how unwise; we regard this alliance or that as absolutely "vital" to the free world; and, of course, we will stand stalwart in Berlin from now until Judgment Day.

. . . in recent years the Congress has not fully discharged its obligations in the field of foreign relations. The reduced role of the Congress and the enhanced role of the President in the making of foreign policy are not the result merely of President Johnson's ideas of consensus; they are the culmination of a trend in the constitutional relationship between President and Congress that began in 1940—that is to say, at the beginning of this age of crisis.

In the past 25 years, American foreign policy has encountered a shattering series of crises and inevitably—or almost inevitably—the effort to cope with these has been executive effort, while the Congress, inspired by patriotism, importuned by Presidents and deterred by lack of information, has tended to fall in line. The result has been an unhinging of traditional constitutional relationships; the Senate's constitutional powers of advice and consent have atrophied into what is widely regarded—though never asserted—to be a duty to give prompt consent with a minimum of advice.

. . . on August 5, 1964, the Congress received an urgent request from President Johnson for the immediate adoption of a joint resolution regarding Southeast Asia. On Aug. 7, after perfunctory committee hearings and a brief debate, the Congress, with only two Senators dissenting, adopted the resolution, authorizing the President "to take all necessary steps, including the use of armed force," against aggression in Southeast Asia.

The joint resolution was a blank check signed by the Congress in an atmosphere of urgency that seemed at the time to preclude debate. Since its adoption, the Administration has converted the Vietnamese conflict from a civil war in which some American advisers were involved to a major international war in which the principal fighting unit is an American army of 250,000 men. Each time that Senators have raised questions about successive escalations of the war, we have had the blank check of Aug. 7, 1964, waved in our faces as supposed evidence of the overwhelming support of the Congress for a policy in Southeast Asia which, in fact, has been radically changed since the summer of 1964.

All this is very frustrating to some of us in the Senate, but we have only ourselves to blame. Had we met our responsibility of careful examination of a Presidential request, had the Senate Foreign Relations Committee held hearings on the resolution before recommending its adoption, had the Senate debated the resolution and considered its implications before giving its overwhelming approval, we might have put limits and qualifications on our endorsement of future uses of force in Southeast Asia. . . .

[From *New York Times Magazine,* 15 May 1966, pp. 29, 103–5.]

Questions for Reflection

How did President Johnson justify U.S. involvement in Vietnam? Were his arguments sensible? What did Senator Fulbright see as the dangers facing the United States in Vietnam? Did the senator also see more general problems with the operation of the federal government in foreign policy? How did Johnson and Fulbright disagree?

ANSWERS TO MULTIPLE-CHOICE AND TRUE-FALSE QUESTIONS

Multiple-Choice Questions

1-A, 2-D, 3-B, 4-B, 5-B, 6-C, 7-D, 8-D

True-False Questions

1-F, 2-T, 3-F, 4-T, 5-T, 6-F, 7-F, 8-T

35 ∽

REBELLION AND REACTION
IN THE 1960s AND 1970s

CHAPTER OBJECTIVES

After you complete the reading and study of this chapter, you should be able to:

1. Account for the rise and decline of New Left protests.
2. Describe the counterculture and its impact.
3. Trace the reform movements for women, Hispanics, Indians, and the environment.
4. Explain Nixon's aims in Vietnam.
5. Assess the impact of the Vietnam War on U.S. society, military morale, and later foreign policy.
6. Explain Nixon's goals in domestic policy and account for his limited accomplishment.
7. Understand the problems plaguing the United States economy in the decade of the 1970s, and describe the various cures Nixon tried.
8. Describe Nixon's foreign policy triumphs in China and the Soviet Union, and explain their significance.
9. Discuss the Watergate cover-up and account for the difficulty in unraveling it.
10. Assess the brief presidency of Gerald Ford.
11. Assess the Carter administration's foreign and domestic policies.

CHAPTER OUTLINE

I. Youth revolt
   A. Sources
      1. Baby-boomers as young adults
      2. Sit-ins and end of apathy
   B. New Left
      1. Student for a Democratic Society
         a. Port Huron Statement
         b. Participatory democracy
      2. Free Speech movement
         a. Berkeley
         b. Quality of campus life
      3. Antiwar protests
         a. The draft
         b. Teach-ins and protests
      4. Growing militancy
      5. 1968
         a. Columbia University uprising
         b. Democratic convention in Chicago
         c. Fracturing of SDS
   C. Counterculture
      1. Descendants of the Beats
      2. Contrasted with New Left
      3. Drugs, communes, hedonism
      4. Rock music
         a. Woodstock
         b. Altamont

5. Cooptation and failure

II. The rights of women and minorities
   A. Feminism
      1. Betty Friedan's *The Feminine Mystique*
      2. National Organization for Women
      3. Federal actions
         a. Affirmative action
         b. *Roe* v. *Wade*
         c. Equal Rights Amendment
      4. Divisions and reactions
   B. Hispanics
      1. United Farm Workers
      2. Chicanos, Puerto Ricans, and Cubans
      3. Political power
   C. Native Americans
      1. Emergence of Native American rights
      2. American Indian Movement
      3. Legal actions
   D. Gays and lesbians
      1. Raid on Stonewall Inn
      2. Gay Liberation Front
      3. Christian fundamentalist reaction

III. Nixon and Vietnam
   A. Reaction in the 1970s
      1. Election of 1968
      2. The "Silent Majority"
   B. Policy of withdrawal
      1. Insistence on Communist withdrawal from South Vietnam
      2. Efforts to undercut unrest in the United States
         a. Troop reductions
         b. Lottery and volunteer army
      3. Expanded air war
   C. Impact of the war on military morale
      1. Military disobedience
      2. Fraggings
      3. Drug problems
   D. Occasions for public outcry against the war
      1. My Lai massacre
      2. Cambodian "incursion"
         a. Campus riots
         b. Public reaction

      3. *Pentagon Papers*
         a. Method of disclosure
         b. Revelations of the papers
         c. Supreme Court ruling
   E. U.S. withdrawal
      1. Kissinger's efforts before the 1972 election
      2. Christmas bombings
      3. Final acceptance of peace
      4. U.S. withdrawal in March 1973
   F. Ultimate victory of the North, March–April 1975
   G. Assessment of the war
      1. Communist control
      2. Failure to transfer democracy
      3. Erosion of respect for the military
      4. Drastic division of the U.S. people
      5. Impact on future foreign policy

IV. Nixon and Middle America
   A. Reflection of Middle American values
   B. Domestic affairs
      1. Status of Nixon in domestic legislation
      2. Continuance of civil rights progress
         a. Voting Rights Act continued over a veto
         b. Supreme Court upholds integration
            i. In Mississippi
            ii. Support for busing
         c. Congress refuses to end busing
         d. Limitation on busing in Detroit
         e. *Bakke* decision
      3. Nixon's Supreme Court appointees
         a. Efforts for Haynsworth and Carswell
         b. Nixon appointments
      4. Effort to fight crime
         a. Preventive detention
         b. No-knock legislation
      5. Proposal for welfare reform
         a. Family Assistance Plan

b. Reasons for rejection
6. Revenue sharing
7. Other domestic legislation
C. Economic malaise
   1. Development of stagflation
   2. Causes
   3. Nixon's efforts to improve the economy
      a. Reducing the federal deficit
      b. Reducing the money supply
      c. Imposing wage and price controls
D. Environmental movement
   1. Recognition of the limits of growth
   2. Impact of the energy crisis
   3. Competition with vested interests
   4. Reasons for opposition to environmental reform
      a. Cost
      b. Loss of faith in governmental efforts
      c. Refusal to accept lesser standard of living

V. Nixon's foreign triumphs
   A. Rapprochement with China
      1. Background to the visit
      2. Benefits of the Nixon visit
   B. Détente with the Soviet Union
      1. Visit to Moscow
      2. SALT agreement
      3. Trade agreements
   C. Kissinger's shuttle diplomacy in the Middle East

VI. Election of 1972
   A. Removal of the Wallace threat
   B. McGovern candidacy
   C. Results of the election

VII. Watergate
   A. Judge Sirica's role
   B. Unraveling the cover-up
      1. Nixon's personal role
      2. Development of illegal tactics
      3. April resignations
      4. Discovery of the tapes
      5. Saturday Night Massacre
      6. Supreme Court decides against the president

7. Articles of impeachment
8. Resignation
C. Aftermath of Watergate
   1. Ford's selection
   2. Nixon pardon
   3. Distrust of leaders and institutions
   4. Shock at the crudity of leaders
   5. Resiliency of U.S. institutions
   6. War Powers Act
   7. Campaign financing legislation
   8. Freedom of Information Act

VIII. Ford presidency
   A. Drift at the end of the Nixon administration
   B. Ford's battle with the economy
   C. Foreign policy accomplishments
   D. Election of 1976
      1. Ford's nomination
      2. Reasons for the Carter rise
      3. Carter's victory

IX. Carter presidency
   A. Carter style and his challenges
   B. Early domestic moves
      1. Appointments
      2. Amnesty for draft dodgers
      3. Administrative reorganization
      4. Environmental legislation
      5. Deregulation of the oil industry
      6. Crisis of confidence
   C. Foreign policy initiatives
      1. Human rights focus
      2. Panama Canal Treaties
      3. Diplomatic relations with China
      4. Camp David Accords
   D. Failure to manage the economy
      1. Emphasis on reducing unemployment
      2. Reversal: the reduction of government deficits
   E. SALT II negotiations
   F. Reactions to the invasion of Afghanistan
   G. Iranian crisis
      1. Background to the seizure
      2. Carter's efforts to help the hostages
      3. Crisis ended

KEY ITEMS OF CHRONOLOGY

Port Huron Statement	1962
Betty Friedan's *The Feminine Mystique*	1963
N.O.W. founded	1966
My Lai massacre	1968
Woodstock Music Festival	1969
Cambodian "incursion"	April 1970
Swann v. *Charlotte-Mecklenburg Board of Education*	1971
Pentagon Papers published	June 1971
Roe v. *Wade*	1972
Nixon's visit to China	February 1972
SALT agreement signed	May 1972
Watergate break-in occurred	June 1972
Last U.S. troops left Vietnam	March 1973
Nixon's resignation	August 9, 1974
Ford pardons Nixon	September 1974
South Vietnam fell to the North	April 1975
Election of Carter	November 1976
Camp David Accords	1978
Bakke v. *Board of Regents of California*	1978
Diplomatic relations with China	November 1978
Seizure of U.S. citizens in Teheran	November 1979

TERMS TO MASTER

Listed below are some important terms or people with which you should be familiar after you complete the study of this chapter. Explain the significance of each name or term.

1. New Left
2. SDS
3. participatory democracy
4. Free Speech movement
5. Weathermen
6. counterculture
7. Betty Friedan
8. N.O.W.
9. Equal Rights Amendment
10. "Silent Majority"
11. *Pentagon Papers*
12. *Swann* v. *Charlotte-Mecklenburg Board of Education*
13. *Bakke* v. *Board of Regents of California*
14. revenue sharing
15. Spiro Agnew
16. OPEC
17. SALT
18. George McGovern
19. Watergate
20. Saturday Night Massacre
21. stagflation
22. Henry Kissinger
23. War Powers Act
24. WIN buttons
25. Camp David Accords
26. Sunbelt
27. conscientious objector
28. Cesar Chavez
29. Vietnamization
30. My Lai massacre

VOCABULARY BUILDING

Listed below are some words or phrases used in this chapter. Look up each word in your dictionary unless the meaning is given here.

1. fissure
2. estranged

3. bastion
4. wrest
5. mandatory
6. berserk
7. rustic
8. bastion
9. pejorative
10. awry
11. ostracism
12. sanctuary
13. complicity
14. contingency
15. ignoble
16. encumber
17. ecology
18. liaison
19. penitent
20. cartel

EXERCISES FOR UNDERSTANDING

When you have completed reading the chapter, answer each of the following questions. If you have difficulty, go back and reread the section of the chapter related to the question.

Multiple-Choice Questions

Select the letter of the response that best completes the statement.

1. The Free Speech Movement attacked
   A. the modern university.
   B. congressional support for the Vietnam war.
   C. movie and book censorship.
   D. Nixon's dishonesty over Watergate.
2. Timothy Leary's credo of "Tune in, turn on, drop out" appealed to the
   A. antiwar movement.
   B. counterculture.
   C. feminists and gay rights advocates.
   D. student radicals of the New Left.
3. At the 1968 national Democratic convention,
   A. Hubert Humphrey won the nomination for president.
   B. Yippies provoked anarchy in the streets.

C. 12,000 police clashed with demonstrators.
   D. all the above
4. In *Roe* v. *Wade* the Supreme Court ruled that
   A. busing for school integration was unconstitutional.
   B. Native Americans were to receive four million acres in Wyoming.
   C. abortion in the first three months of pregnancy was legal.
   D. the Watergate cover-up was sufficient to impeach Nixon.
5. Nixon's new Vietnam policy involved
   A. peace negotiations in Paris.
   B. Vietnamization of the war.
   C. expansion of the air war.
   D. all of the above
6. The Nixon administration's most innovative domestic proposal was
   A. school busing.
   B. the Family Assistance Plan.
   C. revenue sharing with the states.
   D. the Environmental Protection Agency.
7. Causes of the economic malaise of the 1970s included
   A. major tax increases under LBJ to finance the Great Society.
   B. competition in international markets.
   C. labor shortages caused by the Vietnam War.
   D. all of the above
8. During the Watergate crisis, Nixon was *not* accused of
   A. obstructing justice through paying witnesses to remain silent.
   B. defying Congress by withholding the tapes.
   C. using federal agencies to deprive citizens of their rights.
   D. stealing funds from the reelection campaign.
9. Perhaps Gerald Ford's most memorable act as president was
   A. preventing the fall of South Vietnam.
   B. pardoning Richard Nixon.
   C. achieving peace in the Middle East.
   D. rescuing U.S. hostages in Nicaragua.

10. Jimmy Carter's 1976 victory can be attributed to
    A. his strong support among southern African Americans.
    B. the traditional Democratic sweep of the West.
    C. his long career as a national politician.
    D. the large voter turnout in the election.
11. Carter's most significant accomplishment in foreign policy was
    A. retaining complete control over the Panama Canal.
    B. an agreement with OPEC on oil prices.
    C. opposition to the Soviet invasion of Afghanistan.
    D. a treaty between Israel and Egypt.
12. The United States boycotted the 1980 Olympics because of
    A. the seizure of the *Mayaguez.*
    B. the presidential election.
    C. the taking of U.S. hostages in Teheran.
    D. the Soviet invasion of Afghanistan.

True-False Questions

Indicate whether each statement is true or false.

1. Campus turmoil in 1968 reached a peak at Columbia University.
2. The campus protests reached a climax in 1968 at Berkeley.
3. Of all minorities in the 1960s, Native Americans were the most desperate.
4. The Cambodian "incursion" led to widespread rioting on U.S. college campuses.
5. Two years after the Vietnam War ended,

North Vietnam took control of the South.
6. As Nixon had hoped, the Burger Court opposed further school integration.
7. Nixon successfully fought stagflation by raising taxes and cutting the budget.
8. The War Powers Act requires a president to withdraw troops sent abroad after sixty days unless specifically authorized by Congress for a longer stay.
9. Gerald Ford called the fight against inflation "the moral equivalent of war."
10. Jimmy Carter succeeded in negotiating a treaty to return the Panama Canal to Panama.

Essay Questions

1. Compare and contrast the New Left and the counterculture
2. How did the women's movement resemble the reform efforts by Chicanos, Native Americans, and homosexuals?
3. What was Nixon's secret plan to end the Vietnam War and did it work?
4. How did the Nixon administration deal with "stagflation"?
5. How did Nixon try to appeal to the "Silent Majority" with his domestic policies? Did he succeed?
6. Were Nixon's accomplishments in domestic policy more important than his foreign policy achievements?
7. What effects did Watergate have on Americans and their political institutions?
8. How do Nixon, Ford, and Carter rate as presidents?

DOCUMENTS

Document 1. Charges against Nixon

When the House Judiciary Committee completed its investigation and voted the impeachment of Nixon in July 1974, there were three articles that obtained a majority vote of the committee. The heart of the three articles is excerpted here.

Article I. In his conduct of the office of President of the United States, Richard M. Nixon, in violation of his constitutional oath faithfully to execute the office of President of the United States and to the best of his ability, preserve, protect, and defend the Constitution of the United States, and in violation of his constitutional duty to take care that the laws be faithfully executed, has prevented, obstructed, and impeded the administration of justice, . . . Richard M. Nixon, using the powers of his high office, engaged personally and through his subordinates and agents, in a course of conduct or plan designed to delay, impede, and obstruct the investigation of such unlawful entry; to cover up, conceal and protect those responsible; and to conceal the existence and scope of other unlawful covert activities. . . .

Article II. . . . Richard M. Nixon . . . has repeatedly engaged in conduct violating the constitutional rights of citizens, impairing the due and proper administration of justice and the conduct of lawful inquiries, or contravening the laws governing agencies of the executive branch and the purpose of these agencies. . . .

Article III. Richard M. Nixon, contrary to his oath faithfully to execute the office of President of the United States . . . has failed without lawful cause or excuse to produce papers and things as directed by duly authorized subpoenas issued by the Committee on the Judiciary of the House of Representatives on April 11, 1974, May 15, 1974, May 30, 1974, and June 24, 1974, and willfully disobeying such subpoenas. . . . In refusing to produce these papers and things, Richard M. Nixon, substituting his judgment as to what materials were necessary for the inquiry, interposed the powers of the Presidency against the lawful subpoenas of the House of Representatives, thereby assuming to himself functions and judgments necessary to the exercise of the sole power of impeachment vested by the Constitution in the House of Representatives.

[From House, *Report of the Committee on the Judiciary,* 93rd Cong., 2d sess., 1974.]

Document 2. Senator Sam Ervin Explains the Meaning and Consequences of Watergate

Prior to the report quoted above, the Ervin Committee of the Senate had throughout the summer of 1973 treated the U.S. public to weeks of televised hearings at which various Watergate conspirators had testified about the labyrinthine developments of the Watergate affair. In June 1974, shortly before the House Judiciary Committee moved to impeach Nixon, the Ervin Committee made its report. Accompanying the report was a statement from Senator Ervin in which he tried to summarize the Watergate episode in a few paragraphs. Because the report was made prior to the House committee's decision to move toward impeachment of the president, Ervin began his report with a disclaimer to indicate that he was not trying to pass judgment on the president's guilt in the matter. His report is a succinct statement of the Watergate affair and a comment on its implications for the future.

I am not undertaking to usurp and exercise the power of impeachment, which the Constitution confers upon the House of Representatives alone. As a consequence, nothing I say should be construed as an expression of an opinion in respect to the question of whether or not President Nixon is impeachable in connection with the Watergate or any other matter. . . .

I shall also refrain from making any comment on the question of whether or not the President has performed in an acceptable manner his paramount constitutional obligation "to take care that the laws be faithfully executed."

Watergate was not invented by enemies of the Nixon administration or even by the news media. On the contrary, Watergate was perpetrated upon America by White House and political aides, whom President Nixon himself had entrusted with the management of his campaign for reelection to the Presidency, a campaign which was divorced to a marked degree from the campaigns of other Republicans who sought election to public office in 1972. I note at this point without elaboration that these White House and political aides were virtually without experience in either Government or politics apart from their association with President Nixon.

5. Watergate was without precedent in the political annals of America in respect to the scope and intensity of its unethical and illegal actions. To be sure, there had been previous milder political scandals in American history. That fact does not excuse Watergate. Murder and stealing have occurred in every generation since Earth began, but that fact has not made murder meritorious or larceny legal.

What Was Watergate?

Watergate was a conglomerate of various illegal and unethical activities in which various officers and employees of the Nixon reelection committee and various White House aides of President Nixon participated in varying ways and degrees to accomplish these successive objectives:

1. To destroy, insofar as the Presidential election of 1972 was concerned, the integrity of the process by which the President of the United States is nominated and elected.

2. To hide from law enforcement officers, prosecutors, grand jurors, courts, the news media, and the American people the identities and wrongdoing of those officers and employees of the Nixon reelection committees, and those White House aides who had undertaken to destroy the integrity of the process by which the President of the United States is nominated and elected.

To accomplish the first of these objectives. . . .

1. They exacted enormous contributions—usually in cash—from corporate executives by impliedly implanting in their minds the impressions that the making of the contributions was necessary to

insure that the corporations would receive governmental favors, or avoid governmental disfavors, while President Nixon remained in the White House. A substantial portion of the contributions were made out of corporate funds in violation of a law enacted by Congress a generation ago.

2. They hid substantial parts of these contributions in cash in safes and safe deposits to conceal their sources and the identities of those who had made them.

3. They disbursed substantial portions of these hidden contributions in a surreptitious manner to finance the bugging and the burglary of the offices of the Democratic National Committee in the Watergate complex in Washington. . . .

4. They deemed the departments and agencies of the Federal Government to be the political playthings of the Nixon administration rather than impartial instruments for serving the people, and undertook to induce them to channel Federal contracts, grants, and loans to areas, groups, or individuals so as to promote the reelection of the President rather than to further the welfare of the people.

5. They branded as enemies of the President individuals and members of the news media who dissented from the President's policies and opposed his reelection, and conspired to urge the Department of Justice, the Federal Bureau of Investigation, the Internal Revenue Service, and the Federal Communications Commission to pervert the use of their legal powers to harass them for so doing.

6. They borrowed from the Central Intelligence Agency disguises which E. Howard Hunt used in political espionage operations, and photographic equipment which White House employees known as the "Plumbers" and their hired confederates used in connection with burglarizing the office of a psychiatrist which they believed contained information concerning Daniel Ellsberg which the White House was anxious to secure.

7. They assigned to E. Howard Hunt, who was at the time a White House consultant occupying an office in the Executive Office Building, the gruesome task of falsifying State Department documents which they contemplated using in their altered state to discredit the Democratic Party by defaming the memory of former President John Fitzgerald Kennedy, who as the hapless victim of an assassin's bullet had been sleeping in the tongueless silence of the dreamless dust for 9 years.

8. They used campaign funds to hire saboteurs to forge and disseminate false and scurrilous libels of honorable men running for the Democratic Presidential nomination in Democratic Party primaries.

During the darkness of the early morning of June 17, 1972, James W. McCord, the security chief of the John Mitchell committee, and four residents of Miami, Fla., were arrested by Washington police while they were burglarizing the offices of the Democratic National Committee in the Watergate complex to obtain political intelligence.

. . .

The arrest of McCord and the four residents of Miami created consternation in the Nixon reelection committees and the White House. . . . various White House aides undertook to conceal from law enforcement officers, prosecutors, grand jurors, courts, the news media, and the American people the identities and activities of those officers and employees of the Nixon reelection committee and those White House aides who had participated in any way in the Watergate affair. . . .

1. They destroyed the records of the Nixon reelection committee antedating the bugging and the burglary.

2. They induced the Acting Director of the FBI, who was a Nixon appointee, to destroy the State Department documents which E. Howard Hunt had been falsifying.

3. They obtained from the Acting Director of the FBI copies of the scores of interviews conducted by the FBI agents in connection with their investigation of the bugging and the burglary, and were enabled thereby to coach their confederates to give false and misleading statements to the FBI.

4. They sought to persuade the FBI to refrain from investigating the sources of the campaign funds which were used to finance the bugging and the burglary.

5. They intimidated employees of the Nixon reelection committees and employees of the White House by having their lawyers present when these employees were being questioned by agents of the FBI, and thus deterred these employees from making full disclosures to the FBI.

6. They lied to agents of the FBI, prosecutors, and grand jurors who undertook to investigate the bugging and the burglary, and to Judge Sirica and the petit jurors who tried the seven original Watergate defendants in January, 1973

7. They persuaded the Department of Justice and the prosecutors to take out-of-court statements from Maurice Stans, President Nixon's chief campaign fundraiser, and Charles Colson, Egil Krogh, and David Young, White House aides, and Charles Colson's secretary, instead of requiring them to testify before the grand jury investigating the bugging and the burglary in conformity with established procedures governing such matters, and thus denied the grand jurors the opportunity to question them.

8. They persuaded the Department of Justice and the prosecutors to refrain from asking Donald Segretti, their chief hired saboteur, any questions involving Herbert W. Kalmbach, the President's personal attorney, who was known by them to have paid Segretti for dirty tricks he perpetrated upon honorable men seeking the Democratic Presidential nomination. . . .

9. They made cash payments totaling hundreds of thousands of dollars out of campaign funds in surreptitious ways to the seven original Watergate defendants as hush money to buy their silence.

10. They gave assurances to some of the original seven defendants

that they would receive Presidential clemency after serving short portions of their sentences if they refrained from divulging the identities and activities of the officers and employees of the Nixon reelection committees and the White House aides who had participated in the Watergate affair.

11. They made arrangements by which the attorneys who represented the seven original Watergate defendants received their fees in cash from moneys which had been collected to finance President Nixon's reelection campaign.

12. They induced the Department of Justice and the prosecutors of the seven original Watergate defendants to assure the news media and the general public that there was no evidence that any persons other than the seven original Watergate defendants were implicated in any way in the Watergate-related crimes.

13. They inspired massive efforts on the part of segments of the news media friendly to the administration to persuade the American people that most of the members of the Select Committee named by the Senate to investigate the Watergate were biased and irresponsible men motivated solely by desires to exploit the matters they investigated for personal or partisan advantage. . . .

One shudders to think that the Watergate conspiracies might have been effectively concealed and their most dramatic episode might have been dismissed as a "third-rate" burglary conceived and committed solely by the seven original Watergate defendants had it not been for the courage and penetrating understanding of Judge Sirica, the thoroughness of the investigative reporting of Carl Bernstein, Bob Woodward, and the other representatives of the free press, the labors of the Senate Select Committee and its excellent staff, and the dedication and diligence of Special Prosecutors Archibald Cox and Leon Jarworski and their associates.

Why Was Watergate?

Unlike the men who were responsible for Teapot Dome, the Presidential aides who perpetrated Watergate were not seduced by the love of money, which is sometimes thought to be the root of all evil. On the contrary, they were instigated by a lust for political power, which is at least as corrupting as political power itself. . . .

They knew that the power they enjoyed would be lost and the policies to which they adhered would be frustrated if the President should be defeated.

As a consequence of these things, they believed the President's reelection to be a most worthy objective, and succumbed to an age-old temptation. They resorted to evil means to promote what they conceived to be a good end.

Their lust for political power blinded them to ethical considerations and legal requirements; to Aristotle's aphorism that the good of man must be the end of politics; and to Grover Cleveland's conviction that a public office is a public trust.

They had forgotten, if they ever knew, that the Constitution is designed to be a law for rulers and people alike at all times and under all circumstances; and that no doctrine involving more pernicious consequences to the commonweal has ever been invented by the wit of man than the notion that any of its provisions can be suspended by the President for any reason whatsoever.

On the contrary, they apparently believed that the President is above the Constitution, and has the autocratic power to suspend its provisions if he decides in his own unreviewable judgment that his action in so doing promotes his own political interests or the welfare of the Nation. . . .

Antidote for Future Watergates

Is there an antidote which will prevent future Watergates? If so, what is it? . . .

Candor compels the confession . . . . that law alone will not suffice to prevent future Watergates. . . .

Law is not self-executing. Unfortunately, at times its execution rests in the hands of those who are faithless to it. And even when its enforcement is committed to those who revere it, law merely deters some human beings from offending, and punishes other human beings for offending. It does not make men good. This task can be performed only by ethics or religion or morality. . . .

When all is said, the only sure antidote for future Watergates is understanding of fundamental principles and intellectual and moral integrity in the men and women who achieve or are entrusted with governmental political power.

[From Senate Select Committee on Presidential Campaign Activities, *Final Report,* 93rd Cong., 2d sess., 1974, 1097–103]

Questions for Reflection

The U.S. Constitution in Article II, Section 4, states that the President "shall be removed from office on impeachment for, and on conviction of, treason, bribery, or other high crimes and misdemeanors." Do you consider the crimes of which Nixon was accused impeachable offenses? Why or why not?

Why was Ervin so careful to disavow any indictment of the President in his report? Based on the charges of the House Rules Committee in Document 1, which of the actions attributed to others by Ervin might have been charged to the President also?

Who benefited from the Watergate crimes? Were monetary considerations at the heart of the Watergate crimes? Is a President who is dutifully exercising his responsibilities "above the Constitution" with the power to suspend its provisions when he needs to do so? Explain.

What and/or who does Ervin credit with bringing the Watergate conspirators to justice? What does the case suggest about the need for an independent judiciary and a free press? How do you react to Ervin's prescription for preventing future Watergates?

ANSWERS TO MULTIPLE-CHOICE AND TRUE-FALSE QUESTIONS

Multiple-Choice Questions

1-A, 2-B, 3-D, 4-C, 5-D, 6-B, 7-B, 8-D, 9-B, 10-A, 11-D, 12-D

True-False Questions

1-T, 2-F, 3-T, 4-T, 5-T, 6-F, 7-F, 8-T, 9-F, 10-T

36 ⤫

A CONSERVATIVE INSURGENCY

CHAPTER OBJECTIVES

After you complete the reading and study of this chapter, you should be able to:

1. Evaluate the economic policies of the Reagan and Bush administrations.
2. Discuss the U.S. role in Central America in the 1980s and its connections to the Middle East.
3. Understand the causes and results of the Gulf War.
4. Explain Ronald Reagan's political success and the failure of George Bush.
5. Trace the development of the modern computer.

CHAPTER OUTLINE

I. Reagan Revolution
  A. Carter to Reagan
    1. Carter's crisis of confidence
    2. Reagan's message
      a. Optimism
      b. Pride and prosperity
      c. Old-time morality
      d. Public speaking skill
  B. Background of Reagan
    1. Hollywood
    2. Liberal to conservative
    3. Governor of California
  C. Rise to the presidency
    1. Demographic changes
    2. Religious revival
      a. Fundamentalism
      b. Moral Majority
      c. Abortion, prayer, pornography, gender roles
  D. Election of 1980
    1. Reagan victory
    2. Voter apathy

II. Reagan's first term
  A. Domestic policies
    1. Reaganomics
      a. Supply-side theory
      b. Tax cuts
      c. Budget deficits
      d. Budget cuts
      e. "Revenue enhancements"
    2. "Sleaze factor"
    3. Other social policies
      a. Air-traffic controllers' strike
      b. Opposition to ERA and abortion
      c. Affirmative action and civil rights
  B. Foreign affairs
    1. Defense policies

        a. Increased spending
        b. Strategic Defense Initiative
    2. Central America
        a. El Salvador
        b. Nicaragua
        c. Contadora process
    3. Middle East
        a. Iran-Iraq war
        b. Israel, Lebanon, PLO
    4. Grenada

III. Reagan's second term
  A. Election of 1984
    1. Democrats and taxes
    2. Landslide and its effects
  B. Tax Reform Act of 1986
  C. Arms control talks
  D. Iran-Contra affair
    1. Arms-for-hostages reported
    2. Lieutenant-Colonel Oliver North
    3. Congressional hearings
    4. Legal charges
  E. Central America
    1. Support for the Contras
    2. Setbacks in El Salvador
  F. Excesses in business
    1. Leveraged buyouts
    2. Savings and loans
  G. Problems in the economy
    1. Rising debts
    2. Stock market collapse
  H. The left out
    1. Poor
    2. Homeless
    3. AIDS victims
  I. INF treaty with the Soviet Union
  J. Reagan legacy
    1. Unfilled promises
        a. Role and size of government
        b. Budget and deficit
        c. School prayer and abortion
    2. Accomplishments
        a. Redefined national agenda
        b. Prosperity
        c. Nuclear disarmament
        d. Freedom in eastern Europe
  K. Election of 1988
    1. Michael Dukakis as a liberal
    2. George Bush's "kinder, gentler
       nation"

    3. Results
IV. Bush years
  A. Tone of the administration
  B. Domestic affairs
    1. Savings and loan crisis
    2. Deficits, debts, and drugs
        a. Higher taxes
        b. Spending cuts
  C. Foreign policies
    1. Democracy on the march
        a. China
        b. Eastern Europe
            i. End of the Brezhnev
               doctrine
            ii. Romania
           iii. Fall of the Berlin Wall
        c. Chile
        d. South Africa
        e. Soviet Union
            i. Gorbachev reforms
            ii. Coup
           iii. Boris Yeltsin
    2. Panama
        a. Manuel Noriega and drugs
        b. U.S. invasion
        c. Surrender of Noriega
    3. Gulf War
        a. Iraq-Kuwait tension
        b. Iraq invades Kuwait
        c. U.N. Resolutions
        d. Desert Shield
        e. Congressional debate
        f. Desert Storm
        g. Cease-fire

V. Computer revolution
  A. First generation
    1. ENIAC
    2. EDVAC
  B. Second generation
    1. Private corporations
    2. The transistor
  C. Third generation
    1. Microprocessor
    2. Personal computer
    3. Bill Gates
  D. Internet

KEY ITEMS OF CHRONOLOGY

ENIAC	1944
Invention of transistor	1947
EDVAC	1949
Invention of microprocessor	1971
Inauguration of Reagan	January 20, 1981
Attempted assassination of Reagan	March 30, 1981
Economic Recovery Tax Act	August 1981
Stock market collapse	October 19, 1981
INF treaty signed	December 9, 1981
Tax Equity and Fiscal Responsibility Act	September 1982
Bombing of Marine quarters in Beruit	October 1983
Invasion of Grenada	October 1983
Explosion of the *Challenger*	January 28, 1986
Tax Reform Act	September 1986
First Iran-Contra revelations	November 1986
Election of George Bush	November 1988
Invasion of Panama	December 1989
Iraq's invasion of Kuwait	August 2, 1990
Desert Shield begins	August 22, 1990
Desert Storm begins	January 17, 1991

TERMS TO MASTER

Listed below are some important terms or people with which you should be familiar after you complete the study of this chapter. Explain the significance of each name or term.

1. Reaganomics
2. trickle-down theory
3. David Stockman
4. revenue enhancements
5. sleaze factor
6. Teflon presidency
7. Strategic Defense Initiative
8. Sandra Day O'Connor
9. Sandinistas
10. Iran-Contra
11. junk bond
12. INF
13. Resolution Trust Corporation
14. Saddam Hussein
15. Desert Shield
16. Desert Storm
17. transistor
18. nanosecond

VOCABULARY BUILDING

Listed below are some words or phrases used in this chapter. Look up each word in your dictionary unless the meaning is given here.

1. founder (v.)
2. unabashed
3. strident
4. maxim
5. euphoric
6. fortuitous
7. elixir
8. inviolable
9. celestial
10. indulgent
11. plummet
12. calamitous
13. retribution
14. exponential
15. patina
16. arriviste
17. rancorous
18. putsch
19. ballistics
20. cumbersome

EXERCISES FOR UNDERSTANDING

When you have completed reading the chapter, answer each of the following questions. If you have difficulty, go back and reread the section of the chapter related to the question.

Multiple-Choice Questions

Select the letter of the response that best completes the statement.

1. Reaganomics, the policies followed by President Reagan, included
   A. supply-side economics and the Laffer curve.
   B. tax cuts and deregulation.
   C. "voodoo economics," according to George Bush.
   D. all the above

2. In the mid-1980s, the Reagan administration's economic policies benefited from
   A. falling oil prices.
   B. low interest rates.
   C. reduced defense expenses after the cold war.
   D. all of the above

3. The Iran-Contra affair involved
   A. selling arms for hostages in Iran.
   B. Lieutenant-Colonel Oliver North.
   C. secretly supporting the Nicaraguan rebels.
   D. all the above

4. One significant cause of the savings and loan crisis in the 1980s was
   A. the stock market crash of 1987.
   B. inadequate regulation.
   C. leveraged corporate buyouts.
   D. the conservative business practices of the S&Ls.

5. The prosperity of the Reagan years meant that
   A. even the people at the bottom of the economy did better in the 1980s.
   B. after-tax incomes for the top 1 percent of the population went up by 14.2 percent.
   C. homelessness decreased.
   D. all the above

6. In 1989
   A. Chinese authorities crushed the Tiananmen Square demonstration.
   B. the Berlin Wall came down.
   C. Communist rule ended in Poland and Hungary.
   D. all the above

7. One major result of the Gulf War was
   A. peace and stability in the Middle East.
   B. an end to OPEC.
   C. thousands of refugees.
   D. George Bush's popularity and reelection.

8. The key to the development of computers as electronic data processing machines instead of just mathematical calculators was the
   A. silicon chip.
   B. information superhighway.
   C. transistor.
   D. Bill Gates's software company.

True-False Questions

Indicate whether each statement is true or false.

1. Under President Reagan, the national debt nearly tripled.

2. After the attempted assassination, support for President Reagan's programs grew.

3. The Deficit Reduction Act of 1984 reduced personal income taxes.

4. The stock market plunge of October 1987 was partly caused by the rapidly increasing national debt and trade deficits.

5. In 1989, the United States sent military forces into Panama.

6. The leader of Iraq in the Gulf War was Saddam Hussein.

7. Operation Desert Storm involved sending U.S. troops into Romania to support democratic, anti-Communist forces.

8. Bill Gates got his start by inventing the microprocessor.

Essay Questions

1. Was Ronald Reagan a successful president? Explain.

2. Who did the United States support in Central America? Why?

3. Explain why some people consider the 1980s a time of greed and corruption in U.S. life.

4. What happened to the cold war in the 1980s and why?

5. Describe the background and results of the Gulf War of 1990–1991.

6. Through what stages did the computer develop to reach its current widespread use?

DOCUMENTS

Document 1. Moral Majority from a Liberal Christian Point of View

The following excerpt from the *Christian Century* describes several fundamentalist Christian organizations, including the Moral Majority, from a more liberal or mainline Christian perspective.

They share a number of core propositions. The first is that sin and its symptoms are dangerously real in this country. America is suffering from moral decay which, if not stopped, will result in the fall of the country and the rise of atheistic dictatorships. The signs of decay are everywhere: abortion on demand, equal rights for homosexuals, pornography, feminism and drugs, to name but a few. These symptoms, they contend, stem from the philosophy of secular humanism, which holds that God is dead, that people must establish their own moral order, and that individual pleasure is the highest goal.

Furthermore, say these fundamentalist Christians, internal decline is causing the U.S. to lose its position in the world. This nation is a chosen instrument of God, and it carries the major responsibility of implementing God's will in the world. . . .

There is a strong conviction that America's prosperity has resulted from its Christian character: faithfulness to God brings material rewards, and "righteousness exalts a nation." . . .

Next, these interests see the world divided into two main camps. One is the U.S. and its allies—including Israel as God's biblically chosen people—and the other is the godless force of communism, which satanically seeks the total overthrow of the United States. The constant struggle against communism requires the U.S. to maintain its military strength at all times.

Distinct ideas about the role of government in society are also put forward. Reflecting their conservative views, leaders of these right-wing coalitions believe that God ordained government to protect a nation through strong defense and to enforce fundamental laws, but they do not think that the government should regulate the economy, intervene in the parental responsibility for educating children, or help people who can help themselves. They decry the tremendous growth of federal agencies and the incredible increase in the scope of government control that began during the New Deal administration of Franklin Roosevelt. . . .

Finally, these groups believe that Christians have a God-given responsibility to be politically active. In fact, Jerry Falwell has said that the job of a pastor is to save souls, baptize, and get people registered to vote. Failure to register is a sin. If Christians do not act to throw out of office those officials who perpetuate an unchristian, liberal program, the U.S. will crumble and the cause of God's Kingdom will be frustrated. . . .

The core propositions shared by these leaders translate into specific positions on issues, and the groups have made their program abundantly clear. Concerning family issues, they fervently oppose abortion, seek a constitutional amendment to prohibit it and laud the recent Supreme Court decision that government has no obligation to pay for the abortions of women on welfare. They oppose homosexuality and contend that homosexuals should not have the same vocational and housing opportunities that others have. They strongly oppose movements for women's and children's rights. For example, they oppose the Equal Rights Amendment, insisting that it would take mothers out of their homes; they oppose government child-care programs for similar reasons. Concerning education, they are adamant in the belief that parents rather than the government should be in control. They oppose government regulation of private schools, and they would prefer to have the federal government get out of education entirely. They also believe that prayer and Bible reading should be restored in all schools, by law if necessary. They opposed the creation of the new Department of Education on the grounds that it was an attempt to increase government control.

In the area of foreign policy, the groups call for increased military spending to ensure that the U.S. will be militarily superior. They believe that the use of force may be necessary to stop the inevitable communist aggression and that the U.S. must remain loyal to those countries that have sided with it against communism (e.g., Taiwan). . . .we have several serious disagreements with these groups. The first has to do with their explicit link with ideological conservatism and the implicit suggestion that this ideology is more attuned than is liberalism to the principles found in the Bible. The idea that the principles of God's revelation can be neatly subsumed under the rubric of a humanly devised ideology is pretentious. Any full examination of biblical standards will disclose a subtle blend of "conservatism" and "liberalism." The Bible is full of passages mandating a concern for the poor—a focus too often lacking in laissez-faire conservative circles. The Bible does not see government as the satanic evil which the conservatives decry; rather, the government is a divinely ordained instrument.

The point here is not that liberalism is closer to the Bible than conservatism but that we are using the wrong level of analysis when we seek to portray either ideology as more Christian. God's will is not subordinate to ideological predispositions; it supersedes them.

Furthermore, there is evidence that these new groups take an inconsistent view of the role of government. In short, they do not want government intervention when their own freedoms are at stake, but they are willing to use the power of the government to force life-style changes on others. If it is not right to use the government to force one group to tolerate the life style of others, then it is equally wrong to use the government to compel the second group to tolerate the life style of the first. . . .

The issue is not simply the contrasting perspectives of Christians but the claim by these groups that they have the correct, biblical answer and that those who disagree with them are not fit to hold public office because of their immorality. . . . Every group of Christians, not only the conservative ones discussed here, must refrain from the arrogance of presumed omniscience and must adopt an attitude of humility befitting our sinful nature.

Next, the claim that the United States is *the* instrument to accomplish the will of God is suspect. There is no doubt that God could use, and probably is using, this nation for his purposes, but the claim of these groups carries with it a historical and cultural relativism that seeks to interpret God's plan within a framework of flag-waving nationalism. Their claim further excludes God's use of other countries with strong Judeo-Christian foundations or other religious tenets and ignores the possibility that even "godless" nations are instruments which God can use.

Finally, there is a danger in efforts to use ministers in their pulpits to proclaim the politically conservative gospel. Preaching of the Word, not political mobilization or indoctrination, is the central responsibility of pastors. This statement is not meant to deny pastors a political role or to suggest that their sermons must avoid any consideration of political issues or responsibilities, but it must be stressed that political persuasion is not the first obligation of ministers. There is an additional danger: preaching a political gospel may cause or aggravate splits within churches or denominations and thus hinder the effective proclamation of the gospel of salvation in Christ.

[From *Christian Century,* October 8, 1980.]

Document 2. Politically Conservative Analysis of the Moral Majority

Joseph Sobran, a columnist for the *National Review,* offers a positive assessment of Jerry Falwell and the fundamentalist movement in the following selection.

Lately there has been a lot of talk, mostly by worried liberals, about "the electronic church." TV preachers are nothing new: Billy Graham, Herbert W. Armstrong, Oral Roberts, Reverend Ike, and of course Bishop Sheen have long made profitable use of the medium. What worries the liberals, I suspect, is that the evangelicals are now learning to use the mass media to attain political goals.

Regularly cited as among the most sinister of the new TV evangelists is Jerry Falwell, whose conservatism makes no apologies. If he demanded the nationalization of giant oil companies, Falwell would be hailed as an activist who brought social conscience to religion. But what Falwell demands is very different. He demands the preservation of the family—against the attack of government and commercial forces. Hence he is deplored as a threat to the separation of church and state.

I have twice tuned in on this sinister being, who it transpires is about as menacing as the corner grocer.

His method is not to harangue, but to marshall witnesses: in the course of an hour he may show you a documentary film, a U.S. senator, a Christian psychologist, and a kind of chorus line of devout parents with their children, all modestly dressed, perfectly groomed, courteously behaved. Soloists and choirs sing hymns. Falwell seems as much a religious Lawrence Welk as a preacher. What you see is the community he heads, the kind of people he represents, not just himself. It's an epitome and maybe a portent.

Falwell is a sign of the times. Traditionally these people may have been more or less conservative in their politics, but they have carefully kept politics and religion separate. They have, reluctantly, changed. Why?

My guess is that now, for the first time, they feel that politics itself has come to impinge on the sacred. Honest graft they can tolerate. War on morality, on the structure of the family itself, is another matter. They would leave politics alone if they felt it was leaving them alone; but they see that it isn't.

Falwell speaks firmly, calmly, with a glint of humor, about the current tendency of government to foster and accelerate bad trends: promiscuity, divorce, homosexuality, and abortion. Despite liberal propaganda on the subject, I have never heard a Catholic clergyman—not in my church, at any rate—speak as forthrightly against abortion as Falwell does. Though I agree with him, I found myself reacting with shock, as to indelicacy, when he discussed the matter in church. It was not his fault but my custom that caused this reaction. (Gay rights? "The Bible says God created Adam and Eve, not Adam and Steve.")

[From *National Review*, July 27, 1980.]

Document 3. Barry Goldwater's Opinion of the Moral Majority and Politics

Barry Goldwater, the conservative Republican senator and the presidential nominee in 1964, offered his own evaluation of the Moral Majority and the New Right in a 1981 discussion with journalists. It was reported in *Time*.

"I don't like what they're doing," he said. "I don't think what they're talking about is conservatism."

Goldwater accused the Moral Majority and its kind of giving conservatism a bad name. "The religious issues of these groups [abortion, school prayer] have little or nothing to do with conservative or liberal politics," he said. "They are diverting us away from the vital issues that our Government needs to address," such as "national security and economic survival." To drag theological questions into public debate, in Goldwater's view, is dangerously unAmerican. Said he: "One of the great strengths of our political system always has been our tendency to keep religious issues in the background."

Goldwater said he finds the New Right's righteousness especially distasteful, even though he admits he shares many of their moral views. "The uncompromising position of these groups is a divisive element that could tear apart the very spirit of our representative system. I am warning them today: I will fight them every step of the way if they try to dictate their moral convictions to all Americans in the name of conservatism." Said Goldwater "I'm frankly sick and tired of the political preachers across this country telling me as a citizen that if I want to be a moral person I must believe in A, B, C and D. Just who do they think they are?"

[From *Time,* September 28, 1981.]

Questions for Reflection

What has been the role of the church and ministers in U.S. politics, and what is it today? How important are moral questions in politics? Why are moral issues more important at some times than others? How successful has the fundamentalist Christian movement been in achieving its goals? What is your opinion of the Moral Majority?

ANSWERS TO MULTIPLE-CHOICE AND TRUE-FALSE QUESTIONS

Multiple-Choice Questions

1-D, 2-A, 3-D, 4-B, 5-B, 6-D, 7-C, 8-C

True-False Questions

1-T, 2-T, 3-F, 4-T, 5-T, 6-T, 7-F, 8-F

37

CULTURAL POLITICS

CHAPTER OBJECTIVES

After you complete the reading and study of this chapter, you should be able to:

1. Describe the diverse American population in 1990.
2. Explain the election of Bill Clinton in 1992.
3. Discuss the achievements in domestic policy during the Clinton administration.
4. Understand the foreign policies and actions of President Clinton.
5. Analyze domestic politics during the 1990s.
6. Appraise *fin-de-siècle* America.

CHAPTER OUTLINE

I. United States in 1990
   A. Demographic shifts
      1. Aging baby boomers
      2. Growth of "Sunbelt"
      3. Metropolitan growth
      4. Working women
      5. Decline of family unit
      6. African-American poverty
   B. New immigrants
      1. Escalating growth of ethnic groups
      2. Immigrants—legal and illegal
      3. Non-European sources
         a. Asia
         b. Mexico
      4. Ethnic enclaves
      5. Ethnic conflicts

II. Cultural conservatism
   A. Attack on liberal agenda
      1. For decency and propriety
      2. Against affirmative action
   B. Religious right
      1. Christian Coalition
      2. Traditional family values
      3. Political activism

III. Bush to Clinton
   A. Background to 1992 election
      1. New international scene
         a. Gulf War
         b. Collapse of Soviet Union
      2. The economy
         a. Recession
         b. Declining standard of living
      3. Nomination of Clarence Thomas
         a. Sexual harassment charges
         b. Confirmation
         c. Gender gap

4. Republican divisions
  a. Tax increase
  b. Christian Right
B. Democratic nomination
  1. Clinton's background
  2. Primary contests
C. Election of 1992
  1. Economic issues
  2. H. Ross Perot
  3. Results

IV. Domestic affairs in Clinton's first term
A. Initial inconsistencies and problems
B. The economy
  1. Stimulus package approved
  2. NAFTA
C. Health care reform
  1. Background
  2. Universal medical coverage
  3. Opposition successful
D. Passage of Brady Bill
E. Spread of militia movement
  1. Hatred of federal authority
  2. Ruby Ridge incident
  3. Siege at Waco
  4. Oklahoma City bombing
  5. Freemen in Montana

V. Clinton's foreign challenges
A. General policies
  1. Ad hoc approach
  2. Democratic capitalism
B. Support for Yeltsin in Russia
C. The Middle East
  1. Continued negotiations
  2. Israel-PLO agreement
  3. Assassination of Rabin
D. Continuity in Somalia
E. Yugoslavia
  1. Ethnic conflict
  2. U.S. negotiators
  3. Troops as peacekeepers
F. Haiti
  1. Support for Aristide
  2. Refugees
  3. Negotiations and troops

VI. Domestic policies
A. Election of 1994

1. GOP wins control of Congress
2. Repudiation of Clinton
3. Republican initiative
B. "Contract with America"
  1. Newton Leroy Gingrich
  2. Assault on welfare state
  3. Ten-point program
  4. Legislative program
  5. Limited success
C. Legislative breakthroughs in 1996
  1. Raise in minimum wage
  2. Expanded health insurance
  3. Welfare reform
D. 1996 election
  1. Bob Dole
    a. Background
    b. Liabilities
    c. Kemp as running mate
  2. Campaign
  3. Results
    a. Clinton reelected
    b. GOP majority in Congress

VII. Clinton's second term
A. The economy
  1. Prosperity
  2. Budget surplus
    a. Monetarism
    b. Alan Greenspan
  3. Globalization
B. Race relations
  1. Affirmative action
  2. Gerrymandering
  3. *Hopwood* v. *Texas*
C. Scandals
  1. Independent counsel
  2. Whitewater
  3. Allegations of sexual impropriety
  4. House of Representatives votes to begin impeachment inquiry

VIII. America at the turn of the century
A. Conflicting attitudes
  1. Prosperity
  2. Anxiety and self-doubt
B. Threats to cohesion and consensus
  1. Multicultural population
  2. Divisive public discourse
  3. Weakening social fabric

KEY ITEMS OF CHRONOLOGY

Christian Coalition formed	1989
Clarence Thomas named to Supreme Court	1991
Ruby Ridge incident	1992
Clinton administration	1993
Siege at Waco	1993
Brady Bill passed	1993
Middle East agreement	1993
North American Free Trade Agreement	1993
"Contract with America"	1995
Oklahoma City bombing	1995
Personal Responsibility and Work Opportunity Act	1996

TERMS TO MASTER

Listed below are some important terms or people with which you should be familiar after you complete the study of this chapter. Explain the significance of each name or term.

1. Sunbelt
2. Christian Coalition
3. Clarence Thomas
4. H. Ross Perot
5. Family Leave Act
6. NAFTA
7. "Contract with America"
8. Robert Dole
9. Alan Greenspan
10. multicultural

VOCABULARY BUILDING

Listed below are some words or phrases used in this chapter. Look up each word in your dictionary unless the meaning is given here.

1. orthodox
2. dismemberment
3. recession
4. doldrums
5. charade
6. renege
7. rampant
8. paradigm

9. intermediary
10. fractious
11. repudiation
12. insurgent
13. tout
14. contrite
15. acerbic
16. monetarist
17. gerrymander
18. ferocious
19. titillate
20. dormant

EXERCISES FOR UNDERSTANDING

When you have completed reading the chapter, answer each of the following questions. If you have difficulty, go back and reread the section of the chapter related to the question.

Multiple-Choice Questions

Select the letter of the response that best completes the statement.

1. In the 1980s, for the first time, the fastest growing segment of the population was
   A. African Americans.
   B. Hispanics.
   C. gays and lesbians.
   D. Asian Americans

2. For the Bush administration, the most devastating development in the early 1990s was
   A. a long recession.
   B. the survival of Saddam Hussein after the Gulf War.
   C. charges of corruption.
   D. the rise of the Christian Coalition.
3. "Read my lips. No new taxes!" said
   A. Ross Perot.
   B. Ronald Reagan.
   C. George Bush.
   D. Bill Clinton.
4. Anita Hill accused Clarence Thomas of
   A. favoring abortion and gun control.
   B. improprieties in the savings and loan scandal.
   C. sexual harassment.
   D. being a homosexual.
5. Bill Clinton's major legislative accomplishments included
   A. the Family Leave Act.
   B. NAFTA.
   C. the Brady Bill for gun control.
   D. all the above
6. Clinton's most successful departure in foreign policy was in
   A. Chechnya.
   B. Yugoslavia.
   C. Israel.
   D. Haiti.
7. In the 1990s, Alan Greenspan was
   A. a leading advocate of Keynesian economics.
   B. an outspoken Republican critic of Clinton's economic policies.
   C. chairman of the Federal Reserve Board.
   D. opposed to NAFTA, Keogh-IRAs, and budget surpluses.
8. In the mid-1990s, a more conservative Supreme Court
   A. ruled against election districts drawn along racial lines.
   B. strongly endorsed affirmative action programs.

   C. held NAFTA unconstitutional.
   D. all of the above

True-False Questions

Indicate whether each statement is true or false.

1. By 1990 a majority of Americans lived in cities of at least one million people.
2. The Christian Coalition chose to work politically through the Republican party.
3. Bill Clinton's nomination of Clarence Thomas for the Supreme Court was eventually confirmed by the Senate.
4. In his first two years as president, Bill Clinton accomplished virtually nothing.
5. David Koresh and the Branch Davidians were key members of the Christian Coalition.
6. The use of U.S. military forces in Somalia was a thorough success.
7. In the 1992 elections, Republicans gained control of Congress.
8. By 1998, the federal government had a budget surplus.

Essay Questions

1. By 1990 what were the major demographic trends at work in the United States?
2. In domestic policy, what were the successes and setbacks of the Clinton administration?
3. Compare Clinton's foreign policy to George Bush's.
4. What forces contributed to the Republican control of Congress when Clinton was elected and reelected president?
5. Describe the tone and spirit of American society as it approaches the end of the century.

READING

Reading. "The Larger Significance of Michael Jordan"

In considering Michael Jordan as a modern American hero, Jonathan Yardley, a graduate of the University of North Carolina and a Pulitzer Prize–winning literary critic for the *Washington Post,* discusses changes in American culture since World War II.

There is much to be learned about a culture from those persons whom it places upon pedestals, whom it admires and emulates, whom it calls *heroes.* A half-century ago, the great American hero was Dwight David Eisenhower, conquering general of World War II, soon to become president of his country. Today, the great American hero is Michael Jordan, basketball player nonpareil and omnipresent advertising representative.

What does this tell us about ourselves? The transition from "I Like Ike" to "Be Like Mike" encompasses a great deal more than the passage of time. It reflects dramatic changes in American society and culture, ranging from the immense growth in our individual wealth to the decline of our involvement in public affairs, to the rise of the entertainment industry, to our obsession with professional sports, to the impressive—if as yet incomplete—absorption of black Americans into the national mainstream.

All of which is to say that, difficult though it may be to believe, Michael Jordan is a good deal more than Michael Jordan.

It may seem quite enough that he is the most gifted athlete of our time, not merely among basketball players but among athletes in all sports, not merely in these United States but in all the world. It may seem mere icing on the cake that he possesses a gift for the spectacular—a capacity to rise to and beyond any challenge—that borders on the supernatural. Yet there is more to it than that. Michael Jordan transcends sports just as, in another day and in a very different way, Elvis Presley transcended rock 'n' roll. He is a mirror of our outer and inner selves.

Claims such as this should be made, or so it seems to me, with care and trepidation. . . .

Yet the one certainty about Michael Jordan, apart from his extraordinary athletic skills and his irresistible magnetism, is that he must be taken seriously. One reason is self-evident: He occupies a place on the international sporting stage not filled since the retirement of boxer Muhammad Ali. Other explanations require a bit of digging, for they have to do with the ways in which a single individual who has risen far, far above the crowd can come to embody what the crowd reveres and what it desires.

. . . [That] Jordan committed himself to [the University of North Carolina at] Chapel Hill not just as a farm system for pro ball but as a place to learn is something about Jordan I greatly respect and an aspect of him that probably is not well known to the countless fans who esteem him for his obvious talents. . . . Among these are his gift for doing whatever needs to be done to meet the challenge at hand; his sublime physical talents, with which he turns the sweaty basketball court into a place where Nureyev or Baryshnikov would feel at home; his insatiable zest for competition and the pure, irresistible joy he radiates as he engages in it; his willingness to risk failure, as in his abortive baseball career, in order to test himself; his loyalty to his team and his fierce insistence that his teammates reciprocate it; and, by no means least, the sense he conveys of a bright, likable, decent human being underneath all the tinsel of celebrity and image with which he is bedecked.

No, Jordan is not perfect. His well-documented affinity for gambling is not exactly a jewel in his crown. I was sorry to read not long ago that when the NBA auditioned a female referee, Jordan was among those who rode her hardest and, according to one report, tripped her as she ran past the Bulls' bench. Somehow one would like to think that Jordan would have enough competition on the court to render gambling superfluous, and that he could rise above the petty chauvinism of the locker room; indeed, he took a step in the latter direction when, after the NBA decided last fall to hire its first female referees, he welcomed them to the league with equanimity.

Yet even these foibles connect to what it is that we so admire about Jordan. He is a relentless and endlessly zestful competitor who simply cannot resist any tests that fall in his path, indeed goes out of his way to seek them. How else can we explain his gambling, his compulsion to prove himself on the golf course or, for that matter, his presence in the audience at last year's Ryder Cup golf matches in Spain, cheering on his country's team? Apparently, he regards the basketball court on which he competes as a male preserve; this may strike some of us, ostensibly more enlightened, as retrograde, but it is in character for a man who does not believe that challenges should be diluted.

For these reasons, warts and all, Jordan is an American hero. It needs to be emphasized, though, that in the transition from Ike to Mike the word *hero* has gone off on a tangent. Apart from its usage in mythology, its traditional and proper meaning as defined by the excellent *American Heritage Dictionary* is "a person noted for feats of courage or nobility of purpose, especially one who has risked or sacrificed his or her life."

Dwight Eisenhower's service in World War II fits that description. He was courageous as commander in chief of the Allied forces in western Europe, he was the representative and embodiment of a noble purpose, and he was prepared to sacrifice his position, his reputation and his life for that cause. Similarly, any list of true heroes of our age must include Mahatma Gandhi, Martin Luther King Jr., Nelson Mandela, Andrei Sakharov and Winston Churchill.

That list would not, I think, include John Wayne; Mickey Mantle; Diana, Princess of Wales; or Joe Montana. Yet all of these, and many others of similar renown, are routinely described as "heroic" in the press and by the public. To my way of thinking, this diminishes the word, but that is personal bias. What is beyond dispute is that the word has largely lost its traditional meaning.

To say that the transition from Ike to Mike is a transition from hero to celebrity is an oversimplification, but not much of one. Ours is a culture—one we are rapidly exporting to the rest of the world—that honors mere fame far more than it does hard achievement. The struggles of our formative years, struggles that produced such indisputable heroes as George Washington, Abraham Lincoln and Harriet Tubman, are no longer being fought. We are a mature democracy, an imperfect one to be sure, but one rarely placed at risk in circumstances from which heroes emerge. Yet we still want and need heroes, as every society does, so we have redefined the term.

Most of us are, for all the internal self-doubts and tensions that still haunt us, fat and happy, freed by our affluence to seek entertainment and distraction. Our interest in public affairs has declined catastrophically. Only a small percentage of us now vote regularly, and the quality of those who seek public office is, by common consent, a reflection of our indifference. When Lincoln and Stephen Douglas held their famous debates in 1858, people delighted in sitting through hour upon hour of oratory; now we are so complacent about politics that national conventions of the two major political parties are reduced to television sideshows.

Rather than participate in public life and the national defense, we direct our energies toward our amusement. The people whom we most revere are those who most successfully entertain us, whether as motion-picture and television stars, as musicians and performers, as players and coaches in sports, or simply as celebrities in their own, self-perpetuating right, people who are famous, as the saying goes, for being famous.

This is a privilege that unprecedented prosperity has bestowed upon us. The origins of the entertainment culture can be traced back to the phonograph and the radio, both of which made possible for the first time the development of a genuinely mass culture, but until very recently, entertainment was a luxury in which we could indulge only upon occasion. Now it is a daily reality, perhaps a necessity, and certainly, in the minds of many of us, an entitlement.

Sports are central to the entertainment culture, not merely because they provide excitement and glamour and celebrities but because they are an agreeable mixture of fantasy and reality. If on the one hand sports are populated, at the highest levels, by people so far above us as to seem unreachable, on the other hand the results of their contests cannot be determined by scriptwriters. Audience sampling may be used to decide how movies end, but when the Bulls play the Rockets, everything is unknown until the last point is scored. Television and the movies may give us clichés, but sports give us the New York "Miracle" Mets, a perennial cellar dweller, winning the 1969 World Series over the Baltimore Orioles; the New York Jets from the lowly American Football League upsetting the established National Football League's Baltimore Colts in Super Bowl III; and an all-black Texas Western University basketball team prevailing over a still-segregated, all-white University of Kentucky squad in the 1966 NCAA championship game.

This is the world in which Michael Jordan plays, the world in which he is the star of stars. He is a celebrity in the narrowest meaning of the word—famous for being famous—yet he is also a person of real accomplishment, achieved at not inconsiderable risk. Yes, there doubtless are many people who know Jordan only as the most visible spokesman for Nike, just as there are many people who know Joe DiMaggio only as Mr. Coffee. Yet what most of us know is Michael Jordan, his teammates in disarray, taking command of a crucial basketball game all by himself, summoning inner resources at which the rest of us can only wonder, single-handedly defeating the Knicks or the Sonics or the Lakers in displays of individual fortitude that quite literally take the breath away.

Jordan may be said, therefore, to embody both the ancient and the modern definitions of heroic. He is famous, which is often all we require these days in those whom we single out as "role models," yet he is also, like the mythic hero as defined by my dictionary, "endowed with great courage and strength, celebrated for his bold exploits, and favored by the gods." The incalculable popularity he enjoys is therefore an anachronism: In a time when fantasy and imagery flourish, Jordan is admired for the same gritty qualities that made such epic heroes as Odysseus and Ajax, Hector and Achilles, quite literally the stuff of legend.

It seems to me that, amid all the lamentable things that can be said about ourselves and our culture these days, this says something good. We admire Michael Jordan for a few of the wrong reasons but many of the right ones. My own hunch is that the true roots of our admiration lie in what he does and how he does it in his real life as an athlete, and that this speaks favorably for our understanding of what is most important, most worthy of esteem and respect.

There is much in the country today that troubles me. I worry that the entertainment culture may be shoving aside the work ethic, that we prefer fantasy and "docudrama" and "infotainment" to cold reality and rigorous education, that self-discipline is giving way to self-indulgence, that the great struggles in which we once united have left in their wake petty squabbles that divide us. I worry, too, that we admire, even venerate, too many people who do not deserve it.

But I do not worry for a moment over the admiration—adulation, if you will—that we lavish upon Michael Jordan. From time to time I ask myself how many people there are in the public eye whom I admire without significant reservation, and two names always come first to mind: Michael Jordan and baseball's newly crowned ironman Cal Ripkin Jr. I suspect that many other Americans would say the same. What matters about these two men is not that they are athletes but that they have developed their natural gifts to the fullest, that they are steadfast in their loyalties and solid in their convictions, that they work hard and meet the challenges before them, that their presence enriches all of us.

That is neither a classical nor a modern definition of *hero,* but it is an excellent thing to be, worthy of respect and emulation. Still, though the distance from "I Like Ike" to "Be Like Mike" may not really be so great after all, this question remains: In a culture obsessed with mass entertainment and mere celebrity, what sort of "heroes" will we settle for in the future?

[From Jonathan Yardley, "The Larger Significance of Michael Jordan: What Do Our Heroes Show Us about Ourselves?" *Sky,* February 1998, pp. 47–50.]

Questions for Reflection

What does Yardley suggest has happened in American culture between Eisenhower and Jordan? Is Yardley's distinction between heroes and celebrities important? What other people would you suggest as American heroes or celebrities today? As the nation enters a new century, can heroes/celebrities like Michael Jordan perform a unifying role in an increasingly diverse country?

ANSWERS TO MULTIPLE-CHOICE AND TRUE-FALSE QUESTIONS

Multiple-Choice Questions

1-D, 2-A, 3-C, 4-C, 5-D, 6-D, 7-C, 8-A

True-False Questions

1-T, 2-T, 3-F, 4-F, 5-F, 6-F, 7-T, 8-T

PERMISSIONS ACKNOWLEDGMENTS

pp. 156—61: La Wanda Cox, "Could Reconstruction Have Been Effective?" from *Lincoln and Black Freedom: A Study in Presidential Leadership.* Copyright © 1981 by the University of South Carolina Press. Reprinted by permission.

pp. 173–75: Herbert Quick, *One Man's Life.* Reprinted with the permission of Simon & Schuster from *One Man's Life* by Herbert Quick. Copyright © 1925 by Bobbs-Merrill Company, Inc., renewed 1953 by Ella Corey Quick.

pp. 239–41: Walter Lippmann, "The Causes of Political Indifference Today," from the *Atlantic Monthly,* February 1927 issue. Used with permission of the President and Fellows of Harvard College.

pp. 246–48: Charles Kettering, "Keep the Consumer Dissatisfied." Reprinted by permission of *Nation's Business,* January 1929. Copyright © 1929, U.S. Chamber of Commerce.

pp. 255–58: Frank G. Moorhead, "Broke at Fifty-Five," from *The Nation,* May 13, 1931 issue. Reprinted by permission.

pp. 258–61: From *These Are Our Lives* by the Federal Writers' Project, Regional Staff. Copyright © 1939 by the University of North Carolina Press, renewed 1967. Used by permission of the publisher.

pp. 286–89: Arthur M. Schlesinger, Jr., "Origins of the Cold War," from *Foreign Affairs* 46, no. 1 (October 1967): 22–52. Reprinted by permission of Foreign Affairs. Copyright © 1967 by the Council of Foreign Relations, Inc.

pp. 289–92: Barton J. Bernstein, "American Foreign Policy and the Origins of the Cold War," from *Politics and Policies of the Truman Administration.* Copyright © 1970 by Barton Bernstein. Reprinted by permission of the author.

pp. 321–23: William J. Fulbright, "American Foreign Policy," from *The New York Times,* May 15, 1966. Copyright © 1966 by The New York Times. Reprinted by permission.

pp. 341–43: Richard Zwier and Richard Smith, "Christian Politics and the New Right." Copyright © 1980 Christian Century Foundation. Reprinted by permission of the publisher from the October 8, 1980, issue of the *Christian Century.*

pp. 343–44: Joseph Sobran, "Good News," from *The National Review,* June 27, 1980, p. 793. Copyright © 1980 by National Review, Inc., 215 Lexington Avenue, New York, NY 10016. Reprinted by permission of the publisher.

pp. 350–54: Jonathan Yardley, "The Larger Significance of Michael Jordan," *Sky Magazine,* February 1998, pp. 47–50. Copyright © 1998 by Jonathan Yardley. Reprinted by permission of the author.

Diligent efforts have been made to contact the copyright holders of each of the selections. Rights holders of any selections not credited should contact W. W. Norton & Company, Inc., 500 Fifth Avenue, New York, NY 10110, in order for a correction to be made in the next reprinting of our work.